LIVING SCIENCE

OXFORD

LIVING SCIENCE

FUNDAMENTAL PRINCIPLES EXPLAINED

OXFORD
UNIVERSITY PRESS

CONTENTS

Light and sound

Materials

Energy and Forces

Energy

Do you have days when you want to run, jump, shout, sing and be very active? If you do, people will say that you are 'bursting with energy', and they would be right. You need energy to do these things, and all the other actions that you carry out every day.

Every action of any kind needs energy to make it happen – not just here on Earth but throughout the entire Universe. Energy makes your body work so that you can see, hear, think, speak, move and do all kinds of things. Energy keeps all living things – including us – alive. This energy comes from the Sun's heat and from food.

But non-living things use energy too. All machines need a supply of energy to work, and they stop when their energy supply gives out or is turned off. Machines get energy from fuels, such as petrol, or from a supply of power such as electricity or running water.

FROM CORNFLAKES TO CONSERVATION

Many foods have their energy value printed on the packet. It is in kilojoules (kJ), or thousands of joules. A joule is a unit that scientists use to measure energy. It is named after the British scientist James Prescott Joule (1818–1889). He discovered the principle of conservation of energy in the 1840s, which says that energy cannot be destroyed, but changes its form.

What is energy?

Energy makes things happen, and it takes several different forms. The energy in movement is just one of them. Other forms of energy include light and sound, which you use to see and hear things, and heat, which keeps you warm.

Your body has a large amount of stored energy, which keeps it working. Non-living things may contain stored energy too. A battery is a store of electricity, which is yet another form of energy.

◀ Petrol stores a lot of energy. As it burns in this dragster's engine, the petrol's chemical energy changes to heat energy. This heat energy changes to kinetic (movement) energy as the engine drives the car along.

key words

- action
- joule
- kinetic energy
- potential energy

▼ Most of our energy comes through space from the Sun in the form of heat and light. After arriving on Earth, the energy may change its form several times as it is used. Every set of changes ends with the production of heat or light.

Plants use light energy from the Sun to grow. The light energy becomes chemical energy and is stored inside the plant.

The Sun powers the world's weather systems – even when it is not a sunny day! Heat energy makes winds blow and water evaporate into the air to form rain clouds.

Rigs drill for oil on the seabed. Oil is an important source of fuel. It is formed from the remains of living things.

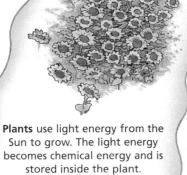

All animals (including us) get their food from plants – or from eating other animals that have eaten plants.

Wind turbines harness the power of the wind and turn their kinetic energy into electricity that will power machines.

Fuels such as oil and coal are burned in power stations. The chemical energy inside the fuels is turned into electrical energy.

The chemical energy in food allows people and animals to move and play. Their bodies change the chemical energy into kinetic (movement) energy.

Electrical energy powers machines, such as high-speed trains. It changes into kinetic energy as the motor turns and drives the train along the track.

Using energy

Energy is needed for an action of any kind to happen. This energy has to come from somewhere. You get energy from food and drink. An electrical machine, such as a radio, gets a supply of electrical energy (electricity) from a power point or a battery.

Although every action needs some energy to happen, it does not use up the energy. Energy cannot be destroyed. Instead, it changes form as the action happens. For example, when you throw a ball, the muscles in your arm take some of your stored energy, which has come from food, and change it into energy of movement. A computer takes electrical energy from a power point and changes it into light energy as a picture appears on the screen.

You need about 10,000 kilojoules of energy every day to keep your body working. Most of this energy comes from your food, and it is about the same amount of energy as there is in a 500-gram box of cereal.

The source of our energy

Our main supplies of energy are food to make our bodies work and fuels to drive our machines. We eat plants, or meat and fish which come from animals that ate plants. So all the energy in our food comes from plants. Our main fuels are coal, oil and gas. All these fuels are the remains of animals and plants that lived millions of years ago. So the energy in fuel comes from plants, too.

But plants are not the original source of this energy. They are just energy stores. The energy that they store comes from the Sun. As plants grow, they turn the Sun's light and heat into stored energy. In fact, the source of almost all the energy on Earth is the rays of heat and light that stream through space from the Sun.

▼ Strip lights use less energy than most light bulbs, which get warm and change much of the electricity they use into heat energy instead of light.

▶ When a jack-in-the-box jumps out at you, it changes energy stored in its spring into energy of movement. The stored energy is also called potential energy.

Waves and vibrations

To a radio wave, your body is like glass! Just as light comes through a window, radio waves and other kinds of wave or ray are streaming through your body right now. You cannot feel them and they cause you no harm, but they bring radio and television programmes to your home.

BRIGHT SPARK
The German scientist Heinrich Hertz (1857–1894) discovered radio waves in 1888. He did this by using a powerful electric current to make a spark, and saw that another spark immediately jumped across a gap in a brass ring nearby. The first spark produced radio waves that travelled through the air to the ring. The waves produced an electric current in the ring, causing the second spark. Radio communications were invented as a result of Hertz's discovery.

Radio and television sets receive radio waves sent out from high masts or satellites. The waves carry sounds and pictures to all sets within range, passing through walls and people on the way.

'Radio waves are electromagnetic waves, a group of penetrating waves. Some of these waves are also called rays. Other kinds of penetrating waves and rays include microwaves, which carry mobile telephone calls, heat rays, which bring you warmth, and light rays, which let you see everything around you.

Sound waves are different kinds of waves that can pass through air and solid materials. They let you hear all kinds of sounds and noises, such as people talking or music playing.

Bringing energy to all

All rays and waves transport energy from one place to another. They spread out from their source in all directions, and bring their energy to everything that they meet.

When you speak, your mouth sends out sound waves. These spread out through the air, and perhaps through thin walls, carrying sound energy. When the sound waves enter the ears of other people, they hear you.

In the same way, rays spread out through space from the Sun. They carry heat energy and light energy to the Earth, giving us warmth and daylight.

Making waves

Water waves, from ripples in a pond to giant breakers at the seashore, also

▲ A good surfer can ride a giant wave for a long way. The surfer is able to stay at the front of the wave and move along with it.

transport energy. If you drop a stone into a pond, the water moves up and down as the stone enters the water. This up-and-down movement, or vibration, travels out across the water surface as a wave. When it meets a floating object such as a toy boat, the wave makes it bob up and down. The energy to make the boat bob comes from the falling stone, and is carried out to the boat by the wave.

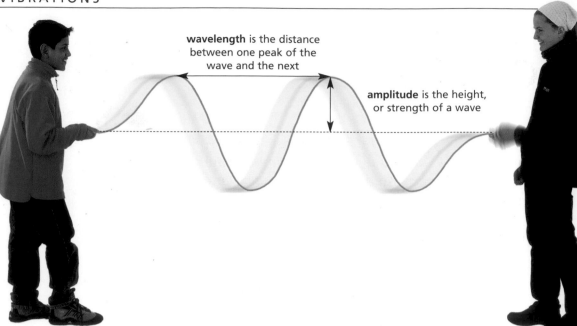

▶ Demonstrate a wave. Tie a rope to a tree or get a friend to hold one end. Hold the other end fairly tightly and move it quickly up and down. A wave travels along the rope. As the wave passes, the rope goes up and down or vibrates at a particular rate. This is called the frequency of the wave.

wavelength is the distance between one peak of the wave and the next

amplitude is the height, or strength of a wave

Light rays, like all electromagnetic waves, move at 300,000 kilometres per second. Sound waves travel a million times slower.

Electromagnetic waves and sound waves transport energy as vibrations just as water waves do, which is why they are called 'waves' or 'wave motions'. Heat rays and light rays are wave motions too, and are sometimes called waves instead of rays.

Every kind of wave has a particular frequency, or rate at which it vibrates. A high-frequency wave vibrates quickly, while lower-frequency waves vibrate more slowly.

Good vibrations

Objects can vibrate in a similar way to water waves. When you twang a stretched rubber band, it moves rapidly to and fro. A swing and a pendulum are other examples of vibration. When objects vibrate, they move to and fro at a regular rate. That is why pendulums and vibrating springs and crystals can be used to control clocks and watches and make sure they keep time.

key words

- frequency
- ray
- vibration
- wave
- wave motion

▶ Strong winds can cause structures to vibrate slowly. In 1940, the Tacoma Narrows Bridge in the United States collapsed because the wind made it vibrate more and more. Bridges like this are now strengthened so that vibration does not build up.

Forces

What lifts a plane from the ground and sends it zooming through the air? An engine moves the plane forwards, and more forces operate under the wings, holding the plane up. Forces are at work everywhere all the time. Many are powerful enough to crush you, others so weak that you cannot feel them.

A force is a push or a pull. You exert a force when you kick a ball or open a book. When anything begins to move, a force starts it off. Forces also make moving things speed up, slow down, stop or change direction. You use a pulling force to stop a lively dog on a lead.

But forces do not disappear when things are not moving. All the parts of a building – the floors, walls and beams – push or pull on each other. These forces exactly balance. If they didn't, a part of the building would begin to move and the whole structure might collapse.

▶ Strong internal forces between the particles inside a pole-vaulter's pole give it elasticity and stop it from breaking. Instead, the pole bends, then springs back to thrust the vaulter into the air.

FORCES

All the forces that make things move or hold things together are composed of a few basic forces. Electrostatic force, magnetic force and the force of gravity are three of these basic forces.

Rubbing a balloon makes it stick to a wall with **electrostatic force.**

Magnetic force between a magnet and steel paper clips enables the magnet to pick up the paper clips.

Gravity is the force that makes things fall to the ground when you drop them.

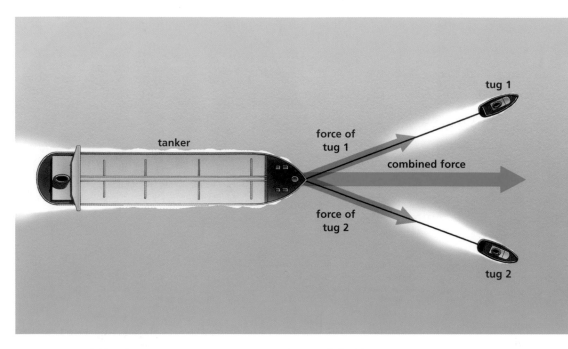

◀ If several forces act on an object, they combine to create one overall force. Here, the forces from the two tugs combine to produce a force that pulls the tanker forwards.

Sources of forces

In people and animals, muscles produce the force to move arms, legs and other body parts. Machines have motors or engines to produce force. Magnets attract other magnets, exerting force that is put to use in electric motors. Springs drive machines such as wind-up clocks or toy mice. When you wind them up, the spring inside stretches and then it contracts to produce a force. This makes the clock hands move round or the mouse shoot across the floor.

Another force – gravity – is present everywhere in the Universe. It makes things fall or roll down slopes. Gravity also makes everything press down on the ground with a force, and this force is their weight.

Adapting or breaking

What happens when forces try to move fixed objects? The objects adapt by changing shape. They may get smaller or bigger, bend, twist or even snap! When you pull a rubber band, you can see it stretch. But many things change shape so little that you cannot see it happening.

▶ On a rollercoaster ride at a theme park the carriages are first raised to a great height, and then released. The force of gravity gives them enough power to complete the ride, even when they loop the loop.

Inside forces

Everything that exists is made up of tiny particles called atoms, or groups of atoms called molecules. Forces between the particles cause them to grip each other and hold things together. These internal forces are strong in hard, tough materials such as steel. But they are weak in liquids and gases, such as air and water. Because the internal forces in liquids and gases are weak, the particles can move about more, and the materials can flow easily.

Motion

Kick a ball. You can feel the force that you use to start it soaring through the air. But why does the ball keep moving through the air? This puzzled people for centuries, for the answer seems unbelievable. The answer is that nothing keeps it moving – it goes by itself.

To get anything moving, a force must push on it or pull on it. But once something is already moving, like a ball soaring or rolling, it does not need a force to continue moving. It carries on of its own accord, moving effortlessly in the same direction and at a constant speed. You continue to move unaided when you slide on some ice or roll along on skates...until you hit a wall!

key words
- accelerate
- brakes
- motion
- speed

Speed, turn, slow or stop

Once an object is moving, it will not speed up (accelerate), slow down or change direction unless another force acts on it. This happens all the time. A soaring ball is slowed by the air, which exerts a backward force called friction as the ball moves through it. The ball also slows down and soon stops rising because the force of gravity pulls it down. At the same time, the force of a gust of wind may blow the ball to one side and change its direction.

If a force pushes or pulls on one side or one end of an object, or if two forces act on both sides or both ends, then the object turns. You grip the ends of the handlebars of a bicycle to turn them.

More weight, less speed

Have you ever tried to push a car to get it moving? Even though the car can roll easily, it needs several people to push it and takes a lot of force to get it going. This is because the car is very heavy. The more you all push, the faster it goes. Slowing and stopping a heavy object needs a lot of force too, so a car has powerful brakes.

▶ When skydivers leap from an aircraft, they accelerate as gravity pulls them towards the ground. But the faster they fall, the greater the friction of the air around them. Eventually the forces of air friction and gravity balance out and the skydiver falls at a constant speed of about 200 kilometres per hour.

Pushing back and moving forwards

How do you jump? You push down on the ground with your legs. But surely, to move upwards, you need a force that pushes you up? Where does that force come from? It comes from the ground, which pushes you up as you push down on it. Forces always act in pairs like this.

Out of this world

Movement is different in space. The Earth, stars, planets and moons were moving as they formed and cannot stop. Space is empty, and there is no air to produce friction and stop them. In the same way, spacecraft and satellites enter space at high speed and, if they do not return to Earth, will continue to move for ever.

You are never at rest. The Earth moves through space, circling the Sun at a speed of 108,000 kilometres per hour, and carrying you along with it.

▼ As the water spurts from a high-power hose, it pushes back on the nozzle. It takes a lot of strength for the firefighters to hold the nozzle steady and stop it pushing them back.

▼ A ride on a bicycle involves several different forces as you start off, speed up, turn, slow down and stop.

You push off and pedal to start moving.
The force of your legs goes to the back wheel, which turns and moves the bicycle forwards. The bicycle speeds up.

You reach a steady speed on the flat.
A backward force called friction comes into action as the bicycle moves. It equals the forward force on the back wheel. There is no overall force so the bicycle's speed is constant.

Travelling downhill, the force of gravity pulls you forwards, and you do not need to pedal.

Travelling uphill, gravity pulls you backwards. You have to pedal hard to produce enough forward force to overcome gravity.

You swivel the handlebars to turn the bicycle. A sideways force moves the front wheel to the side and you change direction.

You apply the brakes.
The brakes produce a backward force on both wheels of the bicycle, and you slow down and stop.

Friction

You pedal hard to get a bicycle up to speed. And yet to stop, all you do is grip the brake levers lightly. How can just a gentle pull of the hands so quickly cancel out all the power you put into pedalling? Friction comes to your aid.

As you brake, blocks in the brakes rub against the rim of each wheel. Tiny irregularities in the surfaces of the brake blocks and the rim catch on each other. This produces a strong force, called friction, that acts to slow and stop the wheel rim.

Friction occurs whenever two objects meet, or when an object comes into contact with a liquid such as water, or a gas such as air. If they are moving, then friction slows or stops them. If they are still but try to move, it may prevent movement from starting.

Using friction

Brakes are just one use of friction. It is also needed for a vehicle to move in the first place. Friction enables the wheels to grip the ground so that they do not slide.

key words

- atoms
- lubrication
- molecules

▶ Cars have powerful disc brakes. A pair of brake pads close and grip a disc attached to the wheel hub, producing a powerful force of friction between the pads and the disc.

All the many things that are held together by screws or nuts and bolts would fall apart without friction. Friction gives the screw a strong grip on the wood around it, or a nut on the metal bolt.

Reducing friction

Friction is not always useful. In moving parts it produces heat, which could damage machines. Oil or grease is used to make the moving parts slippery. This is called lubrication and it reduces friction and heat. This is why you oil the chain on your bicycle.

Lubrication makes a surface smooth because the oil or grease smoothes out any irregularities in the surface. A smooth surface has little friction. Ice is very smooth, which is why you slip on it.

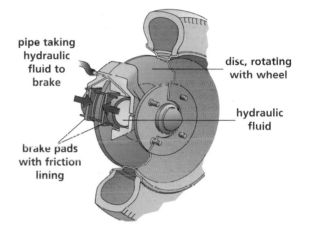

pipe taking hydraulic fluid to brake

disc, rotating with wheel

hydraulic fluid

brake pads with friction lining

◀ The undersides of skis are very smooth so that there is very little friction between the skis and the snow, enabling the skier to move very fast. However, friction comes into play as the skier tilts the skis to grip the snow and change direction.

Machines

Imagine being hungry and thirsty, and having only canned food and drinks in corked bottles – but no can opener or corkscrew to open them. You would have to use your bare hands – a difficult and dangerous business! Every day, tools make all sorts of tasks possible.

▶ Nutcrackers are a kind of lever. The hand is much further from the hinge than the nut, and this magnifies the effort of the hand so that it becomes strong enough to crack the nut.

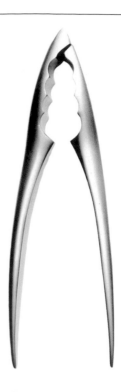

All sorts of tools, such as can-openers, corkscrews, hammers and spanners, are operated by hand. They work by increasing the amount of force you can exert with your hands or fingers. These devices are simple machines.

Powered machines, such as cars and excavators, have engines and motors to produce force. But they may also contain simple machines, such as levers and gears, to increase the amount of force driving the wheels, buckets or other parts.

Greater effort required

Every machine needs a force to drive it, and this driving force is called the effort. The machine magnifies the effort and applies it to a load, which may move.

You can lift the side of a car using a jack. The effort is the light force of your hand turning the jack handle, while the load is the great weight of the car. The jack greatly increases the force of your hand until it is equal to the weight of the car and raises it.

key words
- effort
- gear
- lever
- load
- weight

▲ ▶ Lifting a heavy load of sand into a wheelbarrow takes a lot of effort. This is because your hands and the load have to move the same distance.

The wheelbarrow is a kind of lever. When you lift its handles, your hands move up a greater distance than the load – so you need less effort to raise it.

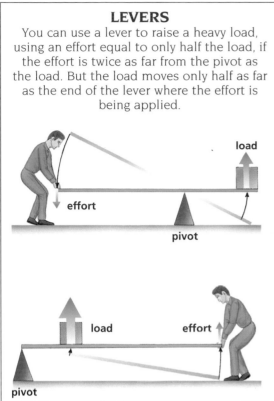

LEVERS

You can use a lever to raise a heavy load, using an effort equal to only half the load, if the effort is twice as far from the pivot as the load. But the load moves only half as far as the end of the lever where the effort is being applied.

The jack works because you have to turn the handle many times to raise the car's wheel just off the ground. Your hand travels a greater distance than the car rises. Simple machines trade force and distance like this. By moving a greater distance than the load, the light effort is magnified to match the heavy load.

Levers and gears

The most common kinds of simple machines are levers and gears. Levers are rods or bars used to move things. You push one end to exert a force at the other end of the lever or another part of it. Pliers, nutcrackers and bottle openers are levers, and pianos, bicycle brakes and excavators use levers. Spanners and screwdrivers are levers that move in a circle.

Car and bicycle gears contain toothed wheels that mesh together or are connected by a chain. The gearwheels are different sizes and rotate at different speeds, so that they can increase or decrease the force. You can ride up a hill in low gear on a bicycle because you pedal more quickly and this increases the force that turns the back wheel.

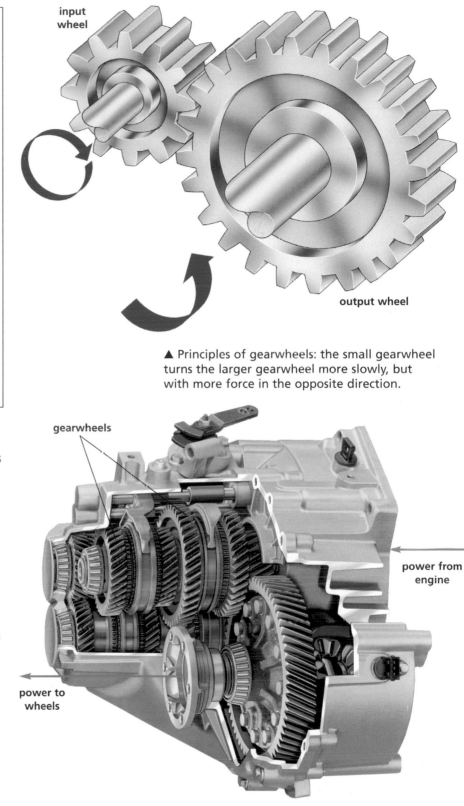

▲ Principles of gearwheels: the small gearwheel turns the larger gearwheel more slowly, but with more force in the opposite direction.

▲ The gearbox in a car connects a shaft from the engine to a shaft that turns the wheels. Changing gear makes different gearwheels connect the shafts so that the engine can turn the car's wheels at different speeds and with different amounts of force.

Pressure

Try to stop the water gushing from a tap by covering the spout – and you will probably end up soaked! That is because the flow of water is too strong to stop.

The water in the tap has a high pressure. It pushes against the inside of the tap with a large amount of force. Water comes out with great force when the tap is turned on.

DOWN DEEP

In 1960, two people descended 11 kilometres to the deepest part of the ocean in an underwater craft called *Trieste*. The pressure of the water there was equal to a weight of just over a tonne on every square centimetre of the cabin (a square centimetre is about the same size as a thumbnail). The cabin had to be very strong to resist this enormous pressure.

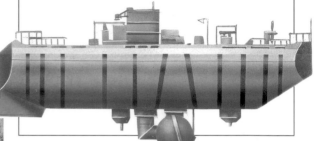

Using pressure

Bicycles, cars and other road vehicles all run on air! The high pressure of the air in the tyres holds the wheel rims above the road surface. Pumps inflate tyres by raising air pressure so that air flows through the valve into the tyre. The valve stops the high-pressure air from escaping.

◀ An excavator works by hydraulics. A pump raises the pressure of hydraulic fluid and sends the fluid through hoses to moving parts such as the bucket, which it drives with great power. The driver controls the fluid's movement to make the bucket scoop up dirt.

Raising pressure

The pressure in a tap is high because the pipe leading to the tap goes back to a tank above it. The weight of all the water in the pipe and tank gives it pressure. If the tank is not higher than the tap, a pump may raise the pressure of the water.

Gases, such as air, also have a certain pressure just as water does. The weight of all the air above you presses in on your body. When you breathe in, the pressure of the surrounding air makes it flow into your lungs.

Solid things exert pressure too. Your weight makes your feet press down on the ground with a certain amount of pressure.

▶ When you suck through a straw, you expand your lungs to lower the air pressure inside them. The outside air pressing on the drink is at a greater pressure, and forces the drink up the straw into your mouth.

air presses down on drink

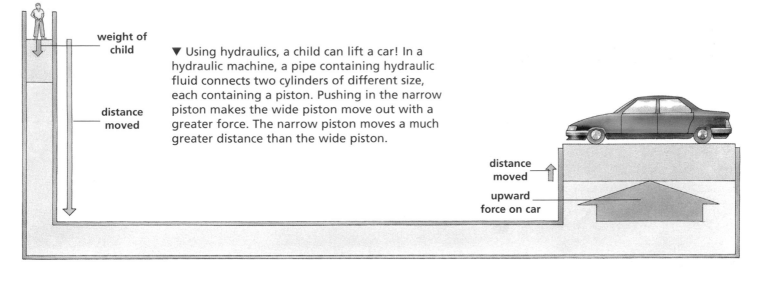

weight of child

distance moved

distance moved

upward force on car

▼ Using hydraulics, a child can lift a car! In a hydraulic machine, a pipe containing hydraulic fluid connects two cylinders of different size, each containing a piston. Pushing in the narrow piston makes the wide piston move out with a greater force. The narrow piston moves a much greater distance than the wide piston.

key words

- hydraulic
- pneumatic
- pump
- valve
- weight

Pumps raise the pressure of water in fountains to make the water spurt upwards. Pneumatic machines, such as road-mending drills, use air pressure, while hydraulic machines, such as car brakes and diggers, use liquid pressure. For both types of machine, pumps produce high-pressure air or liquid to drive the moving parts.

No pressure

Pumps can also remove air from a container to reduce the pressure inside. There is a vacuum in the container when the air has gone. The walls of a vacuum flask contain a vacuum, which keeps food or drink inside the flask hot or cold for several hours.

▶ A diver carries a cylinder of compressed (squashed) air in order to breathe underwater. This limits the time of the dive – it is not safe to breathe high-pressure air for very long.

Floating and sinking

Push an empty plastic bottle with a cap into a bowl of water. Push hard, as the water pushes back strongly. Let go, and the bottle springs back up and floats. It is this force in water that makes things float.

As the bottle enters the water, it pushes aside or displaces water. The weight of this displaced water pushes back on the bottle, forcing it upwards. This upward force overcomes the weight of the bottle and the bottle rises until it floats.

All things that float, such as pieces of wood or hollow objects, get enough upward force from the displaced water to equal their weight.

▶ Even non-swimmers cannot sink in the Dead Sea. The water there is so salty that it gives more upward force than fresh water or ordinary seawater.

To sink, or not to sink

If the weight of an object is always more than the upward force of the displaced water, then it sinks. This is why heavy stones and bricks sink.

◀ The ancient Greek scientist Archimedes once got into a full bath and made it overflow. He realized that immersing an object provided a simple way of measuring its volume. Archimedes' discovery led him to explain why things float.

key words
- displacement
- float
- force
- weight

Solid pieces of metal sink too, but not hollow metal objects such as ships and boats. Submarines and submersibles vary their weight to float, dive and return to the surface.

SUBMARINES

Submarines are ocean-going vessels that can travel on the surface or underwater. Submersibles are smaller vessels, some of which are remote-controlled. Both submarines and submersibles have ballast tanks which can be filled with air or water. To dive underwater, the tanks are filled with water to make the vessel heavier. To return to the surface, water is blown out of the ballast tanks by compressed air. This makes the vessel lighter, and it rises again.

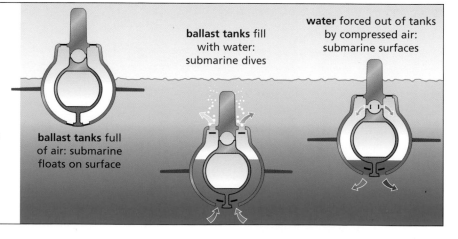

ballast tanks fill with water: submarine dives

water forced out of tanks by compressed air: submarine surfaces

ballast tanks full of air: submarine floats on surface

Flight and flow

A jumbo jet is like 100 cars all in the air at once – it transports about the same number of people and weighs about the same too. How does such a heavy machine stay up? It all depends on how the air flows around it.

▲ Concorde was the fastest airliner ever to have flown. It flew at twice the speed of sound (about 2000 kilometres per hour), more than twice as fast as other airliners.

Aircraft of all kinds and flying animals such as birds or butterflies can fly because they have wings. As the wing cuts through the air, air flowing around it creates a force called lift which pushes the wing upwards. It supports the wing (and everything attached to it) in the air.

Helicopters have wings too. As the whirling blades of the helicopter's rotor cut through the air, they work like moving wings to create lift.

▼ Aircraft wings give an arched cross-section called an airfoil. Air moving over the airfoil produces lift: the faster the aircraft moves, the greater the lift.

How wings work

When you fly a kite, the wind hits its underside and pushes the kite upwards. A wing works partly like a kite. It slopes at an angle so that its underside hits the air. Air is pushed out of its way and the air forces the wing upwards.

Wings also get lift from the way the air flows over them. The top of the wing is curved, so the air moves rapidly up and over. When air moves faster, its pressure drops. The air under the wing has a higher pressure because it moves more slowly, and this higher pressure also forces the wing upwards.

wing   air flow

▼ A glider has no engine, so it is towed along the ground to get up enough speed to take off. Once in the air, it flies at a slight downward angle to keep up enough speed for the wings to generate lift. To regain height, the pilot may fly to a rising air current and circle in it.

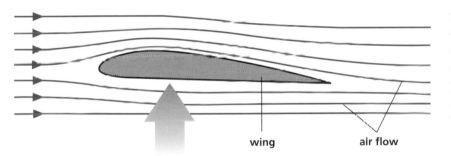

▲ A bird flaps its wings to generate lift, the upward force that holds it in the air, and to propel itself forwards. Once the bird is moving, it may hold its wings out straight and soar, getting lift from the way the air flows around its wings.

Up into the air ... and down again

To take off in the first place, aircraft speed along a runway until they are going so fast that the lift overcomes their weight and they fly. Birds can flap their wings to produce lift to take off from the ground, or simply open their wings and jump off a perch. Helicopters whirl their rotors until the blades generate enough lift, and then they go straight up.

When an aircraft, helicopter or bird is flying level, its lift equals its weight.

key words
- flow
- lift
- streamlining
- weight
- wing

Slowing, or altering the rotors, decreases the lift, and it begins to descend and may land.

Flow and friction

When anything moves through air, the air parts and flows around it. The air rubs against the moving object's surface, producing a force called friction that slows its speed. The same thing happens when an object moves through water. Reducing friction helps to gain speed, and saves fuel.

One way to achieve this is by a streamlined design. Streamlined shapes are narrow and dart-like. A pointed nose or bow makes it easier to cut through the air or water. A smooth surface or skin allows the air or water to rub as little as possible. Streamlining is important for aircraft, cars and ships, and for animals such as fish and birds.

As an airliner takes off and lands, flaps come out from the back of the wings. These flaps are like extra wings. They enable the wings to generate more lift at slow speeds.

◄ The design of an aircraft, such as this jet fighter, can be checked out in a wind tunnel. Air is blown over a model at high speed. The designer studies how the air flows around the model plane, to see how the real aircraft will behave when it flies through the air.

Gravity

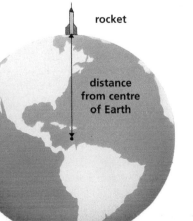

However hard you toss a ball up into the air, it will fall back down. A mysterious force called gravity pulls everything towards the ground. It's mysterious because no one knows why gravity exists – it's one of the great unsolved questions of science.

Gravity pulls whole objects together. If they are free to move, then gravity gets them moving. This is why raindrops, autumn leaves and balls fall towards the ground, the surface of our planet Earth.

Forces and fields

Whenever two objects are near each other, gravity acts between them and tries to pull them together. The strength of the force depends on the mass (the amount of material) in both objects. Because our planet is so massive, there is a strong force of gravity between the Earth and everything that is on or near it.

The Earth's field of gravity extends out into space to the Moon and beyond. Gravity keeps the Moon in its orbit or path around the Earth. In the same way, the Sun's gravity holds the Earth, and all the other planets of the Solar System, in their orbits around the Sun.

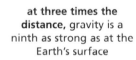

■ key words

- field
- force
- mass
- weight

▼ The force of gravity acting on a rocket is related to its distance from the centre of the Earth. The pull of gravity falls very quickly as the rocket leaves Earth.
At twice the distance from the Earth's centre, gravity is a quarter the strength it is on the Earth's surface.

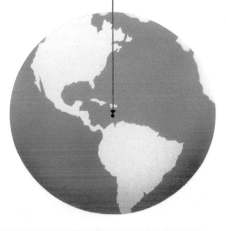

at three times the distance, gravity is a ninth as strong as at the Earth's surface

at twice the distance from the Earth's centre, gravity is a quarter its strength on the Earth's surface

rocket

distance from centre of Earth

▶ If you drop one ball and throw another forward from the same height, both balls take exacly the same time to reach the ground. This is because both balls fall the same vertical distance.

▼ An astronaut floats in space high above the Earth. In space, an astronaut is weightless and is said to experience 'zero gravity'. However, gravity is not zero in space. It is still acting on the astronaut and causes him or her to move in an orbit around the Earth.

▼ Imagine standing on a tower high enough to be outside the Earth's atmosphere. If you threw a ball from the tower, gravity will pull it to Earth (a). But if you could throw the ball as fast as a rocket (b), the curve of its fall would match the curve of the Earth, and the ball would orbit the Earth.

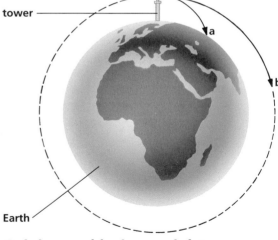

tower

a

b

Earth

Gaining and losing weight

Gravity gives everything its weight. The force of gravity between you and the Earth pulls you down, and your weight is the amount of force that you exert on the ground – or on a weighing machine.

However, if you were to fly to the Moon, you would weigh only a sixth of your Earth weight. This is because the Moon is much smaller than the Earth, and has only about a sixth of the Earth's gravity.

Orbits

Everything, everywhere, is moving. Out in space, satellites, moons, planets and stars are in non-stop motion. Inside the atoms that make up everything, tiny particles are moving non-stop, too. All these things move in the same way – in orbits.

An orbit is a circular or oval path around a centre of some kind. Man-made satellites and the Moon orbit around the Earth, while the Earth and other planets orbit the centre of the Solar System, the Sun. Stars, including the Sun, go round and round the centre of the group of stars which is called the Galaxy.

In every atom, one or more electrons go round the nucleus, a particle at the centre of the atom.

▶ Spacecraft meet in space high above the Earth as a new section called *Unity* (foreground) is added to the International Space Station (centre). The incoming spacecraft fires its rocket engines to go faster and so reach the same orbit as the station.

◀ Tie an object firmly to some string and whirl it around. You pull on the string to keep it in an orbit around your hand. Likewise, gravity between the Sun and Earth pulls on the Earth to keep it in orbit around the Sun.

key words
- orbit
- satellite

A central pull

All orbiting things, from tiny electrons to huge stars, keep to their paths because a force comes from the centre and pulls them into an orbit. Out in space, this force is gravity. Inside atoms, this is electrical force.

Without these central forces, all the satellites, moons, planets and stars would leave their orbits and fly off into space. And all atoms would blow apart as electrons left their orbits.

Reaching orbit

Large rockets launch satellites and spacecraft into Earth's orbit. They must reach orbital velocity – a speed of 28,000 kilometres per hour – to stay in orbit, or they crash back to Earth. Once in orbit a satellite needs no power, because there is no air friction in space to slow it down.

At a speed of 40,000 kilometres per hour ('escape velocity') a spacecraft can escape from Earth's orbit altogether, and go into orbit around the Sun.

Clocks and watches

If you were born on 29 February, you are four years older on every birthday! You have only one birthday every four years. This is because of the way we measure time.

Units of time come from the Earth's movement. One day is the time it takes the Earth to make one turn on its axis. One year is the time it takes the Earth to travel once around the Sun. There are actually 365¼ days in one year. So every four years, we add an extra day (29 February) to make up the difference.

What's the time?

People divide the day into smaller units of time – hours, minutes and seconds. A day has 24 hours, an hour 60 minutes, and each minute 60 seconds. We use clocks and watches to keep track of hours, minutes and seconds.

Clocks and watches all work in the same basic way. A power source, usually a battery or spring, moves hands around a dial or lights up a display. A regulator controls the

● **key words**
- day
- time
- year

▲ Long ago, people used sundials to tell the time. The shadow of the pointer was like an hour hand. Sundials work because the shadow moves round the dial at the same rate as the Earth turns on its axis.

movement of the hands, or the change of numbers in the display, so that the clock or watch keeps good time. The regulator is a spring, pendulum or vibrating crystal that keeps a steady pace.

Scientists measure time very accurately using an atomic clock, which counts vibrations of atoms. It is so accurate that it would be only about one second out after working for a million years.

HOW CLOCKS AND WATCHES WORK

In a mechanical clock or watch, the power to move the hands comes from a coiled mainspring as it slowly unwinds. A small hairspring, which coils and uncoils at a regular rate, controls the speed at which the hands move, so that the clock or watch keeps good time.

In a digital clock or watch, a quartz crystal, powered by a battery, vibrates at thousands of times a second. This accurately controls the change of numbers in the display so that the watch shows the right time.

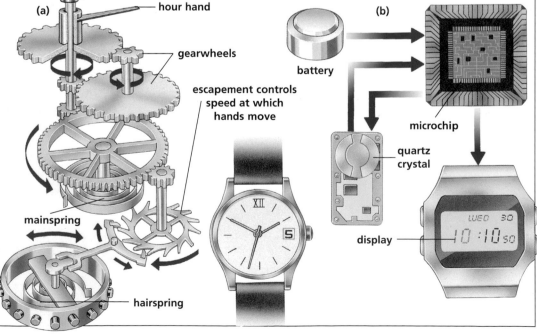

minute hand

(a)
hour hand
gearwheels
escapement controls speed at which hands move
mainspring
hairspring

(b)
battery
microchip
quartz crystal
display

Relativity

If you could travel in a super-fast spacecraft at 99 per cent of the speed of light to the star Sirius and back, 17½ years would pass on Earth before you returned. But time would slow down on the journey. On your return, you would be only 2½ years older!

The theory of relativity says that, to an outside observer, time is seen to slow down for moving things. They have to move very fast – near to the speed of light (300,000 kilometres a second) – for time to slow very much. No spacecraft can move this fast, but fast-moving particles show that relativity really is true.

The ultimate speed limit

Time is not the only quantity to change for fast-moving things. To an outside observer the mass of an object increases as it moves faster, and its length decreases.

The theory of relativity says that the mass of an object would become infinitely great if it moved at the speed of light. Infinite mass is impossible. Therefore, nothing can move at or faster than the speed of light.

Creating energy

Relativity also explains that mass changes into energy. This means that a material can be destroyed and turn into energy, such as heat and light. It explains how the Sun

● **key words**
- mass
- relativity
- speed of light
- time

▼ Einstein worked out his theory of relativity after it had been found that the speed of light is always the same, no matter how fast the person measuring it is moving. If the train driver and the person on the ground both measured the speed of the light coming from the signal, they would get the same result, even though the train is rushing towards the light.

shines. It produces immense heat because gas at its centre is changing into huge amounts of energy.

Nuclear reactors in nuclear power stations work in this way too. They convert a small amount of nuclear fuel into a huge amount of heat energy. The heat is then used to generate electricity.

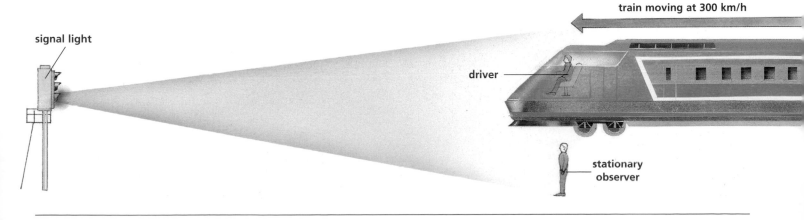

train moving at 300 km/h

signal light

driver

stationary observer

Heat

If you hold the wooden handle of a spade, and then touch the metal, the metal feels colder than the wood, even though the two materials are really the same temperature. This is because of the way heat flows.

Your fingertips are warmer than the metal. Heat flows easily into the metal from them, because metal is a good conductor. As they lose heat, your fingertips get cooler and they feel cold. Heat does not flow easily into wood, which is a poor conductor. That's why your fingertips stay warm when they touch it.

HOW HEAT FLOWS

In a kitchen, heat usually comes from burning gas or electricity. The heat has to flow into food to cook it. Heat flows in three ways – conduction, convection and radiation.

Heat from a gas flame or electric hotplate enters the base of the saucepan. It flows through the metal, and into the water in the pan, by conduction.

Heat flows through the water by convection. Currents of hot water rise from the base of the pan and carry heat to all the water.

Red-hot wires heated by electricity toast bread in a toaster. The hot wire gives out heat rays that heat everything they meet. This kind of heat flow is called radiation.

Gain and loss

Heat is a form of energy, and everything has a certain amount of heat. An object gets hotter if heat flows into it and it gains more heat. If heat flows away, an object gets colder.

Everything is made of atoms and molecules that are moving. When heat flows into something, it makes these particles move faster. When heat is lost, they slow down.

▲ Most materials contract when they get colder, but water expands as it freezes to ice. This makes ice less dense than water, which causes ice to float in water, like this iceberg.

Heating up

Rub your hands together quickly: they soon feel warm. The friction makes the particles in your skin speed up, and it gets hotter. Striking a match produces enough heat in this way to cause the head of the match to burst into flame.

The Sun is our main source of heat. Heat rays radiate out from the Sun. Solar heating systems store the Sun's heat and use it to warm buildings and heat water.

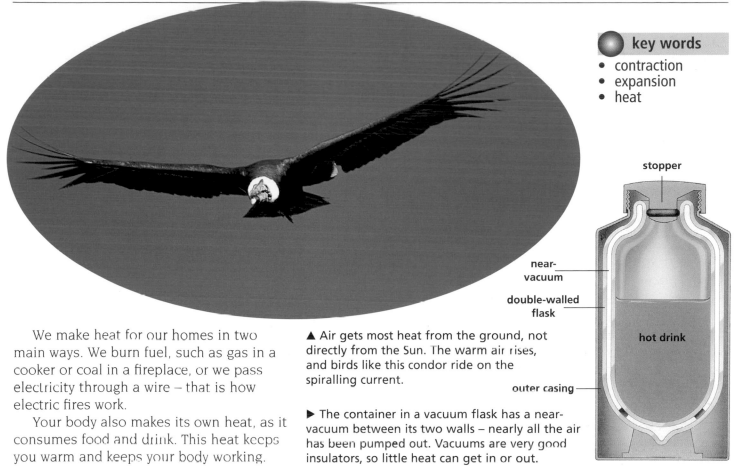

We make heat for our homes in two main ways. We burn fuel, such as gas in a cooker or coal in a fireplace, or we pass electricity through a wire – that is how electric fires work.

Your body also makes its own heat, as it consumes food and drink. This heat keeps you warm and keeps your body working.

Bigger and smaller

Heat not only makes particles move faster. It also makes them move apart, which is why a heated object expands. When Concorde was flying, its hull got very hot and expanded by about 25 centimetres!

In the same way, when something gets colder, the particles slow down and move together, so the object contracts and gets smaller.

Heating a container of gas raises its pressure as the gas particles move faster and strike the container walls with greater force. A car engine burns fuel to make hot gases, and the hot, high-pressure gases drive the engine's moving parts. A jet plane's engine works in the same way. Both of these types of engine are known as heat engines.

▲ Air gets most heat from the ground, not directly from the Sun. The warm air rises, and birds like this condor ride on the spiralling current.

stopper

near-vacuum

double-walled flask

hot drink

outer casing

▶ The container in a vacuum flask has a near-vacuum between its two walls – nearly all the air has been pumped out. Vacuums are very good insulators, so little heat can get in or out.

▶ In this thermograph (heat picture) of a person holding a burger, hotter and colder parts appear in different colours. The hottest parts, such as the burger itself, show up red. Parts coloured blue or purple, such as the bun, are the coldest.

Temperature

Why do you shiver when it's cold, and sweat when it's hot? It is your body's way of keeping itself at the same steady temperature. If your temperature changes too much, you feel ill.

When you measure temperature, the number of degrees tells you how hot or how cold something is. If you are well, your body temperature is about 37°C (degrees Celsius or Centigrade). Shivering makes you warmer, and helps to stop your temperature falling lower in cold weather. Sweating cools you down, and stops your body from overheating.

> **key words**
> - Celsius
> - centigrade
> - Fahrenheit
> - temperature
> - thermometer
> - thermostat

By degrees

A temperature of 37°C is warm. Ice is cold and has a temperature of 0°C, while boiling water has a temperature of 100°C.

Temperatures in degrees Celsius or Centigrade are on the Celsius scale. There is another scale called the Fahrenheit scale. Ice has a temperature of 32°F (degrees Fahrenheit), your body 98°F, and boiling water 212°F.

Thermometers measure temperature. A glass thermometer contains a thin tube in which a liquid moves up and down a scale of degrees to show the temperature. This liquid is usually mercury or coloured alcohol. The liquid rises when it is warmed and drops when cooled. A digital thermometer has a screen that displays the number of degrees.

▶ Temperatures range from absolute zero, the lowest possible temperature, up to temperatures of millions of degrees inside the Sun and other stars. Substances freeze, melt or boil at set temperatures.

◀ A clinical thermometer is a special glass thermometer used to measure body temperature. It has a small range of temperature a few degrees above and below normal, which is about 37°C or 98°F.

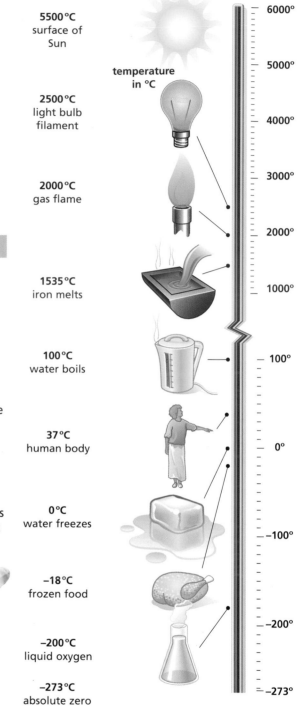

temperature in °C

5500°C
surface of Sun

2500°C
light bulb filament

2000°C
gas flame

1535°C
iron melts

100°C
water boils

37°C
human body

0°C
water freezes

−18°C
frozen food

−200°C
liquid oxygen

−273°C
absolute zero

6000°

5000°

4000°

3000°

2000°

1000°

100°

0°

−100°

−200°

−273°

Keeping warm

A heating system keeps the rooms of a house at a comfortable temperature. It contains devices called thermostats that detect and control the room temperature. The thermostat switches the heating on if the room is too cool, and off when it gets too hot.

Electric kettles also have thermostats. They switch the kettle off when the water gets to the temperature at which it boils.

Refrigeration

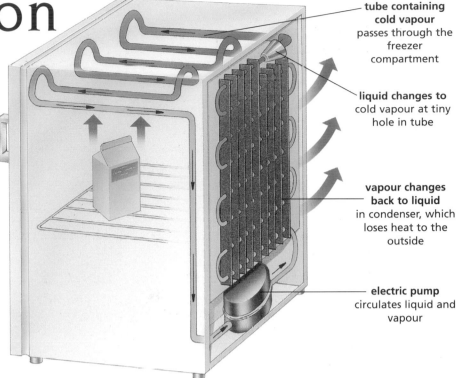

tube containing
cold vapour
passes through the
freezer
compartment

liquid changes to
cold vapour at tiny
hole in tube

vapour changes
back to liquid
in condenser, which
loses heat to the
outside

electric pump
circulates liquid and
vapour

Wet your finger and blow on it. Your finger gets cold before it dries. Refrigerators work in a similar way to keep food and drinks cool.

Blowing air over a wet finger makes the water quickly evaporate or dry up. Water loses heat as it evaporates. It takes this heat from your finger, which gets colder.

Refrigerators and freezers use evaporation to remove heat from food and drinks. A refrigerator cools food and drinks to a temperature just above freezing. This keeps them fresh for a few days, because bacteria do not multiply so fast at low temperatures, so the food does not decay. In a freezer, food is frozen to a temperature of about −18°C, and this preserves it for a long time, because bacteria cannot multiply at all below freezing.

How a refrigerator works

Inside a refrigerator is a tube containing a liquid called a refrigerant. The liquid

key words

- evaporation
- liquid
- refrigerant
- vapour

▼ The cold tubes of a refrigeration system pass through the base of an ice rink to keep the ice frozen.

▲ A refrigerator takes heat from inside the freezer compartment, and transfers it to the warm condenser outside. Cold air descends from the freezer compartment to cool the whole interior.

passes through a tiny hole inside the tube, which makes it evaporate and become a vapour. It gets very cold, and takes heat from inside the refrigerator so that the contents are cooled.

The tube, now containing cold vapour, goes to the rear of the refrigerator. The refrigerant changes back into a liquid, which makes it gain heat. The heat taken from the food warms the tube, which is why the back of the refrigerator is warm. Then the liquid refrigerant returns to the inside to evaporate and cool again.

Freezers and air conditioning units work in the same way as refrigerators.

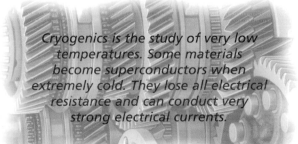

Cryogenics is the study of very low temperatures. Some materials become superconductors when extremely cold. They lose all electrical resistance and can conduct very strong electrical currents.

Fuels

If you could take the energy from just one litre of petrol and use it to power yourself, then you would be able to cycle over 500 kilometres! Petrol is just one of several energy-rich fuels that we use to produce power.

Just about every time you switch on a light, use a heater, cooker or a powered machine, or take a ride in a car, bus, train or plane, you are causing fuel to burn.

We depend on machines like these, so we need an abundant source of energy to power them. Fuels are the most useful energy source we have. They contain a lot of energy that we can release as heat energy simply by burning them. Fuels provide much more energy than other energy sources such as solar power and wind power.

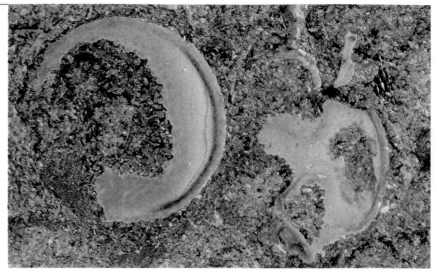

▲ In this slice of coal, the yellow areas are the leaves of some of the plants that formed the coal.

1 Oil and gas formed from tiny sea creatures that died millions of years ago. and sank to the seabed.

2 Layers of rock gradually built up over the sea creatures. Heat and pressure under the earth changed their remains into liquid oil and gas.

1 The forests that formed coal grew in the Carboniferous Period, about 300 million years ago. In swampy areas, the trees and plants decayed very slowly.

2 The rotting plants formed a layer of spongy material called peat.

3 The peat was slowly buried under layers of mud and sand. It formed a soft coal called lignite.

▶ Coal, oil and gas are known as fossil fuels because they are the remains of things that lived millions of years ago. Coal is the remains of ancient forests that grew millions of years ago. Oil and gas are found where there were seas long ago.

4 After millions of years underground, the lignite was squashed into layers of hard coal.

Heat is power

Some heaters and cookers burn fuel like gas to make and use heat directly. Cars and most other kinds of transport have engines that burn petrol or other fuel. Even electric trains, lights and other electrical machines use fuel – the electricity that powers them comes mostly from power stations that burn fuel such as coal.

The main fuels are coal, crude oil or petroleum, and natural gas. These are known as fossil fuels. Petrol and diesel for engines come from crude oil.

Another important fuel is nuclear fuel. It produces huge amounts of heat energy, and is used in nuclear power stations to generate electricity.

An energy-hungry world

We burn fuels in huge quantities, but this produces smoke, fumes and waste gases that pollute the air, causing illness and damaging buildings. One product of burning fuels is carbon dioxide, an invisible gas that enters the atmosphere. Rising levels of carbon dioxide are causing global warming, a gradual rise in temperature at the Earth's surface that could bring about serious damage in the future.

The waste from nuclear fuel is very dangerous to health, and storing this waste is also a cause for concern.

key words
- burning
- fossil fuels
- heat
- nuclear fuel
- pollution

THE FUTURE OF FUEL

Fuels come from deposits underground, which will eventually run out. Although new deposits may be found in the future, it makes sense to try to use up less fuel so that the deposits will last longer.

Using cars with smaller engines, and insulating houses to reduce heat losses, are two good ways of cutting back on fuels. Using less fuel also helps to reduce pollution and global warming.

We can also tackle the problem by finding alternative sources of fuel. Renewable resources include energy from the Sun, which will not run out for another 4500 million years.

▼ In hot countries, people may collect cow dung and then dry it in the Sun to produce a fuel.

3 The liquid oil and gas slowly moved upwards through tiny holes in the rocks above them.

4 Eventually the oil and gas reached a rock layer that they could not pass through, and deposits collected.

Coal

A century ago, many cities were full of grimy, dark, black buildings. They were coated with soot – black powder from the smoke from coal fires. Nowadays, cities are much cleaner as smoke no longer fills the air. But coal remains an important fuel.

Coal is a hard, black substance made of carbon. It catches fire and burns fiercely when strongly heated. It is found in deposits underground and at the surface of the ground. Coal formed over millions of years from the remains of trees and plants.

Peat is coal at an early stage of its formation. It is brown and softer than coal, and is found at the surface, not deep underground.

key words

- bitumen
- coke
- opencast
- steam engine

▲ This massive excavator cuts coal from a huge opencast mine.

Mining coal

If the deposits of coal are at or near the surface of the ground, the coal is dug out in vast pits called opencast mines. Huge excavating machines strip off any soil covering the coal, and dig out the coal beneath.

Coal often lies in seams or layers deep underground. At underground mines, shafts go down to the seams. Miners take lifts down to the seams, and then dig tunnels through the seams as they remove the coal. They use cutting machines to dig out the coal. Conveyor belts take the coal back to the shafts, where lifts raise it to the surface buildings.

Industrial power

Coal brought the people of the 17th and early 18th centuries comfort at home, the means to travel widely, and lots of useful goods and products. It powered steam locomotives on railways, and ocean-going passenger ships. Factories burned coal to power steam engines and to produce heat for manufacturing products. People used coal and peat to heat their homes, burning them in open fires that could also heat running water for warm baths.

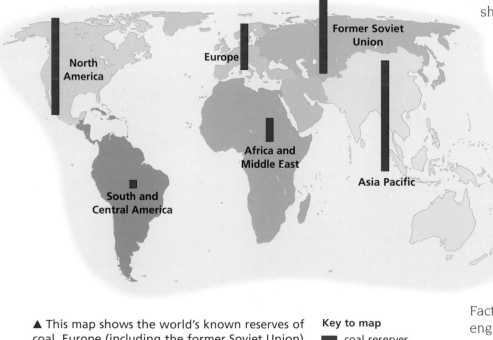

North America

Europe

Former Soviet Union

Africa and Middle East

Asia Pacific

South and Central America

▲ This map shows the world's known reserves of coal. Europe (including the former Soviet Union) has about a third of the world's coal, while North America and Asia each have about a quarter. These reserves should last for several hundred years.

Key to map
■ coal reserves

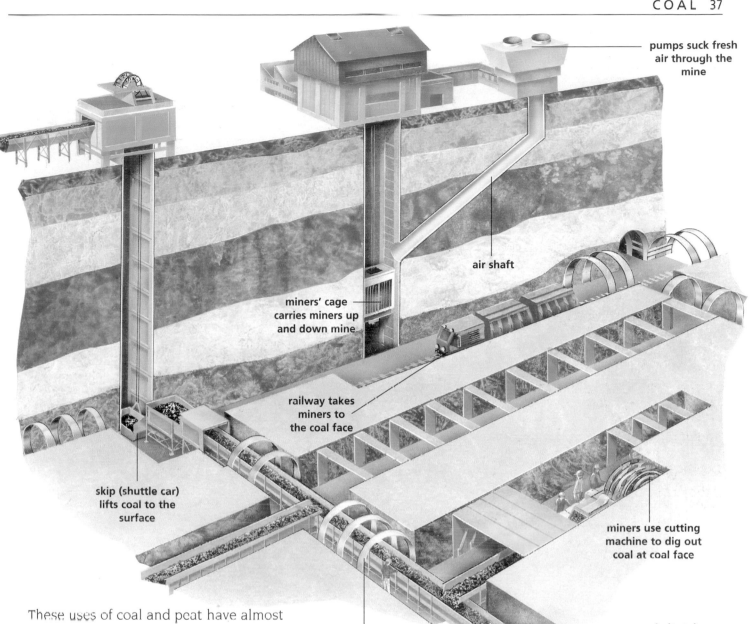

pumps suck fresh air through the mine

air shaft

miners' cage carries miners up and down mine

railway takes miners to the coal face

skip (shuttle car) lifts coal to the surface

miners use cutting machine to dig out coal at coal face

supports hold roof and sides of tunnels in place

conveyer belts take coal to shaft

These uses of coal and peat have almost disappeared as new and cleaner sources of energy – oil, gas and electricity – have replaced them.

Useful products

Peat is now used mainly for growing garden plants, but coal is still an important source of power. Many power stations burn coal to raise steam to drive electricity generators. Factories making products such as cement burn coal to provide the heat for the manufacturing process.

Coal also provides useful products for industry. Heating coal without air produces coke, which is used to make steel. Bitumen for surfacing roads comes from coal, and coal also contains chemicals used to make dyes, drugs and plastics.

▲ An underground coal mine is a maze of tunnels. Some lead from the main shaft to the seams or layers of coal. Other tunnels are formed as the miners cut away the coal deposits. The tunnels may be many kilometres long: in coastal areas, they may extend out under the seabed.

Did you know that you can use coal products to wash yourself? Coal is not only used as a fuel. Coal is also a source of chemicals that can be processed to make soap and dyes, as well as medicines, pesticides and other products.

Oil and gas

If you could dig deep, far below the ground you might find a liquid, so dark and so precious that it is sometimes called 'black gold'. It is crude oil. It is a valuable fuel that powers transport and machines, and it also contains a whole range of useful chemicals.

Crude oil, often called petroleum or simply oil, lies sealed in cavities in rock deep under the land and under the seabed. In these deposits, there may also be large quantities of natural gas, mainly methane.

Oil and gas deposits formed over millions of years from the buried remains of animals and plants that lived in ancient seas.

Drilling for oil

Experts search for deposits of oil and gas by studying the layers of rock deep beneath the land and seabed. They locate cavities where deposits are likely to lie. But the only way to be sure is to drill for oil or gas.

On land, a drilling rig is set up. This lowers a sharp drill into the ground. In soft ground, the drill can dig down 60 metres every hour.

key words
• gas
• oil
• refinery
• rig
• terminal

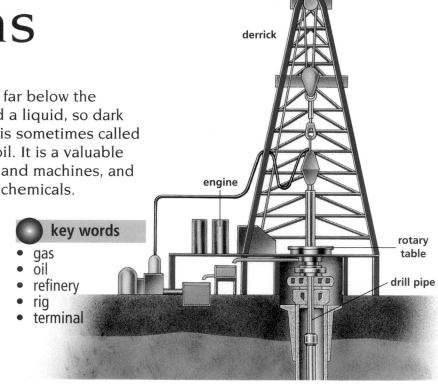

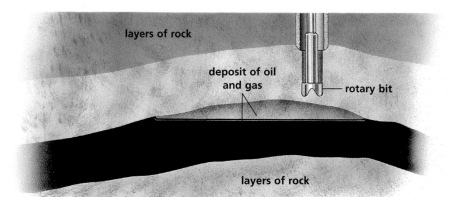

▲ An oil rig drills a deep shaft into the ground to find a deposit of oil or gas. The deposit may be hundreds of metres down.

At sea, a drilling rig is built on tall legs that go down to the seabed. If the water is too deep, the rig floats at the surface. The rig sends a drill down through the water to the seabed, and drills down into it.

◀ Saudi Arabia and other countries of the Middle East have about 65 per cent of the world's known reserves of oil. The United States has about 5 per cent and Europe, including Russia, about 7 per cent. These reserves are expected to last for about 50 more years.

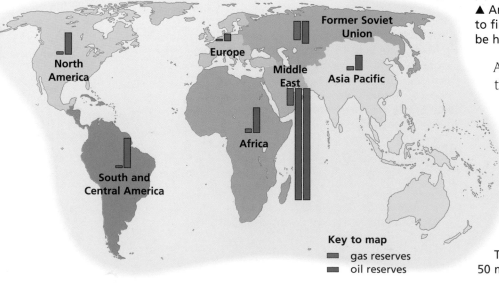

Key to map
 gas reserves
 oil reserves

Striking oil

If the drill meets a deposit, the oil or gas flows back up the shaft or is pumped up. The shaft becomes an oil well or gas well.

On land, the oil rig is taken down and the top of the well is fitted with pipes to take the oil or gas away. At sea, the rig is removed and a production platform towed out to the drilling site. This may be a huge tower that stands on the seabed and supports a platform above the water. Or the production platform may float. Pipes go down from the platform to the oil well on the seabed.

▼ At an oil refinery the crude oil is separated into many different products. The main ones are fuels (such as liquid petroleum gas (LPG), petrol, paraffin and diesel), lubricating oils, and bitumen for surfacing roads.

▲ Oil deep below the seabed flows up shafts to a production platform. There the oil is treated to remove water and also waste gas, which may burn off in a flare. The oil is piped or sent by tanker to a refinery, which may also receive oil pumped up from oil wells on land.

Using oil and gas

Tankers and pipelines carry the oil to oil refineries. The crude oil contains lots of useful substances, including diesel, petrol and kerosene. At the refinery, these different substances are separated out.

Tankers and pipes take gas to gas terminals, too. There the gas is purified and then piped direct to homes and factories, or bottled for use in places with no direct gas supply. In homes, gas is used for cooking and heating. It is also used as a source of heat for industry, and some power stations burn gas to produce electricity.

▶ After refining, products such as liquid petroleum gas (LPG) and petrol are stored in huge tanks before being pumped into road tankers, oil drums or canisters for delivery.

The world's production of oil is about 30,000 million barrels per year (one barrel is 159 litres of oil). This is enough oil to fill approximately 10 million public swimming pools.

Water power

The sight of a mighty waterfall like Niagara Falls is awesome. The water roars as it strikes the river or rocks far below. Can such enormous power be harnessed? In fact, a fifth of the world's electricity comes from water power.

Not all power stations burn fuel. The most powerful ones are hydroelectric, which means they generate electricity from water. The power station at the Itaipu Dam on the River Paraná, Paraguay, for example, generates over 12,500 megawatts of electricity – twice as much as the biggest coal-powered plants.

Hydroelectric power stations do not use up the water or turn it into something else. Flowing or falling water has energy, and a hydroelectric station changes some of the energy into electricity. When the water comes out of the power station, it moves less fast, because it has given up some of its energy.

● **key words**
- hydroelectric
- pumped storage
- tidal power

▲ A waterwheel turns as water flows from a channel over the blades mounted on the wheel. The turbines in hydroelectric power stations work in the same basic way, but produce more power.

Electricity from water

High dams are built across river valleys to create large reservoirs or artificial lakes that can supply people with water. A dam may contain a hydroelectric power station. Water from the reservoir flows down through the dam to drive the station's turbines, which in turn drive generators that produce electricity.

Hydroelectric stations are also built without high dams. They take water from fast-flowing rivers or are fed with water piped down from high lakes.

Many rivers flow too slowly to be used for generating electricity, or their valleys are not deep enough to be dammed. Hydroelectric stations are built mainly in mountainous regions with heavy rainfall, such as Switzerland, Norway, Sweden and

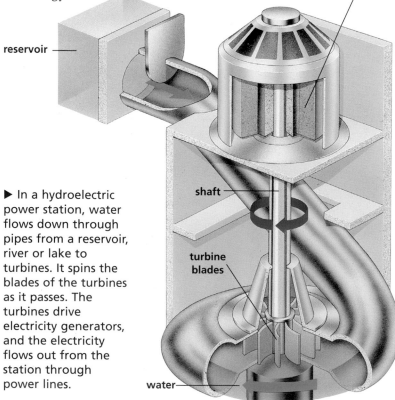

electricity generator

reservoir

shaft

turbine blades

water

▶ In a hydroelectric power station, water flows down through pipes from a reservoir, river or lake to turbines. It spins the blades of the turbines as it passes. The turbines drive electricity generators, and the electricity flows out from the station through power lines.

THE THREE GORGES DAM
The world's largest hydroelectric project is under construction in the region of the Three Gorges on the Yangtze River, China. Plans call for a dam 185 metres high and 2 kilometres long to create a reservoir extending 600 kilometres along the valley. When completed in 2009, the dam will generate about 18,000 megawatts of electricity – about 10 per cent of China's total electricity needs. But the project will drown 19 cities and displace almost 2 million people.

▶ At the mouth of the River Rance in northern France is a tidal power station. As the tide rises and falls, water flows rapidly into and out of the river. The water passes through turbines in a barrier across the river, and the turbines drive electricity generators. The power station generates 240 megawatts of electricity.

In 1968, the building of the Aswan High Dam in Egypt began to create a large lake that would drown the ancient temple at Abu Simbel. So, before the lake rose, the whole temple and its magnificent statues were cut out of the rock and rebuilt above the final water line.

Canada. Some large rivers have been dammed to provide power and also to prevent the rivers from flooding. These great dams include the Aswan High Dam across the River Nile in Egypt, and the Three Gorges Dam across the River Yangtze in China.

Clean and everlasting

Water power is a clean source of power. Unlike the burning of fuels, tapping the energy in flowing water does not pollute the air and cause global warming.

Furthermore, hydroelectric power stations are not using up a valuable source of energy. The water in rivers and lakes is constantly replaced by fresh rain.

Hydroelectric power stations produce about 20 per cent of the world's electricity. Building more hydroelectric stations would save fuel and reduce pollution and global warming. However, building in mountainous regions is difficult and costly.

Much of electricity generated there would be lost as it would have to travel a long way to cities. Most large rivers are not suitable for damming, and the creation of large reservoirs can cause hardship to the people who have to move away from the land that is to be drowned.

◀ The generator hall of the hydroelectric power station at Hoover Dam, USA. The huge electricity generators are driven by water turbines below the floor of the hall.

Renewable resources

In a tiny desert village in Rajasthan, India, an ordinary-looking lamp post shows how energy use is changing. This village has no electricity supply, but the lamp stores the Sun's energy by day to light the village at night. In the future, all people will need everlasting sources of energy like this.

We need energy sources to power all our machines and for cooking and heating in our homes. The Sun's energy, or solar energy, is one of several renewable energy sources that produce energy all the time.

At present we mainly use fuels to produce energy. Once burned, fuels are finished – they are not renewable. Our sources of fuel will run out in the future, and people will then depend on renewable energy.

Energy crisis

The world's known reserves of oil and gas are likely to run out by 2050. Today's nuclear power stations may have closed by then. Few new nuclear power stations are

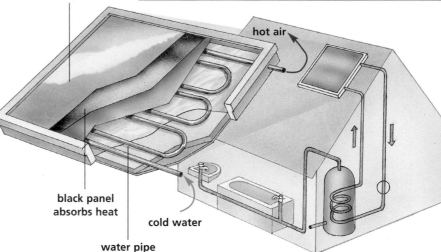

glass traps heat

hot air

black panel absorbs heat

cold water

water pipe

▼ This experimental car is powered by the Sun. It is covered with solar cells that use sunlight to generate electricity and power the car's electric motor. Solar cells are likely to become an important source of energy in the future.

▲ Inside a solar heating panel is a layer of black material, which gets hot when the Sun shines on it. The material heats water flowing through a pipe in the panel. The hot water goes to heat the house or supply hot water to taps. Using solar heating cuts electricity or fuel costs.

being built, as many people consider them too dangerous, although scientists hope that power from nuclear fusion will soon be a reality. Coal will remain the only available fuel, and it could be used to make other fuels such as petrol. Known coal reserves will last for hundreds of years.

Using more renewable energy will cut back on fuel and make reserves last longer. Unlike fuels, renewable energy does not cause pollution and global warming, and it will reduce this damage too.

Everlasting energy

There are five main kinds of renewable resources. Hydroelectric power stations,

◀ This wind farm has rows of giant turbines. The wind spins the blades of each rotor, which drives an electricity generator at its hub. The photo has been 'cross-processed' to show the structure of the turbines more clearly.

More to come

Renewable resources do not produce much energy and are unlikely ever to meet all our energy needs. The International Energy Agency has forecast that by 2010, 3 per cent of all our energy will come from hydroelectric power and only 1 per cent from other renewable resources. Coal, oil and gas will provide 90 per cent of our energy.

One reason for this is that generating electricity by solar power is costly. But as the fuels needed to produce electricity become rarer, they will also be more expensive. Then the use of solar power should increase.

which generate electricity from flowing water, produce the most energy.

Solar power taps the Sun's energy in two ways. Solar panels, often on roofs of houses, face the Sun and absorb solar rays of heat and light. Some panels tap the Sun's heat to warm a house or provide hot water. Photovoltaic panels or solar cells turn the Sun's rays into electricity, which may be stored in a battery for use later.

Geothermal power taps the energy inside the Earth. In some places, underground rocks are very hot. Water is heated by piping it through the hot rocks. In Iceland, most homes are heated in this way.

Wind turbines tap the energy of moving air. The wind turns the blades of the turbine, which drive an electricity generator. Wind turbines line high ridges or coasts in windy regions. Wind power is being used in many countries, particularly Germany, India, Denmark and Spain.

Wave machines of various kinds tap the energy of water as it rises and falls in waves and convert the energy into electricity. This renewable resource is still undergoing development.

▼ Geothermal power stations may be built where hot rocks lie close to the surface, for example in volcanic regions. Hot water in the rocks is brought to the surface through a bore hole. There the hot steam drives steam turbines that power electricity generators.

electricity generator

steam turbine

steam separator

steam cools to water

hot water rises through bore hole

cold water returned to ground

cooling tower

Engines and turbines

Have you ever had a machine in your mouth? You probably have – when you were at the dentist's. Inside a dentist's drill is a tiny turbine whizzing round thousands of times a second. It is powered by a stream of air.

Engines, turbines and motors drive most machines and make parts move. Engines burn fuel, while turbines require moving air, steam or water.

Heat engines

Most engines use heat. They burn fuel, such as petrol, in air they suck in. The hot gases produced expand rapidly, and make the parts of the engine move. Petrol and diesel engines in road vehicles and trains, and jet engines in aircraft, work in this way. All these engines are called internal-combustion engines as they burn fuel inside the engine.

In steam engines, hot steam drives the moving parts. Fuel is burned in boilers outside the engine to produce the steam, so these engines are called external-combustion engines.

key words

- external-combustion engine
- internal-combustion engine
- piston engine
- turbine

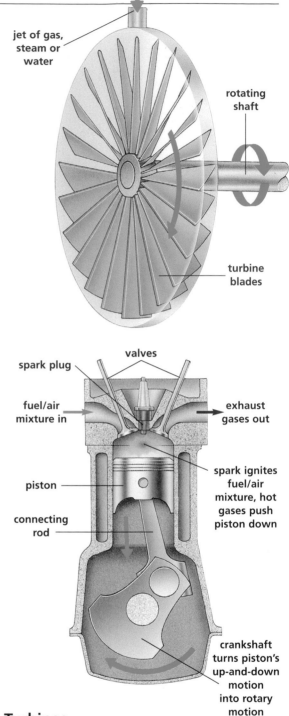

jet of gas, steam or water

rotating shaft

turbine blades

spark plug

valves

fuel/air mixture in

exhaust gases out

piston

spark ignites fuel/air mixture, hot gases push piston down

connecting rod

crankshaft turns piston's up-and-down motion into rotary motion

▶ A turbine (top) produces circular or rotary motion directly. A piston engine (bottom) produces up-and-down motion, which is changed into rotary motion by the crankshaft.

Turbines

A turbine works rather like an old windmill or waterwheel. It has blades that spin round when driven by a moving gas or liquid. Wind turbines use moving air, and water turbines in hydroelectric power stations are driven by moving water. Steam turbines in other power stations are driven by heated steam.

◀ The jet engine of an aircraft is a gas turbine. The blades of the turbine can be seen in the centre of the picture.

Steam engines

You boil a kettle of water to make a cup of tea or coffee – power stations boil water on a far greater scale. This generates the supply of electricity that comes to your home and makes your kettle work.

When water boils, it produces a large amount of hot steam. This steam has a lot of energy. Most power stations burn fuel to boil water, and the hot steam goes to huge steam turbines that drive the generators.

Steam turbines

Inside the turbine are sets of blades fixed to a central shaft. The steam drives the blades around, turning the shaft with great power. The turbine shaft drives an electric generator, and the electricity flows through power lines to homes.

Some large ships are powered by steam turbines, which drive the ship's propellers.

key words

- piston engine
- steam locomotive
- steam turbine

STEAM POWER

The steam engine was developed into a powerful, efficient engine by the British engineer James Watt (1736–1819) in 1769. He improved a slow and inefficient engine invented in 1712 by Thomas Newcomen. Units of power are called watts in honour of his achievement.

Steam trains

The steam engines in old locomotives were piston engines. A coal-fired boiler in the locomotive raised steam, which went to cylinders by the wheels. Inside each cylinder, the steam pushed a piston backwards and forwards and the piston drove a connecting rod and crankshaft that turned the wheels.

Steam piston engines once powered factories and ships, too.

◄ The fastest steam locomotive was *Mallard*, which reached a record speed of 203 kilometres per hour in 1938. It is now in the National Rail Museum in York, England.

A steam turbine can produce a huge amount of power. A large steam turbine generates as much power as all the engines in about 20,000 family cars.

◄ The steam turbine in a power station has several sets of blades all fixed to a central shaft. The steam enters the first set at high pressure and, having turned the blades, leaves at lower pressure. The next sets of blades work at lower pressure. In this way, the turbine uses up nearly all of the energy in the hot steam.

hot steam at high-pressure

fixed turbine blades

cooler, low-pressure steam

rotating turbine blades

Petrol and diesel

Foresters need chainsaws that are powerful enough to cut down big trees, but also light and portable. Only one kind of engine is suitable for the saw – a petrol engine. It carries its own fuel supply and is light yet powerful.

Petrol and diesel engines power all sorts of vehicles, from cars and motorcycles to diesel trains, boats and small aircraft. Being light and portable, petrol engines are also used to drive machines such as lawnmowers and chainsaws.

Inside a petrol engine

A petrol engine contains one or more cylinders in which a piston moves up and down. It produces power by burning petrol in the cylinders. The intense heat causes air in the cylinders to expand violently, driving down the pistons. The pistons turn a crankshaft, which drives the wheels, propeller or other mechanism.

The petrol engine in a car is a four-stroke engine. The piston repeats a cycle of four movements in which it goes up and down twice. Motorcycles and other light machines often have simpler, two-stroke engines. The piston repeats a cycle in which it goes up and down once.

Diesel engines

A diesel engine works in the same way as a petrol engine, except that it needs no spark plug to ignite the fuel. The air is strongly compressed, which causes it to heat up. Fuel is then added, and it immediately ignites in the hot air.

▲ A chainsaw has a rotating chain lined with sharp teeth that cuts into the wood. It is driven by a small but powerful petrol engine, and can cut through a thick trunk or branch quickly and easily.

key words

- catalytic converter
- diesel engine
- four-stroke
- petrol engine
- two-stroke

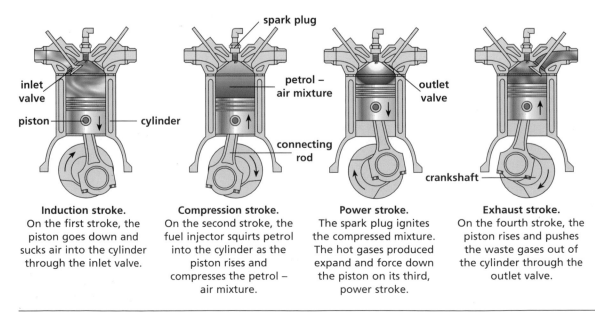

inlet valve
piston — cylinder
spark plug
petrol – air mixture
connecting rod
outlet valve
crankshaft

Induction stroke. On the first stroke, the piston goes down and sucks air into the cylinder through the inlet valve.

Compression stroke. On the second stroke, the fuel injector squirts petrol into the cylinder as the piston rises and compresses the petrol – air mixture.

Power stroke. The spark plug ignites the compressed mixture. The hot gases produced expand and force down the piston on its third, power stroke.

Exhaust stroke. On the fourth stroke, the piston rises and pushes the waste gases out of the cylinder through the outlet valve.

◀ A four-stroke petrol engine repeats a cycle of four strokes, or movements, in which the piston goes up and down the cylinder twice. Car engines usually have four cylinders, each on a different stroke at any time.

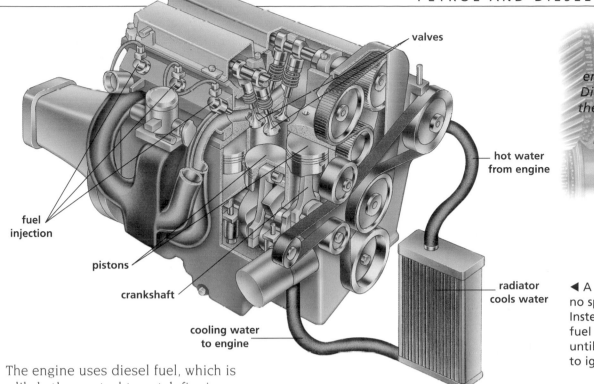

valves

fuel injection

pistons

crankshaft

cooling water to engine

hot water from engine

radiator cools water

The German engineer Rudolf Diesel developed the diesel engine. He patented his invention in 1892.

◀ A diesel engine has no spark plugs. Instead, the injected fuel is compressed until it is hot enough to ignite by itself.

The engine uses diesel fuel, which is less likely than petrol to catch fire in a crash. Diesel engines are simpler in construction, more robust and more fuel-efficient. Unfortunately, they cause more pollution than petrol engines.

Outside the engine

Around a petrol or diesel engine are several systems that make the engine work.

The injection system controls the supply of fuel to the cylinders, squirting in more when the vehicle needs to go faster. In petrol engines, the ignition system makes the fuel ignite at the right moment to give the most power.

The exhaust system leads waste gases away from the cylinders into the atmosphere. The fuel ignites with a bang, and the exhaust system has a silencer that reduces this noise. The waste gases are polluting, and the catalytic converter in the exhaust system makes most of the polluting gases harmless. It does not remove carbon dioxide, though, which causes global warming.

▼ In Thailand, many boats have a petrol or diesel engine and propeller mounted at the end of a long steering handle. This makes it easy to turn the boat quickly. However, the boats are very noisy.

Jet engines

▼ B-58 bomber. Flames roar from the engine of this jet fighter. They come from the afterburner, which burns more fuel in the exhaust to increase power when needed.

Only two centuries ago, it could have taken you a whole day to travel to the nearest city – the fastest stagecoach could not top 300 kilometres in a day. Nowadays, an airliner covers this distance in 20 minutes! Every large city in the world is no more than a day's journey away.

Most airliners cruise at speeds of up to about 1000 kilometres per hour. Supersonic aircraft can travel up to three times as fast. The jet engine makes economical high-speed travel possible. It produces great power without being very heavy.

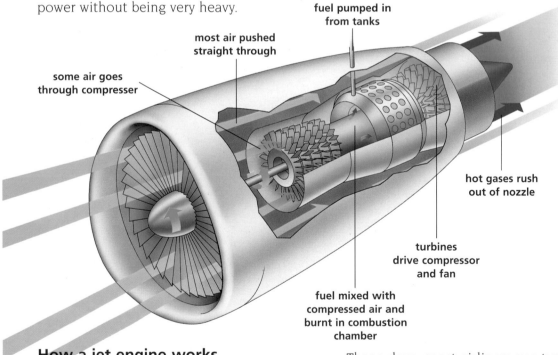

some air goes through compresser

most air pushed straight through

fuel pumped in from tanks

hot gases rush out of nozzle

turbines drive compressor and fan

fuel mixed with compressed air and burnt in combustion chamber

◄ Inside a turbofan jet engine. A huge fan sucks in air. Turbofan engines are much more efficient than turbojets. Some of the air is compressed, then heated in the combustion chamber to increase the pressure even more. This jet of hot air then shoots out of the back of the engine, turning a turbine to power the compresser and the fan as it goes. The rest of the air drawn in by the fan goes around the chamber and out of the back adding an extra 'push' of cooler air.

How a jet engine works

There are three main types of jet engines – turbojets, turbofans and turboprops. A turbojet engine is the basic model. It sucks in air at the front, burns fuel to heat the air, and expels the hot gases from the rear of the engine. The gases leave the engine in a powerful jet, thrusting the engine – and the aircraft – forwards with a strong force.

These days, most airliners use turbofan engines, in which a large outer shell surrounds the jet engine. A turbofan engine produces more power because more air flows through it. The shell surrounding the engine also makes it less noisy. Turboprop engines are often used in helicopters. The turbine drives a shaft connected to the rotors.

key words

- compressor
- turbine
- turbofan

Rockets

The most exciting part of a firework display comes as rockets zoom up into the night sky and burst high above in cascades of colour. All spacecraft get to space and travel there in the same way. Only a rocket engine can carry them up and out into space.

The rocket engines of a spacecraft, such as the space shuttle, work in the same way as a firework rocket. They both burn fuel called a propellant very quickly to produce huge amounts of hot gases. As these gases rush out from the exhaust of the engine or tail of the rocket, they exert a powerful force on the engine or rocket and drive it forwards or upwards.

Beyond the air

Most kinds of transport have engines that burn fuels, such as

▶ The *Ariane* rocket is a huge rocket that launches a payload such as a satellite into space. It has three sections called stages that fire in turn. When its fuel is used up, each stage falls away and the next stage takes over. Only the payload and third stage reach space. Using stages saves fuel.

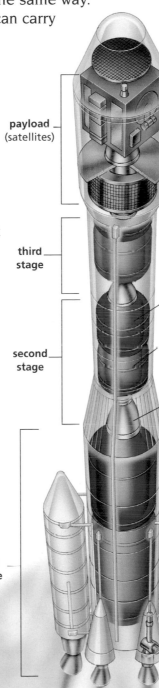

payload (satellites)

third stage

liquid fuel

liquid oxygen

second stage

motor

first stage

booster rocket (solid fuel)

▲ Firework rockets carry a cluster of stars that burn in bright colours. These ignite and burst out when the rocket uses up its solid fuel and is high in the air.

petrol, diesel fuel or paraffin. Fuels need a gas called oxygen to catch fire and burn. This oxygen comes from the air.

Rockets are different. They carry their own oxygen, and so can work beyond the atmosphere where there is no air.

Rocket fuels

Firework rockets and many space rockets that launch spacecraft use fuel made of powder. In this solid fuel is a substance containing oxygen, which enables the fuel to burn. A solid-fuel rocket engine continues to burn until the fuel is used up.

In all spacecraft and many rocket launchers, two liquids are pumped to the engine, where they catch fire and burn. In most liquid-fuel engines, one liquid is liquid oxygen and the other is a liquid fuel such as liquid hydrogen.

Liquid-fuel rocket engines can run for an exact time, then shut down and start again later. This enables spacecraft to change orbit in space, and to return to Earth.

key words

- firework
- propellant
- satellite
- spacecraft
- stage

Electricity and Electronics

Electricity

Blasting out of the sky like a jagged laser beam, a bolt of lightning strikes a tree, scorching it to a blackened crisp. The power of a lightning strike is spectacular and dangerous. What is this strange, violent energy that comes from the sky?

The answer is that lightning is a form of electricity. During a thunderstorm, clouds can store up electricity. When enough electricity has built up, it zaps down from the clouds to the ground in the form of a lightning strike.

Electric power

Lightning is one way in which electricity occurs in nature. But it's man-made electricity that powers much of today's world. Without it, we would have no commonplace gadgets such as personal stereos, computers, televisions, toasters, programmable dishwashers and mobile phones. So what exactly is this stuff called electricity that we all depend on so much?

Charging about

All substances are made of tiny particles called atoms. In the middle of each atom

FRANKLIN'S EXPERIMENT

In 1752, the American statesman and inventor Ben Franklin (1706–1790) undertook a very risky experiment. He flew a kite with a salty thread (which electricity could flow through) near thunderclouds. He managed to get electric current to leak down the thread to charge a Leyden jar – a very early form of battery. This proved that lightning was another form of electricity. Others who tried to copy Franklin's experiment were not so lucky – at least two were struck by lightning and killed.

▼ Lightning over a city. Metal rods called lightning conductors, mounted high on buildings, have been used for hundreds of years to help lightning strikes leak harmlessly to earth.

there is a core called a nucleus. Around this nucleus is a cloud of very light particles called electrons. Electricity results from the behaviour of the electrons, which possess a strange property called electric charge.

No-one knows exactly what electric charge is, but we know there are two kinds: positive and negative. Electrons have a

(a)

electrostatic charge

drum

(b)

light beam

lamp

charge remains in dark area

(c)

toner

(d)

toner transferred to paper

(e)

heated rollers fix image

USING STATIC TO MAKE COPIES

Static electricity plays an important part in the photocopying process. First, a drum inside the photocopier is charged with static electricity (a). Then light is shone on the image being copied. The light reflects onto the drum, and in the bright areas it makes the drum lose charge (b). There is now a pattern of charge on the drum, a copy of the pattern of light and dark on the original image. An ink powder called toner is now spread on the drum, but it only sticks to the charged areas (c). This toner pattern is then transferred from the drum to a piece of paper (d) and fixed by two heated rollers (e).

negative charge. They are attracted towards positive charges (the nucleus of an atom is positively charged) and forced away from, or repelled, by other negative charges.

Atoms have a balance of electric charge, because the positive charges in the nucleus balance out the negative charges of the electrons. But some substances can accept extra electrons, while others lose electrons quite easily. So objects can become electrically charged. This is known as static electricity. Charge cannot build up on materials such as metals because they let electrons flow through them. We call a flow of electric charge 'current electricity'.

Passing on the charge

If you have ever received a small electric shock after walking across a thick carpet and grasping a metal door handle, you will have experienced the effects of static electricity. Static electricity will also make a balloon stick to the wall after you have rubbed it on your hair.

In static electricity, electrons create a stationary charge. For example, when you rub the balloon on your hair, loosely held electrons in your hair are rubbed off on to the balloon. The object that loses the

key words

- atom
- charge
- current
- electron
- static electricity

▶ The charge on a balloon can make your hair stand on end.

electrons (your hair) builds up a positive charge, while the object that gains the electrons (the balloon) builds up a negative charge. The balloon will then stick to the wall because its negative charges are attracted to positive charges in the wall. Similarly, when you walk across a fluffy carpet, loose electrons in the carpet hop on to your body, charging you up. You don't feel this until you grab a metal door handle. Then the electron charge is released into the metal through your hand, and you feel a small shock. You may also hear a crackle, as this electricity makes a spark as it jumps to the metal.

▶ Doctors use the electrical signals made by the brain to find out whether people have certain illnesses.

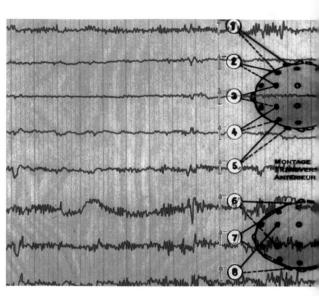

Interestingly, lightning involves both static and current electricity. During a storm, electrons build up inside the lower surface of clouds to make a static electric charge. When the attraction between the negatively charged cloud and the positively charged ground (or even another cloud) is great enough, electrons flow through the air in a searing current that makes the air glow. This is what we call lightning.

Electricity and magnetism

Electricity is very closely related to magnetism. That's because both depend on the way electrons behave. A material can be magnetic if many of its electrons spin in the same direction. When an electric current moves through a wire, it also creates a magnetic field around it. And moving a wire through a magnetic field can produce an electric current in the wire. Both these effects are used in many of the electric machines that we use every day.

Current affairs

In current electricity, electrons are made to flow through a material such as a metal wire. A battery, or another power supply such as mains electricity, pushes electrons through the wires. This flow of electrons creates an electric current. As electric current passes through metal wires, it can power a light bulb, turn a motor or do many other useful jobs.

▲ The high electric current that flows through an electric arc-welder creates a high-temperature 'spark' that is hot enough to melt metal. It can be used to cut through pieces of metal or to join them together.

Our bodies are full of electricity. The 10 billion nerve cells in your brain work by sending messages in the form of bursts of electricity (impulses) to each other. Reading this page will have set off hundreds of impulses as your nerves sent messages from your eyes to your brain.

Conductors and insulators

The ring of an electric cooker glows brightly when electricity is passing through it. But if the ring were made of wood instead of metal, it would not work. That's because some materials do not let electricity pass through them.

▶ These ceramic (pottery) insulators are placed between high-power electricity cables and the pylons that support them. They stop electricity from flowing into the pylon itself.

Materials that let electricity pass through them are called conductors. Materials that don't are called insulators.

Conductors

Conductors are usually made of metal, or at least mainly of metal. Silver and copper are two of the best conductors. Copper is most widely used for electrical wiring.

Metals are good conductors because they have many spare electrons (the tiny particles that move round atoms). These electrons are free to move. They can be made to move by a battery or by mains electricity. When electrons move, or flow, they create an electric current.

Insulators

Insulating materials such as concrete or rubber hold on tightly to their electrons, so the electrons are not free to move. Materials that resist the flow of electricity

key words

- conductor
- electron
- insulator
- semiconductor
- superconductor

▼ The small disc in this photo is a magnet. It is repelled so strongly by the superconductor below that it hovers in mid-air. New trains called maglevs use superconductors and magnets in this way to make the train hover above the track.

can be very useful. Wall sockets and plugs are made of thick plastic, which is a good insulator. This stops us from getting electric shocks.

Special conductors

Electrically, some materials are between conductors and insulators. Materials like this are called semiconductors. Silicon is the best known. Semiconductors can be treated with chemicals to change how well they conduct electricity.

Other materials called superconductors conduct electricity incredibly well at low temperatures. They are also strongly diamagnetic – they strongly repel magnets.

Batteries and cells

There's a car accident, and someone who saw the crash uses their mobile phone to call an ambulance. Minutes later, the injured are being rushed to hospital. The time saved by using a mobile phone could help to save their lives.

Portable gadgets like mobile phones and portable TVs can be extremely useful. But to be portable, they have to get their power from batteries. A battery is a clever collection of chemicals that can react together to make electricity.

Electrical chemistry

How does a battery release electrons? It does so through a carefully chosen pair of chemical reactions. A battery can have one or more parts, called cells. Each cell has two pieces of metal (the electrodes) dipped in a chemical called an electrolyte.

key words

- battery
- terminal
- cell
- electrode
- electrolyte

▼ Solar power. Out in space, satellites cannot be serviced or refuelled. Many of them rely on huge solar panels to generate the electricity they need to work.

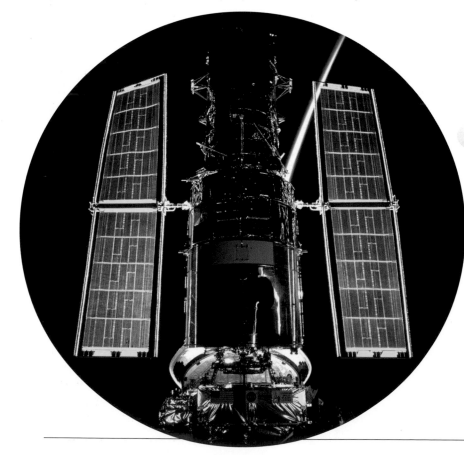

BATTERY VARIETY

Different types of battery use different chemicals to produce electricity. A car has a powerful, rechargeable lead-acid battery (a). The electrodes are made of lead compounds, while the electrolyte is an acid. A personal stereo uses an alkaline battery (b). In this the electrodes are powders, mixed with an electrolyte to make a paste.

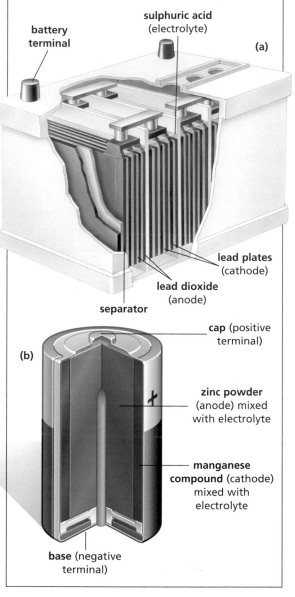

battery terminal

sulphuric acid (electrolyte)

(a)

lead plates (cathode)

lead dioxide (anode)

separator

cap (positive terminal)

(b)

zinc powder (anode) mixed with electrolyte

manganese compound (cathode) mixed with electrolyte

base (negative terminal)

When a battery is connected up, chemical reactions takes place between the electrodes and the electrolyte. At one electrode (the negative terminal or anode), there is a chemical reaction that produces electrons. These electrons can then flow as electricity. At the other electrode (the positive terminal or cathode), another chemical reaction uses up electrons.

Dissolving away

The chemical reactions that happen at the anode and the cathode of a battery affect the materials that they are made of. The anode slowly dissolves away, while the cathode becomes encrusted with chemicals. In some kinds of battery this process cannot be reversed, and the anode eventually wears out. This is what happens when a battery goes flat. But in a rechargeable battery, the chemical reactions that make the battery work can be reversed by connecting the battery up to an electricity supply and running it in reverse. This is what happens when you use a charger to recharge a battery.

▲ The electric motor that drives this experimental car is powered by a fuel cell instead of a battery.

GALVANI AND VOLTA

In 1791 an Italian anatomist called Luigi Galvani (1737–1798) was probing a dead frog's nerves with tools made of different metals. He noticed that when he did this, the frog's leg muscles twitched. Alessandro Volta (1745–1827) at the University of Pavia heard about Galvani's discovery. Volta worked out that the twitching was caused by electricity. The metal instruments were acting like electrodes in a battery, while the fluids in the frog's body were the electrolyte.

Alessandro Volta

This discovery inspired Volta to developed the voltaic pile, in 1799. The pile was a battery with a number of cells, each with one electrode of zinc and one of silver, with a layer of card soaked in salt water between them. This was the world's first-ever battery.

Volta's pile

Luigi Galvani

Solar cells and fuel cells

Batteries are not the only portable sources of electric power – solar cells and fuel cells can also make electricity.

A solar cell makes electricity using sunlight. Inside the cell are special materials that release electrons when they are bathed in light. Solar cells are used, for example, in space probes and satellites. At present they are not very efficient – they can only turn about 15 per cent of the light that falls on them into electrical energy. But scientists hope to make better solar cells in the future.

Fuel cells make electricity using hydrogen as a fuel. A chemical reaction in the fuel cell turns the hydrogen into water, at the same time producing electrons that can flow in a circuit. But hydrogen is difficult and dangerous to store, so engineers are now trying to make fuel cells safe. Fuel cells are more powerful than batteries, and scientists hope that they can soon be used to power cars. Tiny fuel cells may also be used to power personal stereos and tiny 'wearable' computers.

Circuits

Have you ever wondered how flicking a switch on the wall can cause a light bulb to glow on the other side of the room, as if by magic? When you press the switch, a lever brings two pieces of metal together inside the switch. This opens a pathway for electric current to travel along – like lowering the drawbridge for people to enter a castle. Electricity gushes into the light bulb, making it burn brightly.

The path that the electric current flows along is called a circuit. A torch, for example, contains a simple circuit that has three components parts – a battery, a light bulb and a switch. These are joined together in a loop by strips of metal, which conduct electricity.

All electrical equipment and gadgets depend on circuits, which may have different components connected in different ways, depending on the job the piece of equipment does. Whether you are adding numbers on a calculator, watching TV or heating food in a microwave oven, an electric circuit is doing the work for you.

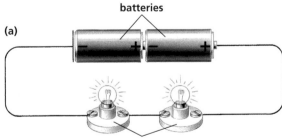

batteries

(a)

bulbs

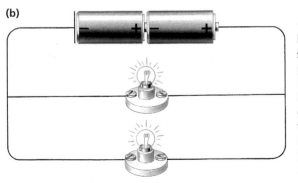

(b)

▶ A torch is an example of a very simple but very useful circuit. A bulb is connected to a battery and a switch. Pushing the switch on lets electrons travel, and the bulb lights up.

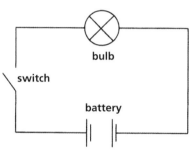

bulb

switch

battery

▲ This circuit diagram shows the torch circuit very simply, using symbols for the bulb, the battery and the switch.

◀ Two identical light bulbs connected in series (a) and in parallel (b). The bulbs in series glow brighter, because each is getting the full current from the batteries. But if one bulb blows in the series circuit, neither bulb will work.

Going with the flow

All circuits need a supply of electricity. The supply will set electrons (tiny particles found in atoms) moving around the circuit.

Electrons carry an electric charge, so as they move they produce a flow of electricity called a current. Current is measured in amperes (amps). If there is a break in the circuit, the current will stop flowing. Electricity does not flow through a circuit by itself. It needs a 'push', or energy, to keep it moving. We call this energy the voltage of the circuit. Voltage is measured in volts (V).

The power used by a device is a measure of how fast it uses energy. Power is measured in watts (W). A bar of an electric fire uses about 1000 W.

Electric power can come either from a battery or from a mains socket. A battery produces direct current (DC): this means

reflector

bulb

positive terminal

switch

connection to bulb from negative terminal

that the current flows one way around the circuit. Mains electricity is alternating current (AC). Alternating current flows first one way round the circuit, then the other, changing direction many times per second.

Resistance

Some electrical components reduce – or resist – the flow of current through a circuit. We say that they have a resistance. When a current flows through a light bulb, for example, the atoms in the bulb's filament – the coiled wire inside the bulb – resist the flow. This causes the atoms to get hot, making the filament glow. Resistance was discovered by Georg Ohm in 1826, and is measured in ohms.

Components called resistors are put into circuits to help control the flow of current through the circuit.

OHM'S LAW

The German scientist Georg Ohm (1787–1854) is best remembered for working out Ohm's Law. He discovered that the voltage across a conductor – such as a strip of metal or a wire – and the current flowing through it, always vary in the same proportion. So if you double the voltage, you double the current. This is incredibly useful, because it lets you predict the current you will get for a particular voltage.

Series and parallel

When there is more than one component (part) in a circuit, they can be connected in one of two ways: in series or in parallel. If the components are in series, each gets the full amount of current. But if one component breaks, the circuit does not work. When components are wired in parallel, each one gets less current, but if one part breaks, the others can still work.

When there is a current of 1 ampere in a circuit, more than a million, million, million electrons flow through it every second.

key words
- battery
- circuit
- current
- resistance
- voltage

▼ Machines like TVs and radios have very complicated circuits with lots of parts. Instead of connecting all the parts with wires, the components are fastened to a circuit board, which has tiny silver tracks connecting them in the right order.

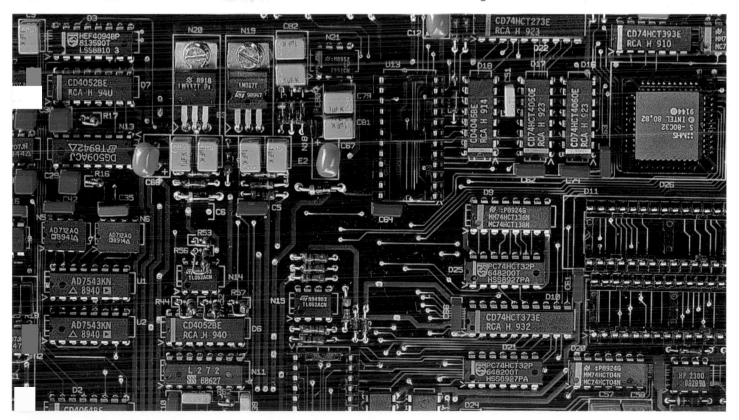

Magnetism and electromagnetism

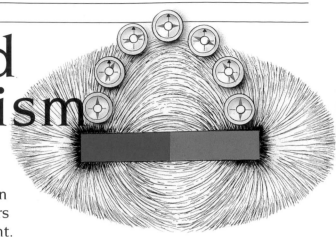

Without magnetism many things we take for granted today would not exist. The electricity that powers all the electrical items in your home, for example, comes from generators that use huge magnets to create electric current. And in many televisions, the picture is moved and changed many times each second by magnets inside the TV tube.

▲ If you scatter tiny iron filings around a magnet, they line up along the lines of magnetic force around the magnet. More filings collect at the poles than anywhere else. A compass needle will also point along the lines of magnetic force.

Magnetism is a force that is found in nature and has been known about for thousands of years. Before scientists discovered how it worked, it was thought to be a magical power. Magnetism is closely related to electricity and can do important work for us.

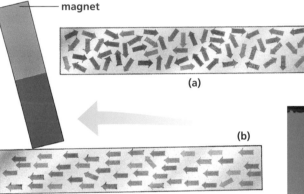

magnet

(a)

(b)

Quite repulsive

A magnet can attract other objects or repel other magnets (push them away) without touching them. All magnets are surrounded by an invisible magnetic field, where their magnetism can be felt. The field is strongest in two places on the magnet, called the north and south poles. On a bar-shaped magnet, the poles are at either end.

▲ A magnetic material like iron contains many tiny magnetized areas called domains. If the material is not a magnet, these domains point in different directions (a). But by rubbing another magnet on the material, the domains can be lined up, and it becomes a magnet (b).

◄ A compass needle is a small bar magnet whose north pole lines up with the Earth's magnetic field, showing us where north is.

Magnets can only attract things that also contain magnetic materials. Iron is the most common magnetic material. An iron-rich rock called magnetite, or lodestone, was one of the first natural magnets discovered. Other magnetic materials include nickel and cobalt. It is the arrangement of the electrons (the tiny particles inside atoms) in a substance that makes it magnetic or not.

Perhaps the best-known use for magnets is in compasses. Compass needles always point to the north. But why? The answer was found by William Gilbert, an English scientist, in 1600. He discovered that a compass needle is in fact a magnet, and that the Earth itself has a magnetic field, with one magnetic pole near the North Pole, and the other near the South Pole.

MICHAEL FARADAY

Michael Faraday (1791–1867) has a special place in the history of physics and engineering because his discoveries led to so many inventions. He was a classic experimenter rather than someone who got bogged down in theory.

Faraday invented the first electric motor, and discovered the theory of electromagnetic induction. This showed that a magnet pushed into a coil of wire generated an electric current in the coil. Modern electric generators all use induction to make electricity. Faraday also discovered that an electric current in one wire can cause a current to flow in another wire.

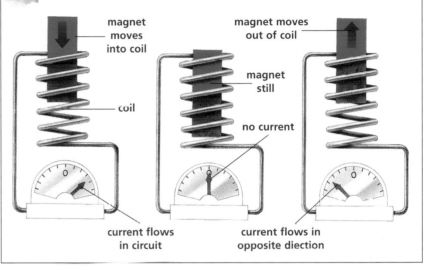

magnet moves into coil

coil

current flows in circuit

magnet still

no current

magnet moves out of coil

current flows in opposite diection

key words

- generator
- induction
- magnet
- motor

◀ Powerful electromagnets can be turned on to pick up scrap metal, then turned off to dump the metal. Similar electromagnets are used to lift and dump old cars into crushers.

Electrickery

Because magnetism depends on the behaviour of electrons, there are strong connections between electricity and magnetism. This was first noticed in 1820, by the Dane Danish scientist Hans Christian Oersted, who saw that a current flowing through a wire made a nearby compass needle move. Later, André Ampère in France discovered that electric currents in wires can attract or repel each other, just like magnets.

Today, these principles are used to make a powerful type of magnet called an electromagnet. An electromagnet is made by passing an electric current through a coil of wire, usually wound around an iron core. When the current is switched off, the electromagnet loses its magnetism. Electromagnets are used in many electrical machines, such as generators and motors. In the home, small electromagnets work electric doorbells.

Generators

What does a rock star playing an electric guitar have in common with a power station? They both use electric generators. When the musician belts out some power chords on the electric guitar, the guitar uses tiny generators to convert vibrations from the strings into electrical energy.

Generators are machines that produce (generate) electricity. They convert mechanical energy – the energy of motion – into electrical energy. The small dynamo that makes electricity for bicycle lights is a generator, driven by one of the bike's wheels. Giant spinning turbines drive the generators in power stations, which make mains electricity for our homes.

The principle behind the generator is called electromagnetic induction. It was discovered by the English scientist Michael Faraday in 1831. He found that he could produce an electrical current in a wire if he moved the wire in a certain direction near a magnet. The same happened when he moved a magnet near a wire – again, in a certain direction only. (The wires had to be

key words
- coil
- dynamo
- generator
- induction
- magnet

cap **bicycle tyre**

iron

rotating magnet

fixed coil

electric current lights bulb

▲ A dynamo produces enough electricity to power the lights on a bicycle. The movement of the bicycle tyre turns the cap, which spins a magnet inside the dynamo. Around the magnet is a fixed coil. Current flows in the coil as the magnet turns.

▼ The outer part of this generator is a large electromagnet. The hole through the centre is where the coil will go.

part of a closed loop called a circuit, because you don't get a current in a wire that's not connected to anything.)

Building generators

Some generators work by moving coils of wire in a magnetic field. In some generators the coil spins on a shaft surrounded by magnets. As it spins, electricity flows through the coil. However, in a bicycle dynamo, and in the large generators used in power stations, the coil is fixed. Down the centre of it runs a shaft carrying a magnet (in a power station generator, a powerful electromagnet is used). As the magnet spins, electric current is generated in the coils.

Generators normally produce two-way, or alternating current (AC), which is why they are often called alternators. If one-way, or direct current (DC), is needed, generators must be fitted with a switching device to keep the current flowing in only one direction.

Electric motors

Electric motors power most of the machines we use in our homes, and most machines in industry, from drills and printing presses to trains and milk floats. In fact it probably won't be long before electric motors, using a new type of battery called a fuel cell, are powering the latest cars.

Electric motors work in the opposite way to electricity generators. They convert electricity into energy to make things move, whereas generators use movement to make electricity. The English physicist Michael Faraday made the world's first electric motor in 1822. He showed that electric current could be used to move a wire in a magnetic field.

How motors work

An electric motor is built in much the same way as a generator. It has a set of wire coils, wound round a block called an armature, and mounted on a shaft, or rotor. Magnets or electromagnets around the armature create a magnetic field.

When electric current is fed into the wires of the coils, the shaft of the motor rotates. The rotating shaft can then be used to drive machines.

Electric motors may be driven by direct (one-way) current or alternating (two-way) current. Direct current machines need a switching device called a commutator to keep the rotor spinning in the same direction.

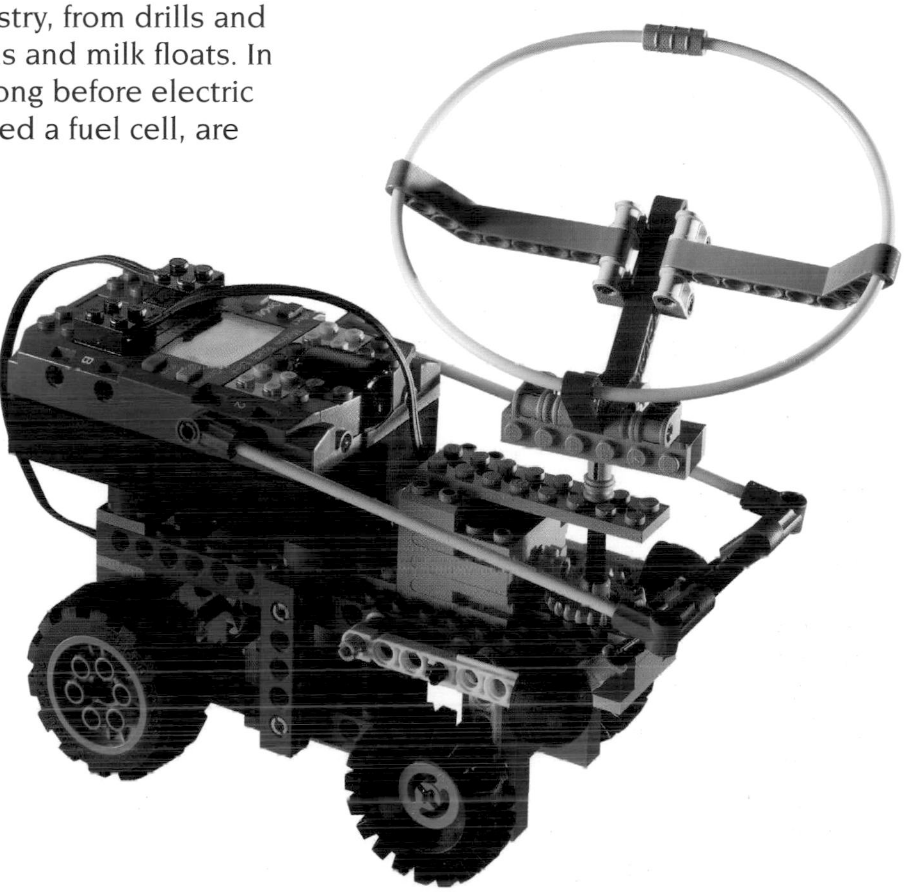

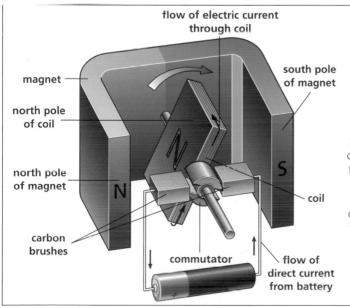

▲ Many toys today have electric motors in them. The motor in this vehicle drives the wheels and also turns the radar aerial.

A SIMPLE MOTOR

This diagram of a simple direct-current (DC) motor shows a motor with just one turn of the wire coil. When current passes through the coil, it creates a magnetic field around the wire. This magnetic field interacts with the field between the poles of the permanent magnet. The coil turns until its own poles are next to the opposite poles of the magnet, because opposite magnetic poles attract each other. At this point, the commutator, which connects the coil to the battery, reverses the direction of the current flowing through the coil. The magnetic field around the coil is reversed, forcing the coil to make another half-turn.

Diagram labels:
- flow of electric current through coil
- south pole of magnet
- magnet
- north pole of coil
- north pole of magnet
- N
- S
- coil
- carbon brushes
- commutator
- flow of direct current from battery

key words
- coil
- electromagnet
- generator
- magnet
- motor

Power stations

Switch on your TV and it flickers into life. But have you ever considered where it gets its power from? Huge, fuel-hungry power stations dotted around the country make electricity and send it to our homes through cables. One power station generates enough electricity to supply thousands of homes.

Most modern power stations make electricity by burning fuel to heat water. Heating water creates steam, which is used to turn the blades of giant turbines – just as blowing on a child's toy windmill makes it spin round. The spinning turbines drive huge machines called generators, which produce electricity.

Choice of fuels

There are several types of fuel that a power station can use to heat water. Those most

▶ White, cloud-like plumes of water vapour rise from cooling towers at a power station in Cheshire, UK.

key words
- fossil fuels
- generator
- nuclear energy

often used in today's power stations are coal, gas, oil or nuclear fuel. Coal, gas and oil are known as fossil fuels, because they formed from the remains of plants and animals over millions of years.

In conventional power stations, fossil fuels are burned to heat vast quantities of water. In nuclear power stations, however, nuclear fuels such as uranium are used to make electricity. The uranium is not burnt

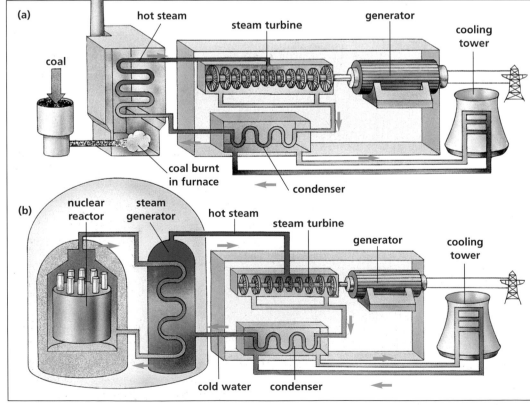

POWER STATIONS
A coal- or oil-fired power station (a) contains a furnace, where the fuel is burned to heat water and make steam. The steam drives a turbine attached to an electricity generator. The steam is turned back into water in a condenser, then goes back to the furnace to be heated again. The condenser is cooled with cold water, which is then itself cooled in a cooling tower.
In a nuclear power station (b), the energy to heat the water and make steam comes from a nuclear reactor. The reactor heats the water in the steam generator through a heat exchange system, so that no radioactivity can get into the steam powering the turbines.

in a furnace. Instead, its atoms are broken apart in a process called nuclear fission. This process creates large quantities of heat, which is used to produce high-pressure steam.

Burning fossil fuels in power stations creates pollution that causes damage to the Earth's atmosphere. It may cause acid rain, for example. Nuclear power stations cause no air pollution, but they produce wastes that are radioactive (give off dangerous radiation).

Alternative energy

Because using fuel to make electricity damages the environment, scientists have found different (alternative) ways of generating electricity. Hydroelectric power stations are one way of doing this. They use the power of the water that cascades down a waterfall or a dam, to turn a turbine – without making harmful waste materials.

▲ Some people think they are an eyesore, but wind farms provide energy without damaging the environment.

▼ A model of what was probably the world's first power station, built by Thomas Edison (1847–1931). Edison invented light bulbs in 1879, and realized that many people would want electric light in their homes. He decided that he would have to set up power stations to provide electricity for them. So he designed the first power station at Pearl Street in New York. The station was 'switched on' in 1882.

Wind is also a harmless source of power. Armies of giant windmills – called wind farms – are springing up both on land and at sea. The propellers of the windmills spin round and turn generators when the wind blows. The electricity the windmills generate can also charge batteries, which then supply power when the wind drops.

Power from the sun is another great hope for the future. At present solar power is expensive, but scientists are trying to find ways of producing it more cheaply. Geothermal energy is also being examined. This involves using the tremendous heat trapped in the Earth's crust – perhaps 15 kilometres below ground – to heat water and drive turbines.

Electricity supply

Stretching all over the country, thousands and thousands of kilometres of cables carry electricity to factories, offices and homes. These cables are carried by tall pylons (towers) or buried underground. They join many power stations in a vast network, called a national grid.

Power stations produce electricity at a voltage (electrical pressure) of about 20,000 volts. It is alternating current (AC), which means that the current changes direction many times per second.

But it is not economic to transmit (send) electricity over long distances at 20,000 volts. Too much power would be lost. If the electricity is transmitted at a much higher voltage, the power losses are much lower.

All change!

The kind of electricity produced by power stations is called alternating current (AC). AC does not travel through the cables in one direction only, but changes direction many times a second. It is easy to change the voltage of AC electricity, using a device called a transformer. At the power station a 'step-up' transformer boosts the generated voltage to as much as 500,000 volts. The power travels along high-voltage cables (which lose much less power) to where it is needed.

▶ A simple transformer. A voltage applied to the primary coil produces a voltage in the secondary coil. If the secondary coil is smaller than the primary coil, the transformer reduces the voltage (step-down). If the secondary coil is bigger, the voltage is stepped up.

half primary voltage

primary voltage

primary coil

iron core

secondary coil (half size of primary coil)

500,000 volts

step-up transformer

pylon

power station

boiler

town

low voltage (about 240 volts) for homes

11,000 volts

turbine

generator

factories

step-down transformers

medium voltage for factories and offices

step-down transformers

high voltage for heavy industry and railways

▶ Electricity is carried across the country from power stations by overhead cables. The voltage is changed by transformers as the power is distributed to homes and factories.

Of course, we don't want electricity coming into our homes at 500,000 volts! Other transformers are used to 'step down' the voltage to more useful levels: several thousand volts for factories, and about 240 volts for homes. This process normally happens at local substations.

Electricity in the home

We call the electricity that comes into our homes 'mains electricity'. It travels to where it is needed along circuits. There are separate circuits for different things. One may carry heavy current to drive an electric cooker. Another will power the sockets we use to plug in things like dishwashers and TVs. A third circuit powers the lights.

Occasionally a broken machine might use more electricity than is safe, and could catch fire. To prevent this, plugs are fitted with fuses. These are thin pieces of wire that melt when too much current flows through them, so breaking the circuit.

A circuit-breaker is another safety device that we have in our homes. This cuts off the electricity automatically if the amount of current flowing in a circuit gets too high.

▼ Pylons bring high voltage electricity to the transformers (centre) in this electricity substation.

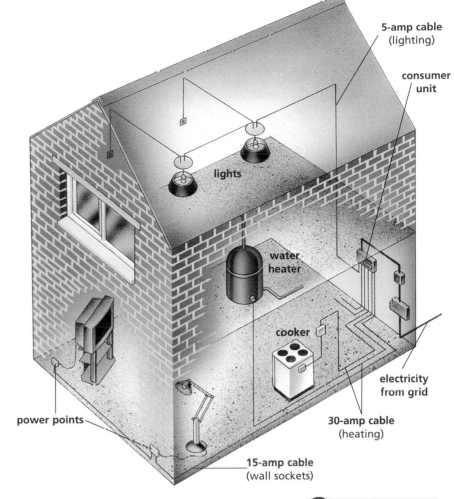

5-amp cable (lighting)

consumer unit

lights

water heater

cooker

electricity from grid

30-amp cable (heating)

power points

15-amp cable (wall sockets)

▲ The wiring in a house. In many houses, the main cable branches out to several circuits at the consumer unit. The power points are usually all connected to the same cable, called a ring main.

key words

- voltage
- power station
- alternating current
- transformer
- fuse

Powerful plug-ins

Companies that supply electricity keep a constant check on how much electricity people are using. Sometimes, more electricity is being used in an area than is available. The electricity company will then connect to other power stations in the grid and use some of their electricity.

Electricity supply is now a big international business. This means that different countries can share electricity if they have some to spare. At peak times, for instance, when everybody is using electricity, Britain can use power from France.

Electronics

Mobile phones, pocket computers and many other devices have been made possible by the incredible advances in electronics since the mid-20th century. Of all the devices invented since then, none has matched the impact of the transistor.

The transistor is at the heart of electronics. This is the branch of electrical engineering involving small-scale devices. Where electrical engineers tend to look at heavy currents in large devices, electronics engineers are concerned with light currents in small devices.

More from less

One of the most important jobs an electronic circuit does is to make a small signal into a bigger one. This is called

THE FIRST TRANSISTOR

In 1947, three scientists working at the Bell Telephone Laboratories in New Jersey, USA, made an important breakthrough in electronics. John Bardeen (1908–1991), Walter Brattain (1902–1987) and William Shockley (1910–1989) used a semiconductor called germanium to make the world's first transistor. The three scientists shared the Nobel Prize for Physics in 1956.
The invention of the transistor, shown below resting on a fingertip, made it possible to build much smaller and more reliable electronic circuits.

▼ A transistor on a fingertip.

a single transistor

aluminium (for electrical connections

layers of treated silicon form circuit components

silicon wafer

whole microchip

electronic circuits

microchip

plastic base

connector pins

microchip on base

▲ The transistors and other devices on a microchip are made up of layers of silicon, treated in different ways to have different electrical properties. A final layer of aluminium 'tracks' connects the devices together. The complete microchip is fastened to a plastic base, which has connector pins.

amplification. When you turn up the volume on your hi-fi, you are amplifying the electrical signal that produces the sound.

Early amplifiers used big, fragile devices called valves to amplify signals. The development of the transistor, a small 'sandwich' made of semiconducting material, was an important step in electronics. Transistors provided amplification from a very low-powered device the size of a peanut.

The first transistor radios appeared in 1955. Soon transistors were being used in all sorts of gadgets, such as TVs and hi-fis. Transistors also helped to make equipment in spacecraft much lighter.

In the 1970s integrated circuits (microchips), containing many transistors and other parts on one tiny chip of silicon, began to replace individual transistors. Now there are millions of transistors in the microchip circuits used in computers.

Capacitors and diodes

Capacitors and diodes are two other devices used in electronic circuits.

A diode conducts electricity easily in one direction, but resists the flow of electricity in the other. It is an important part of many circuits.

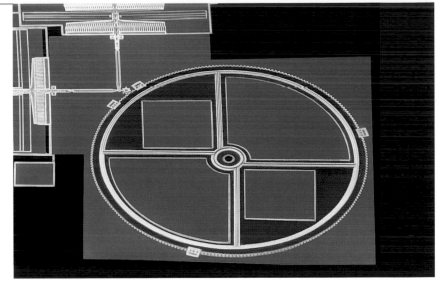

A capacitor stores electric charge between two conducting plates. It takes a certain amount of time for a capacitor to charge up. So capacitors are important components for making timers.

Capacitors can also be used in filtering circuits. These get rid of signals you don't want. When you turn up the bass and turn down the treble on your hi-fi, you are using filtering circuits.

▲ Future electronic devices may include minute motors like this one, etched on to a wafer of silicon. Two 'microengines' at top left (green and yellow) turn a tiny gear (centre), which is smaller in diameter than a human hair.

television

radio

digital music player

LOGIC GATES

As well as working as amplifiers, transistors can be used to switch signals on and off. This makes them particularly useful for circuits called logic gates, which are central to computers. An OR logic gate, for example (a), has two inputs. An electrical pulse can pass through the 'gate' if there is a signal from either or both inputs. A NOT gate (b) lets a pulse through if there is no input, but doesn't let it through if there is an input. These and other logic gates can be combined to make circuits that can work out simple sums. A computer's central processor has thousands of such circuits.

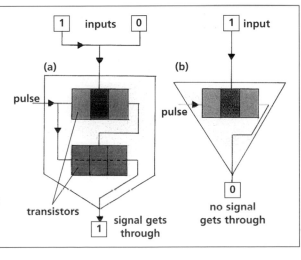

▲ Radios, TVs, personal stereos and many other devices we use every day rely on electronics to work.

key words
- amplifier
- capacitor
- diode
- filtering
- logic gate
- transistor

Communications

'That's one small step for a man, one giant leap for mankind', said the US astronaut Neil Armstrong in 1969, as he took his first steps on the Moon. Radio signals beamed Armstrong's words and TV pictures live to Earth, and they were broadcast around the world.

The Moon landing broadcasts were a triumph of modern communications. But today, people can communicate in many more ways than in 1969, using mobile phones, faxes, emails and satellite links.

▶ A sound or a picture can be recorded as an analogue signal – an electrical copy of the sound or image. This signal changes smoothly. But modern communications are mostly digital. In a digital signal, the sound or picture is 'sampled' (measured) at regular intervals. The string of measurements is the digital signal.

Reaching out

However different they are, all communication systems have one thing in common. They turn a message – made up of spoken words, music, text or pictures – into something that can be sent (transmitted) in some way. This is called a 'signal'. At the receiving end, the signal is turned back into the message.

One of the first long-distance communication systems, invented in 1790, was the semaphore tower. Semaphore

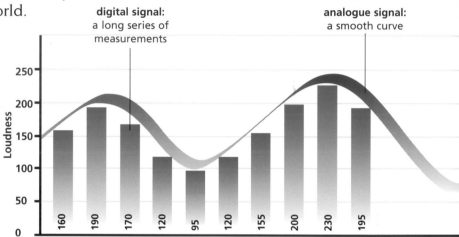

digital signal: a long series of measurements

analogue signal: a smooth curve

towers had two long wooden arms that could be moved to different positions. Each position of the arms stood for a different letter or number. Using semaphore, messages could be sent between distant hilltops many kilometres apart. But semaphore was very slow.

Going electric

Communications speeded up after the discovery in 1821 that an electric current flowing in a wire can make a compass needle turn. This led to the invention of the telegraph, which could send messages both further and faster than semaphore.

◀ Digital phone calls can be transmitted as flashes of light, through cables made of optical fibre. Today, most telephone networks use fibre, as they can carry more calls.

▶ A type of semaphore signalling was used by sailors for many years to communicate between ships. The sailors signalled using two flags, one in either hand.

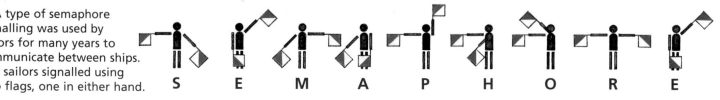

S   E   M   A   P   H   O   R   E

Telegraphs sent different electric currents down the wires. At the receiver, these made needles point to different letters or numbers.

The telegraph became faster with the invention of a springy switch called a telegraph key, which could send messages in Morse code. This coded letters and numbers as mixtures of short 'dots' or longer 'dashes' of electric current.

Sounds and waves

The invention of the telephone in 1876 made it possible for people to actually speak to each other, rather than sending messages by code. As with the telegraph, the messages were sent as electrical signals along wires.

Radio waves can also carry communications. Television, radio, telephone and Internet signals can all be sent this way. Radio waves travel in straight lines. This means that over long distances radio signals do not follow the curved surface of the

▼ Some mobile phone masts are made to look like trees so that they blend into the environment.

Earth. Satellites circling in space can be used to send such signals around the world. The satellite receives a signal – such as a TV sports broadcast – then re-transmits it to another part of the Earth that could not be reached otherwise.

Calls on the move

Mobile phones transmit messages using radio-type waves called microwaves. Special masts with aerials that can send and receive mobile phone transmissions are dotted all over the country. A call from a mobile usually goes to the nearest of these masts. If the receiving phone is a mobile too, the signals travel through the telephone network to the mast nearest to the receiving phone. This mast then transmits the call via microwaves.

Modern mobiles and television networks send very clear digital signals. These turn a normal, or analogue signal, into a stream of numbers.

SAMUEL MORSE'S CODE

The US inventor Samuel Morse (1791–1872) became interested in the telegraph in the 1830s. He eventually developed the system of dots and dashes that became known as Morse code. He demonstrated the code for the first time in 1844.

Although Morse code was punched into paper tape at the telegraph receiver, operators found they could decode it much quicker by simply listening to the noise made by the tape punch.

▶ The alphabet and numbers 1 to 10 in Morse code.

A ●—	B —●●●	C —●—●	D —●●
E ●	F ●●—●	G ——●	H ●●●●
I ●●	J ●———	K —●—	L ●—●●
M ——	N —●	O ———	P ●——●
Q ——●—	R ●—●	S ●●●	T —
U ●●—	V ●●●—	W ●——	X —●●—
Y —●——	Z ——●●	1 ●————	2 ●●———
3 ●●●——	4 ●●●●—	5 ●●●●●	6 —●●●●
7 ——●●●	8 ———●●	9 ————●	10 —————

key words

- telegraph
- semaphore
- message
- transmission
- digital
- analogue

Telephones

Mobile phones have given people the freedom to make calls from just about anywhere. As a result, they have helped save many lives. Stranded mountaineers, people on sinking boats – even hot-air balloonists in trouble – have all used mobiles to call for help.

Mobiles are a very recent invention. But telephones were invented more than a hundred years ago. Telephones have changed a great deal since the early days, but the way the telephone system works is still basically the same. So just what happens when you make a phone call?

Current voices

When you punch in a phone number, the telephone sends the number to a place called an 'exchange'. The exchange connects you up to the person you want to contact.

When the person you are ringing picks up the phone, you speak into the handset. A microphone in your handset changes

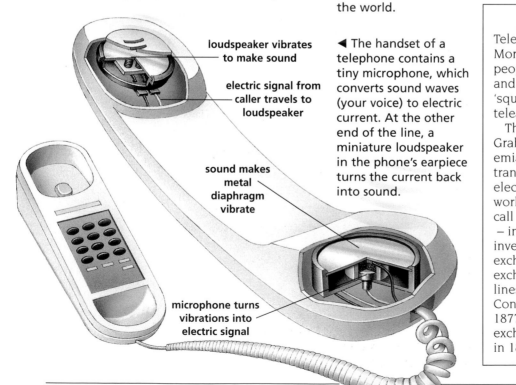

► Our telephones and mobiles are part of a huge communication network that carries information all over the world.

◄ The handset of a telephone contains a tiny microphone, which converts sound waves (your voice) to electric current. At the other end of the line, a miniature loudspeaker in the phone's earpiece turns the current back into sound.

loudspeaker vibrates to make sound

electric signal from caller travels to loudspeaker

sound makes metal diaphragm vibrate

microphone turns vibrations into electric signal

ALEXANDER GRAHAM BELL

Telephones were developed because the Morse code of the telegraph did not let people talk to each other. So engineers and scientists wondered how they could 'squeeze' human voices down the telegraph wires.

The problem was solved by Alexander Graham Bell (1847–1922), a Scot who had emigrated to Canada. He experimented with transmitting sound by electricity and made the world's first telephone call – to his assistant – in 1876. Bell also invented the telephone exchange. The first exchange, with just 20 lines, was installed in Connecticut, USA, in 1877. Britain's first exchange opened in 1879.

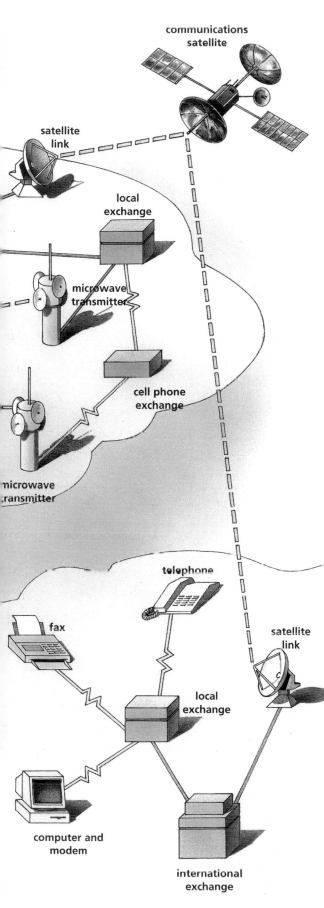

communications
satellite

satellite
link

local
exchange

microwave
transmitter

cell phone
exchange

microwave
transmitter

telephone

fax

satellite
link

local
exchange

computer and
modem

international
exchange

sound waves from your voice into an electric signal. This signal is then sent through the telephone system to the other phone. At the receiving end, the electrical signal drives a tiny loudspeaker in the handset, which reproduces your voice.

But why are telephone exchanges necessary? It's because if every phone in the world was connected to every other, we would be awash in wires. Instead, each phone is connected to a local exchange, which connects in turn to other exchanges.

Early exchanges used operators who plugged your line into the one of the person you were calling. But that was only possible when there were few telephone users. As phones became more popular, automatic exchanges were introduced.

Light fantastic

In modern phone networks, the sound of your voice is not only sent down electrical wires – it is transmitted in many other ways. Many telephone cables are now made up of optical fibres, which can carry more calls than wires. Instead of transmitting the sound of your voice as electrical signals, optical fibres carry the voice information as tiny pulses of light.

Phone networks also use radio waves and microwaves to send information from place to place. Radio links, called relays, are used particularly in places where it's hard to put up telegraph poles. Satellite links, and undersea optical fibre cables, are used to connect phones across the oceans. Telephone networks are also used to transmit information over the internet and to send faxes.

Phones of the future

Modern mobile phones can do much more than just make calls. They can send faxes and emails, store phone numbers and other information, and connect up with your computer and, to a limited extent, the internet.

Soon videophones will let people see each other using built-in cameras and small video screens. You will also be able to use them to watch other kinds of videos, and to surf the Internet.

▲ A videophone allows two people to have a conversation and see each other at the same time.

Faxes and modems

Did you know that you can squeeze pictures down your telephone line? A fax machine lets you do just that. And phone lines can carry other information besides voices and pictures.

Phone lines are useful for sending documents to people by fax. But if you have a modem and internet connection, you can also use a phone line for surfing the web and keeping in touch by email.

Fax is short for facsimile, which means 'identical copy'. Fax machines turn an image or document into information that can be sent down a phone line. Modems can also send information down a phone line – in this case, computer data. A computer with a modem can send faxes, too.

Sending and getting faxes

Once a fax machine gets through to the machine it is sending to, light sensors inside it scan across the page in a series of

▶ Sending and receiving a simple image via a fax. Telephone lines were designed originally only to carry voice signals, and this means that the speed at which a fax can work is limited.

key words

- document
- fax
- modem

◀ Missed the post? Birthday wishes are just one kind of message that can be sent anywhere in the world over the internet. The picture and text are stored on computer as digital information. A modem converts this information into packets of electrical signals that can be sent down the phone line.

0 0 1 1 1 0 0 0 0 0 0 0 0 0 0 0 1 1 1 0 0

light sensors

sending fax

Light sensors change blacks and whites of image into electrical 0s and 1s.

thin lines. Scanning turns the pattern of light and dark on each line of the original into electrical signals, which are sent through the telephone system to the receiving fax machine. This machine takes the signals one line at a time. It sends them to a line of tiny heating elements. Where the original document was dark, the heating element is turned on. Where it was light, the element is turned off. Heat-sensitive paper moves past the heating elements, and where the elements are on, the paper turns black. Gradually, the pattern of light and dark on the original document is drawn at the receiving fax.

0 0 1 1 1 0 0 0 0 0 0 0 0 0 0 0 1 1 1 0 0

heating elements

receiving fax

Heat-sensitive paper turns black where it is heated.

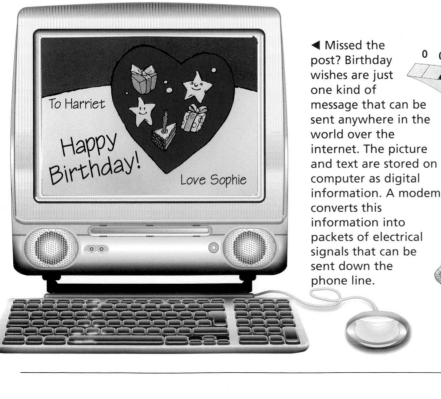

Radio

It is 12 December 1901. In St John's, Newfoundland, on the east coast of Canada, a team of people are struggling to raise a long aerial into the stormy skies. Supported by balloons and kites, the aerial is at last raised. Miraculously, it picks up faint signals – the letter S in Morse code. The signal comes from Poldhu in Cornwall, England. It is the first international radio broadcast.

The driving force behind the first transatlantic radio transmission was the Italian inventor Guglielmo Marconi. He had been experimenting with sending radio, or 'wireless', messages for six years. In December 1901 he proved that radio could be a new way for the whole world to communicate.

Today, radio stations in every country broadcast programmes to billions of people. And two-way radio links connect mobile phones, aircraft with airports, ships with the shore, and spacecraft with Earth.

🔵 key words

- broadcast
- radio waves
- sound signal
- transmitter
- wireless

▲ Clockwork radios work without an electricity supply or batteries. The clockwork spring turns a generator, which makes electricity.

How radio works

In a radio studio, microphones make an electrical 'copy' of the sound being recorded. This is called a sound signal. The sound signal is combined with a more powerful signal called the carrier wave. The combined signal goes to a transmitter, a metal antenna on a tall mast that sends out the signal as radio waves. The radio waves travel through the air to your radio receiver, where an electrical circuit, called a demodulator, extracts the original sound.

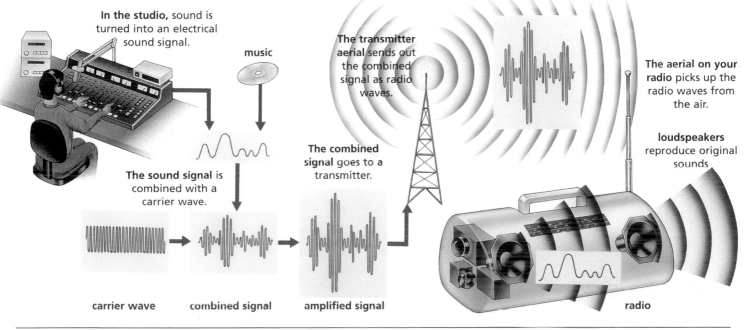

▼ How a radio broadcast reaches your radio at home.

In the studio, sound is turned into an electrical sound signal.

music

The transmitter aerial sends out the combined signal as radio waves.

The aerial on your radio picks up the radio waves from the air.

The sound signal is combined with a carrier wave.

The combined signal goes to a transmitter.

loudspeakers reproduce original sounds

carrier wave   combined signal   amplified signal   radio

Television

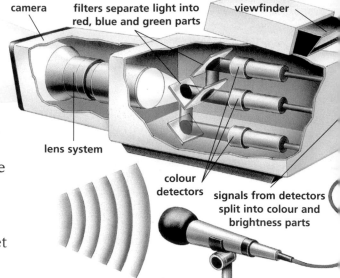

camera   filters separate light into red, blue and green parts   viewfinder

lens system

colour detectors

signals from detectors split into colour and brightness parts

When we watch television, we can cheer our favourite sports teams from our living-rooms, or hear news of earthquakes and wars on the other side of the world. We can watch movies, soaps and music videos, too. Satellite, cable and digital TV have added hundreds of extra TV channels. Soon, interactive TV will let us take part in programmes from home.

But have you ever wondered just how those pictures and sounds get on to your TV set? Television is a system that sends and receives pictures and sounds. A television camera records the pictures; a microphone records the sounds. The camera changes the images from light rays into electrical signals. These are sent to your TV set (television receiver). The receiver changes the electrical signals back to light again.

On camera

To make a TV picture, the camera focuses the scene being filmed onto three light-sensitive microchips called charge-coupled devices (CCDs). Each CCD is sensitive to a different type of light: one to red light, one to green and one to blue.

Each CCD has millions of tiny 'wells' sunk into its surface. When light falls on the CCD, each well becomes electrically charged, with a charge equal to the brightness of the light at that point. Together, the three CCDs produce an electric 'picture' of the brightness of red, blue and green light throughout the scene.

A TV camera does not capture a moving scene as whole pictures. Instead, it scans across the scene in a series of lines. The camera scans a complete set of lines 25 times each second.

Sending the pictures

To get the action to your home, the electric 'pictures' from the camera and the sound information from the microphone are collected together into a TV signal. The signal is combined with a carrier wave, a powerful electric current that can be used to create radio waves.

The carrier wave, carrying its TV signal, can be used to send out radio waves from a transmitting aerial on a high TV mast. Your TV aerial then picks up these radio waves. The signal may also travel to your home as flashes of light along an optical cable. Satellite TV programs are beamed up to a communications satellite in orbit around Earth. The satellite then sends a signal back to Earth, which is picked up by your satellite dish.

▲ A TV camera captures a moving scene and sends a TV signal to your home via a transmitting aerial or an optical cable.

BAIRD'S BOX

John Logie Baird (1888–1946), a Scot, was the first person to make a moving television picture. He used a mechanical way of scanning each line of his TV picture, using a spinning perforated disc invented by a Greman scientist, Paul Nipkow. In the UK, the BBC set up the world's first public TV broadcasting company using Baird's device, but it was soon replaced by a better, electronic system.

key words
- CCD
- CRT
- electron beam
- radio waves
- scanning
- transmission

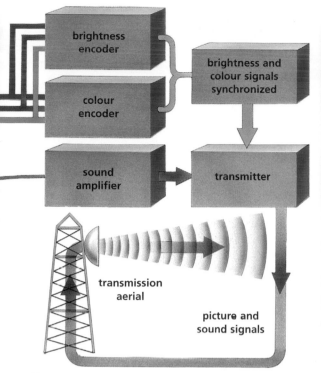

On screen

Many TVs still use a glass cathode-ray tube (CRT) to display pictures. At the narrow end of a CRT are three electron 'guns'. Each fires a beam of electrons at the TV screen, which is coated with a material called phosphor. Where the beam hits the screen, the phosphor glows. The three electron guns light up red, green and blue phosphor dots on the screen.

▲ A television programme being filmed in front of a studio audience. Using lighting, sets and special effects it is possible to create all kinds of different scenes in a TV studio.

The TV signal controls the red, blue and green electron guns. As the beams scan across the screen, the TV signal changes the strength of each beam, recreating the pattern of light and darkness in the original picture. Although the picture is only in three colours, different mixtures of the three make other colours, in the same way that paint colours can be mixed.

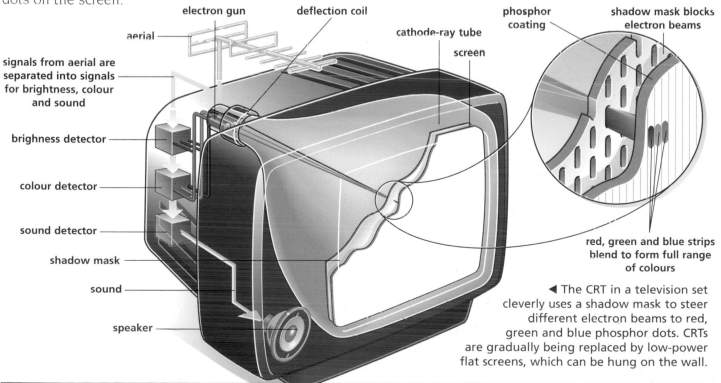

◀ The CRT in a television set cleverly uses a shadow mask to steer different electron beams to red, green and blue phosphor dots. CRTs are gradually being replaced by low-power flat screens, which can be hung on the wall.

Video equipment

Home videotaping means you don't have to rush home to watch your favourite TV programmes. By simply setting a timer, you can watch what you want, anytime. And portable cameras, with video recorders built in, let you make your own home movies. But how does videotape work?

TV pictures can be recorded on magnetic tape in the same way that sound is recorded on a tape recorder. The main machine used is called a video cassette recorder (VCR), in which the tape is normally on a cassette. But TV pictures contain too much information to fit on an ordinary audio tape. The tape would have to run so fast that it would snap.

Tilted drums

The answer to this problem is to use wider tape, and tape heads (the part that 'reads' the tape) that spin rapidly rather the stationary ones used for sound recording.

The heads in a video machine are on opposite sides of a circular drum that is tilted slightly in relation to the direction that the tape moves in. During recording or playback, the tape wraps around the drum. As the drum spins very fast, it 'wipes' thin diagonal stripes of the TV signal on to the slowly moving tape. This is called helical scanning.

▶ Just the batteries of an early video camera were bigger than this tiny palmcorder. Miniature microchips and tiny mechanical parts make today's video cameras unbelievably small.

◀ Editing TV programmes has been made easier by computers.

key words
- helical scanning
- recording
- VCR

Digital rivals

Traditional video tapes are being replaced by machines such as DVD players, which record videos digitally. These store the information about the pictures and sound in the same way that a computer stores information on its hard disk.

With digital video recordings it is easy to edit TV programmes or home movies. You can record digital pictures on to computers, then cut and paste the footage where you want it, just like the text in a word processor!

▼ Inside a video recorder, the tape runs over the spinning video head drum and past the audio (sound) head. The sound track is recorded along the top of the tape. The video head records the pictures as diagonal tracks across the tape, resting side by side like fallen dominoes.

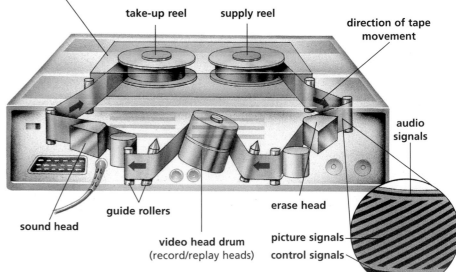

video cassette

take-up reel

supply reel

direction of tape movement

audio signals

sound head

guide rollers

erase head

video head drum (record/replay heads)

picture signals

control signals

Computers

Thud! You feel the wheels of your aircraft touch down on the runway – but you're surprised that you've landed already. Outside, the fog's so thick you thought you were still up in the clouds. So how did the pilots manage to land the aircraft without seeing the runway? Well, they had a computer to help them.

Computers are very good at storing and handling information (data). The internet provides a vast store of data that we can all tap into from a computer at home.

Computers are also very good at controlling all kinds of machines, from dishwashers to the space shuttle. In industry, computers are at the heart of control systems that run everything from car assembly lines to oil refineries.

How computers work

But what exactly is a computer? It is an electronic machine that works under the control of a list of instructions called a program. The computer takes in data, which is called an input. It processes the data in a central processing unit (CPU). The CPU contains one or more microchips, or microprocessors. A microprocessor is basically a calculator that performs a few simple types of sums very quickly.

The result of all the processing is called the computer's output. The computer is called the hardware, while the program is the software.

Only two numbers

Most computers are digital computers. This means they handle all their data in the form of binary numbers. The two numbers in binary are simply 0 and 1 (the decimal system we count in runs from 0 to 9). Binary is easy for a computer to deal with. The

▲ Tiny notebook computers like this one can link to the internet over mobile phone networks.

▼ In older aircraft, the pilot controlled the plane using mechanical links from the cockpit controls to the plane's engine, flaps and rudder. But in airliners like this Airbus A340, computers can control the aircraft by sending electrical signals to the engine, flaps and rudder.

microprocessor contains millions of tiny electronic switches equivalent to miniature transistors, which can be turned on or off. 'On' can represent the 1 in a binary number, and 'Off' can represent the 0. Using these simple numbers, the microprocessor is able to do sums at lightning speed.

It's not just calculations that a computer uses binary numbers for. Words, pictures and sounds are all created, changed and stored digitally using binary numbers. In a word processing program each letter and number is coded for by a particular binary number. Pictures are broken up into tiny dots (pixels), and the brightness and colour of each pixel is coded as a binary number. Sounds can also be coded for in a similar way.

Total recall

The computer's software is stored in a memory of some kind. A computer has two kinds of memory, stored on microchips. The software that controls how the

serial processing

instruction 1   instruction 2   instruction 3   CPU   results

parallel processing

instruction 1 → CPU
instruction 2 → CPU → results
instruction 3 → CPU

▲ Serial processing – working on one piece of data at a time – is slow but cheap, while parallel processing is fast but expensive.

computer's various pieces of hardware operate is stored in a memory that cannot be interfered with. This is called the Read-Only Memory, or ROM.

Before the computer starts up a program, the software will be sitting on a disk. When the computer software is running, this software will be copied into another memory, where it can be used much faster than from a disk. This memory is called the Random Access Memory, or RAM.

In operation

The operating system (OS) is a piece of software that controls how the user works the computer. Most systems use a lot of

▼ A timeline of some of the important events in the history of computing.

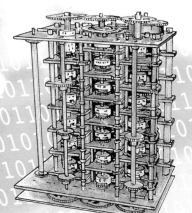

1830s
British mathematician Charles Babbage (1791–1871) designs a machine to calculate numbers correctly. Although it was not built, his Difference Engine contained ideas used in computers today.

1890s
American Hermann Hollerith (1860–1929) develops a machine that uses punched cards to calculate the results of the 1890 US census. In 1896 Hollerith sets up the company that later becomes IBM.

1940s
The ideas of British mathematician Alan Turing (1912–1954) lead to the development of computers like the Colossus, which helps crack German secret codes in World War II.

1951
Univac-1 (above), the world's first commercial computer, is designed by John Mauchly (1907–1980) and J. Presper Eckert (1919–1995). Mauchly and Eckert built ENIAC, the first electronic computer, in 1946.

'windows' and small pictures called icons, which represent different programs. You point to them, then click using a hand-held device called a mouse. Older operating systems, like those in early PCs, had a rather boring screen in which you entered commands, such as 'run word processor,' using a keyboard.

Call an architect

The way computers process data can be chosen to best match the task in hand. In a serial processor, a microprocessor carries out the first part of the task it has to do, then the next part, then the next, and so on. In a parallel processor, software divides up a task and splits it between many microprocessors, which all work on it at the same time.

Parallel processing is very fast, but also very expensive. Some parallel processors are so fast that they are called supercomputers.

Supercomputers are used for very special projects like weather forecasting or making computer models of the surface of the Sun. They might be used to predict hurricanes – which could save lives, if they help raise the alarm in time. Supercomputers are needed for such jobs because so many

▲ Computers can be built into many gadgets. This electronic 'pen' can scan text into its

things happen at once in weather systems that only a very powerful computer can hope to keep track of them.

Future ideas

The microchips in today's computers are made up of thousands of tiny transistors, made from silicon. But future machines could use even smaller parts, capable of even greater speeds. Some scientists want to use single chemical molecules (groups of atoms) as computer on/off switches. Meanwhile, others think that single atoms, or even parts of atoms, could be used to make 'quantum' computers.

● **key words**

- binary numbers
- hardware
- microprocessor
- program
- software

1968
'Mainframe' computers beginning to be used in large businesses.

1976
The first supercomputer, the Cray-1, is built. Modern supercomputers are used for weather forecasting, complex maths and physics problems, and animation in modern films.

1981
IBM produce the IBM PC, with software provided by American Bill Gates (born 1955). The machine is a success for IBM, and for Gates's company Microsoft.

1998
A team of researchers at IBM build a very simple quantum computer. Quantum computers work using single atoms or even electrons. They have the potential to be enormously more powerful than ordinary computers.

Microchips

Computers might be powerful, but the bits that do all the hard work are tiny. The 'brains' of a computer are made of microchips, each one a flat sliver of silicon smaller than a fingernail. Microchips can contain millions of unbelievably small electronic parts.

But it's not just computers that use microchips. You'll find them in almost every electronic gadget you can think of. In a car, they may help control the braking system. They could even be in your toaster, controlling how brown the toast gets. But what has made microchips so popular?

Cool, cheap, light and fast

The electronic circuits that were used before microchips were invented used lots of separate parts all wired together. These included transistors, which switch signals on and off, resistors, which oppose currents, and diodes, which let current go one way only.

But in large electronic circuits the wiring gets hot and can burn out. And all those separate parts are quite big – a

▲ This magnified photo of a single microchip shows how all the parts have been packed into the smallest possible space, so that none of the expensive silicon is wasted.

 key words
- dopant
- silicon
- transistor

▲ Each tiny square on this silicon wafer is one microchip. The wafer measures about 30 cm across.

transistor is about the size of a jelly bean – so conventional circuits need a lot of space.

Microchips overcome these problems by using laser light and special chemicals to 'grow' tiny circuits on a thin wafer of very pure silicon. The special chemicals, called dopants, are used to alter the electrical properties of the silicon in different ways, making tiny areas that behave like transistors, or resistors, or diodes. No wires are needed – the different parts can be grown side by side. The result is a tiny circuit that stays cool. And because all the parts are so close, the chip works very fast.

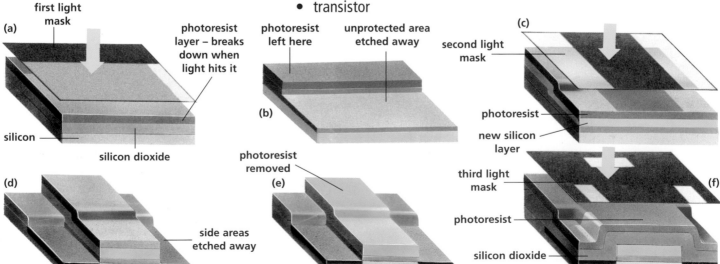

(a) first light mask

photoresist layer – breaks down when light hits it

silicon

silicon dioxide

(b) photoresist left here   unprotected area etched away

(c) second light mask

photoresist

new silicon layer

(d)

side areas etched away

(e) photoresist removed

(f) third light mask

photoresist

silicon dioxide

A chip off the block

To make a chip, the circuit first has to be designed. Engineers have to design chips using computer design software because there are simply too many components to draw by hand. The first microprocessor chip had 2300 transistors, but today's chips can have more than 30 million!

Once it has been told what the microchip should do, the designer's computer works out which components are needed and how they should connect up.

Laser stencils

The microchip is made in several layers, so when the design is correct, a picture of each layer is printed onto a series of glass 'masks'. These masks are used like stencils. The first mask is placed over the silicon wafer, then a laser is shone through it.

The wafer is coated with a tough coating that is sensitive to light. The areas where the laser hits the coating are changed, and can be washed away with an acid. Dopant chemicals are then injected into the chip. Where the coating has been washed away the dopant can reach the silicon below. In this way, the different dopants can be placed on exactly the right areas to form the electronic circuit.

Making contacts

Components in the chip are connected together by metal tracks laid down after the circuit parts have been made on top

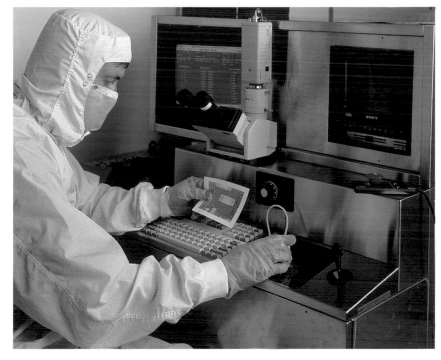

▲ The slightest impurity can ruin a microchip, so the people who make them and test them have to wear special suits and masks, and work in dust-free 'clean rooms'. The chips are made in a vacuum, so that the dopants do not become contaminated by impurities in the air.

of the chip. There can be many layers of these connectors, separated by glass 'insulator' layers.

When the chip is finished, it is sawn off the wafer and placed in a plastic package. Thin wires are stretched from the chip to contacts that stick out of the package. The chip is then tested – if it works, it is ready to be soldered onto a circuit board.

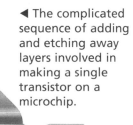

aluminium electrical contacts

finished transistor

(g)

◄ The complicated sequence of adding and etching away layers involved in making a single transistor on a microchip.

THE FIRST MICROCHIPS

The American Jack Kilby (born 1923), working for the company Texas Instruments, was the first to develop an integrated circuit. In 1964 he worked out how to make more than one transistor in a sliver of a material called germanium. By 'growing' the transistors together at the same time, he found he could connect them together internally without wires. In 2000 Jack Kilby was awarded the Nobel Prize for Physics, for his part in developing integrated circuits.

Around the same time another American, Robert Noyce (1927–1990), working for Fairchild Semiconductors, made a similar microchip from silicon. Silicon ultimately became the standard microchip-making material.

Hardware

O ne day, scientists will be able to make plastic computers that can be rolled up and put in your pocket. These computers will have colour screens made of an amazing bendy plastic that makes light when electric current passes through it.

magnetic heads read disks

The computer's hard disk drive is actually a number of disks, one on top of the other. Each one has its own recording and playback head. Using a number of disks makes storing and retrieving data much faster.

hard disk drive stack

Plastic computers and screens are still some way off. In the meantime, we must make do with rigid screens.

The computer and screen are part of what is called computer hardware. This contrasts with the software – the programs and instructions that run the computer.

The main computer unit is the box that contains all the electronic circuits that make the computer work, such as the processing and memory units. These are circuit boards carrying microchips and other parts. The main computer unit also has sockets to plug in to other hardware, and a power supply. It also contains one or more disk drives.

processing unit

external disk drives

Window on a computer's world

The screen (called a monitor or VDU) helps us keep a check on how the computer is working, and displays information and pictures.

The older type of monitor uses a cathode-ray tube (CRT). These tubes are big and take up a lot of desk space.

Most new computers have flat-screen monitors. They use only a third of the power of a CRT and take up much less space. But they are more difficult and expensive to make. Laptop screens use liquid crystals to form an image. These work in much the same way as the display on a digital watch.

▶ Laptop computers have to squeeze everything into a small space. There's no place for a mouse – you move your finger on a screen-shaped touch pad instead.

printer

Keyed up

Information is typed into a computer using a keyboard. Pressing a key on a keyboard connects two metal contacts. This makes electric current flow, so the computer knows which key has been pressed.

A mouse makes a computer easier to use. Instead of having to type everything, you can point and click anywhere on the screen. A simple mouse has a ball inside it that rolls as you move the mouse around. Rollers around the ball sense the ball's movement, and pass this information to the computer. Some mice now use a laser instead of the ball.

▶ Computer screens based on CRTs are bulky and use a lot of power. Newer flat screens use low power but are more expensive.

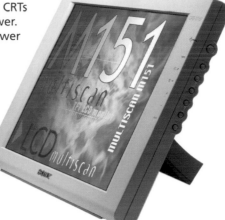

flat-screen monitor

Hitting a key on the keyboard makes an electrical contact, which causes a signal to go to the computer. Microchips in the computer change the keyboard signals into letters on the screen.

keyboard

electrical contacts

buttons

mouse

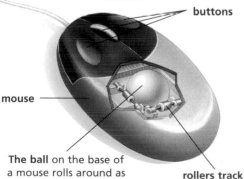

The ball on the base of a mouse rolls around as you move the mouse. Rollers around the ball sense these movements, and send signals to the computer telling it where the mouse is.

rollers track movement of mouse ball

◀ A cutaway view of a computer and some 'peripherals': devices that are not part of the computer itself. Peripherals such as the keyboard are input devices: they feed information into the computer. Output devices, such as the screen and printer, display information from the computer. Parts such as disk drives are input/output (I/O) devices.

● **key words**
- keyboard
- magnetic disk
- mouse
- optical disk
- screen

If you like computer games, you can plug in a joystick. This not only lets you steer, say, a starship around the screen, but it also has extra buttons that make games more fun.

Going for a spin

Disks are a good way of either storing data or taking it from one computer to another. There are two main types of disk. Magnetic disks, like a computer's hard drive or a floppy disk, store data as patterns of magnetism. Optical disks, like CDs or DVDs, store data (or music) in the form of tiny pits in the shiny surface. Optical disks can store hundreds, or even thousands of times more information than a floppy disk.

Disks store all sorts of things – including pictures. Digital cameras take pictures that are stored in memory chips or on a tiny floppy disk. They can be used directly in computer files. For pictures that already exist on paper, you can use a scanner to copy the image into the computer.

To get copies of documents out of the computer, you need a printer. Printers simply turn the text or pictures on the screen into tiny dots on paper. The dots can be made of ink or, in a laser printer, a powder called toner.

Microchips will soon be able to store as much data as a computer hard drive. So hard disks will one day be replaced by cards containing memory chips.

Software

If you want to bake a really delicious chocolate cake, it's best to follow a recipe. If you follow the instructions carefully, the cake should be great! A computer program can also be thought of as a recipe. It is a list of instructions that makes the computer do the job you want it to.

▲ Electronic games have been popular since people first began making personal computers. Modern games have sophisticated graphics that can simulate whole environments.

Computer programs can do really useful things, like control a space rocket, manage your washing machine cycle or change the traffic lights.

A computer's programs are part of its software. The software of a computer is every bit as important as the hardware (the physical parts like the screen and keyboard). If the software is wrong, the program won't work – just like a recipe.

Home on the range

The range of software is staggering. We are all used to word processors, which let us type letters and get them right before we print them out or email them. But PCs can also run programs that let you store information (databases), programs that do calculations (spreadsheets), programs that

▼ There are many types of computer program. Some are lists of things to do, while others, like this one, describe how a web page should look. Web pages are usually written in Hyper Text Mark-up Language (HTML). The HTML code on the right makes the page shown on the left.

play music or sounds, ones that let you draw pictures or modify photographs – and of course computer games. There are also many other kinds of software used in science and industry.

One kind of program that has to be designed with extra care is safety-critical software. This is the software that operates aircraft, cars or medical equipment. If safety-critical software goes wrong, people can get hurt.

Not all software is useful. Computer viruses are pieces of software that invade computer systems and cause problems.

BILL GATES AND MICROSOFT

In the early 1980s, IBM designed a revolutionary computer, the IBM PC (personal computer). It was small enough to sit on a desk. But their computer had no software – so IBM turned to a tiny firm called Microsoft for help. This company was run by a young American called Bill Gates. Microsoft supplied MS-DOS – the MicroSoft Disk Operating System – for the IBM PC. With every PC sold making money for Microsoft, the firm soon became a huge corporation, and is now the world's leading software maker.

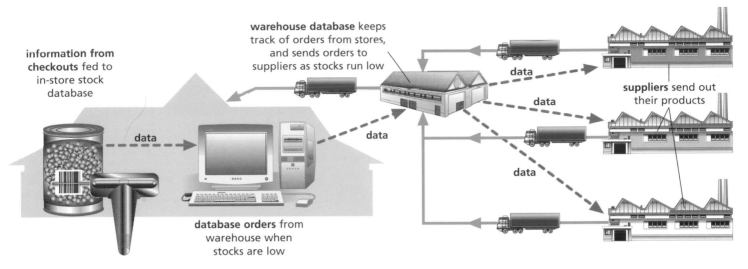

information from **checkouts** fed to in-store stock database

warehouse database keeps track of orders from stores, and sends orders to suppliers as stocks run low

suppliers send out their products

data

data

data

data

data

database orders from warehouse when stocks are low

Some viruses just display cheeky messages, while others erase certain types of file, like pictures or music files. Some viruses erase everything on your computer. Viruses are often spread by email. To fight them, it's important to have up-to-date anti-virus software that stops them working.

▲ Databases are important programs for many businesses. In a supermarket, databases keep track of what needs ordering at the store, at the warehouse, and at the supermarket's many suppliers.

◀ Complex software is used to control much of the engine management, and even gear changes, in Formula One racing cars.

key words

- application
- bug
- computer language
- computer virus
- database
- program
- software
- spreadsheet

Mind your language

Software is written in a computer language. There are many languages – BASIC, Java, and Fortran are a few examples. Each is good at different things. For example, BASIC is a simple language that beginners can learn. Java is a more complex language that makes internet programs work on many different types of computer. Fortran is a more specialist scientific language. Programmers choose the language for the job in hand.

Some programs can be very long. The program that guides a space rocket into orbit, for instance, can be many thousands of lines long. That's because there are many different pieces of equipment to control, and many pieces of information that need including in the program.

Computer processors cannot understand programs directly. The words and figures in a program have to be converted first into digital instructions that the computer processor can understand. This is done using a system called a compiler.

Bugs and debugging

Because a program is a list of instructions, any mistake in the commands can stop the program working. This could be serious if the software is controlling, for example, the engines on an aeroplane or a computer that does blood tests. So errors, known to computer programmers as 'bugs', have to be removed. Debugging (getting rid of bugs) can take as long as writing the program in the first place.

Computer graphics

© Disney Enterprises, Inc

Animated movies like *Toy Story* and *A Bug's Life* were made entirely on computers. To make computer graphics appear to move naturally, a computer has to make about 24 pictures for every second of the movie. And each picture is made up of millions of coloured dots called pixels. This needs a lot of computing power.

It took about 35 years after the invention of computers for the technology to become good enough to make computer movies. But movies are only one of many areas where computers are being used to design things.

© Disney Enterprises, Inc

► A CAD drawing of a future NASA space shuttle that might use a magnetic track to speed its take off.

◄ The characters Woody and Buzz Lightyear from the *Toy Story* movies were created on computer. Extremely fast, powerful supercomputers are needed to create a full-length animated film.

key words
- Computer Aided Design (CAD)
- pixel
- simulator

Planes, trains and cars

If you travel in a car, train, bus or plane, the vehicle has almost certainly been designed on a computer. The same goes for bridges, buildings and even clothes.

There are many advantages to designing things on a computer. The main one is that you can try many different designs until you have one that is just right. And the computer can make sure that you use the least amount of material to make, say, a new style of jacket. So you save money.

What a CAD

Designing things with the help of computers is called Computer Aided Design (CAD). This takes advantage of the fact that it is easy to save pictures of things in a computer's memory.

Using a CAD system, drawings are made on the computer screen using a special pen that you press on a rectangular pad called a graphics tablet. This uses the pressure of the pen tip on the pad to draw on the computer screen. A mouse could also be used. But if you already have a hand-drawn picture of a car, you can use an image scanner to capture it on the computer.

The pixels (dots) that make up the drawing are saved as a number of digital 'bits' in the computer's memory and displayed on the computer's screen. The software then lets you do things like show the design from a different angle, or colour it differently. Designs drawn with a CAD system can be printed out as plans for making

▶ Astronomers can use computers to put together information from different types of telescope into a single picture. In this picture of the remains of an exploded star, the blue parts came from an X-ray telescope, the green from an optical telescope and the red from a radio telescope.

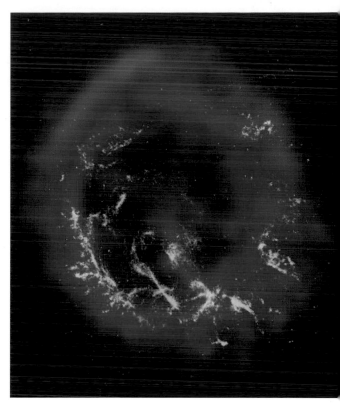

▼ Engineers usually work out their designs in three dimensions, then produce plans on paper. But using rapid prototyping, they can now make solid models of objects from computerized plans. The printer works by building up the object in thousands of thin layers.

something, or they can be used to control the machines that are used to make the parts. With a technique called rapid prototyping, it is even possible to print out a solid, three-dimensional model of the object in rubber, wax, plastic, metal or a material similar to plywood.

Applying physics

But drawing is only part of the design. Computers also let you check, for example, how a bridge design will stand up to high winds or very low temperature. This is called simulation. Computer simulations save money, as engineers don't have to build the design to see how it behaves. If the simulation shows problems, they can be corrected before anything is built.

Simulation using computer graphics is also useful for teaching. Airline pilots 'fly' a computerized flight simulator before they fly a real plane.

Computer images also help scientists to understand things. Molecules are too small to see, but models of them can be drawn on computers and studied to see how they might be useful. And radio telescope images of space can be cleaned up so that far-off galaxies can be seen more clearly.

Virtual reality

You are in a building you have never been in before. You move into a room to explore it. But suddenly, the floor disappears and you are falling. Looking up as the room disappears above you, you see the blackness of space. This is the kind of experience that you can have when you enter the world of virtual reality.

Virtual reality (VR) involves creating a three-dimensional environment inside a computer's memory. It can be a room, a cave, or a shopping mall. The idea is to let people explore that space by looking around it and walking around it in as natural a way as possible, listening to sounds they might hear, even feeling things that they might touch. Virtual reality lets designers get a feel for buildings or cars that have not even been built yet. Players of computer games can use virtual reality to reach a new level of realism.

adjustable headpiece

tiny video screen (one for each eye)

lens system

surround-sound headphones

▶ VR helmets have a screen for each eye and surround-sound speakers. Sensors tell the computer when you move your head.

key words

- graphics
- sensors
- virtual reality

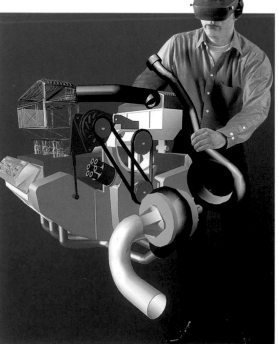

◀ Using VR, engineers can 'walk around' their design ideas, getting a sense of how they will look – and even feel – without having to build them. This picture shows an engineer with a virtual model of an engine.

In your head

To get you inside the 'space' in the computer, VR systems use a head-mounted display that contains two tiny computer monitors, one for each eye. The images are slightly different in each, to create a three-dimensional effect.

But the really clever thing about a VR helmet is that when your head moves, the graphics you see move too. Magnetic sensors in the helmet tell the computer how much you move, so it can change the image correspondingly. This makes you feel that you are in the environment. Speakers in the helmet let you hear sound all around you for added realism.

You can use a 'data glove' to help make VR even more authentic. When you 'push' on something, tiny balloons in the glove inflate, pressing on your hand. It feels like you've really pushed something!

Researchers are working on adding 'thought control' to VR systems. Using brainwave sensors inside a VR helmet, people will be able to control or change what they listen to, by just thinking about it.

Internet

The internet connects you to people, businesses and organizations all around the world. You can listen to faraway radio stations, download music from new bands, or play computer games. And you can find out almost anything you might want to know.

Few inventions have changed people's lives as much as the internet. Long-lost families have been reunited by it. Some people have found life-saving information on it. All these amazing developments have been made possible by a communications network that goes all over the world.

What is the internet?

The internet is a vast network of computers, connected to each other in a variety of ways. The original internet was a small computer network, set up in the 1960s by American military scientists who wanted a reliable way of communicating with each other in emergencies. The network soon grew, as scientists realized how useful it could be.

Many large organizations are connected directly into the internet. But smaller users, such as people with PCs at home, connect to organizations called Internet Service

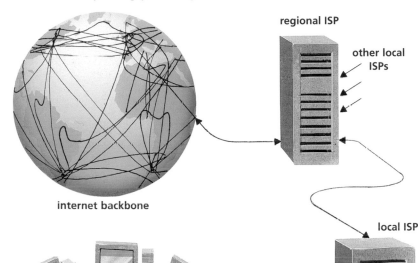

regional ISP

other local ISPs

internet backbone

local ISP

company with small network

home internet user

▲ Computers connect to the internet via an ISP. ISPs around the world are connected by the internet's 'backbones'. These are fibre-optic cables carrying information that span the globe.

Providers (ISPs). The ISPs run special 'server' computers that pass on internet information.

Email and web pages

Sending messages by electronic mail (email) is one of the most popular things on the internet. All you need is a modem (a device that connects your computer to the telephone network) and an email program. You can write messages as long or as short as you like. And you can 'attach' all sorts of other computer files – a picture, a movie, a sound file or a computer program.

▼ The internet is now available on some mobile phones. Accessing pages is slow, but phones are getting faster all the time.

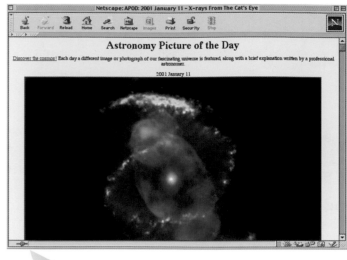

The internet also has billions of pages of information in the form of 'web' pages. To help you find your way around all this information, there are websites called search engines that help you find the pages you're interested in. If you are interested in dinosaurs, for instance, you can enter the word 'dinosaur', and the search engine will give you a list of sites on that subject.

Another very useful internet idea is the newsgroup. This lets people with a common interest send emails to whole bunches of like-minded people. There are many thousands of such groups on an area of the internet called the usenet.

▲ How a search engine works. Suppose you want to find out about a website you have heard of, Astronomy Picture of the Day. Typing in 'astronomy picture of the day' gives a list of websites with these words in. And clicking on the first site in the list takes you to the website itself.

Internet shopping

The internet is also becoming important for business. Home shopping sites let you order groceries with an email and have them delivered. You need never go to a supermarket again.

But the net also threatens businesses such as record companies. A lot of music is now available on the internet, and people can make digital copies of songs and swap them for free. So bands and record companies constantly try to stop this 'piracy' happening.

▶ When you send an email to a friend, it goes first to a computer called an email server. This then sends the message via the internet to your friend's email server. Here, your email is stored in an electronic 'postbox' until your friend looks at their emails.

reply

email message

email server

your computer

your 'post box'

🔵 **key words**
- email
- internet
- modem
- world wide web

world wide web

friend's server

email message

friend's computer

friend's 'postbox'

reply

THE WORLD WIDE WEB

The world wide web was invented to make scientists' lives easier. They needed a quick way of telling others around the world what research they were doing – and a quick way to see what research others were doing. So Tim Berners Lee (born 1955) and his colleagues at the European Particle Physics Laboratory (CERN) in Switzerland, invented the Hypertext Transfer Protocol (http). This makes it possible to look at pages of information from an internet server on a PC. The web took off so fast after its launch in 1992 that it contained more than a billion pages by 2000.

Robots and AI

'Shape shifter' robots can design themselves – and even recycle themselves. A computer designs the robot's parts, which are then 'printed out' by a machine called a 3-D printer. When the robot has finished the task it was built for, it melts itself down, and the plastic is used for another robot.

A robot is an automatic machine that does jobs under the control of its computer brain. The great advantage of a robot is that it doesn't make mistakes or get tired, and it can work just about anywhere.

Robot workers

Robots are used to do jobs that are too dangerous or boring for people to do. In factories, robots carry out tasks that have to be done over and over again, 24 hours a day. Robots are also used for dangerous

tasks like getting broken or worn-out parts from nuclear reactors, or finding and disarming bombs.

The basic parts of a robot are a controller (the robot's 'brain'), sensors (these tell the robot about the outside world) and effectors (its 'hands').

▼ One way artificial intelligence researchers test out their ideas is to build robotic football players. But robot footballers aren't going to take over from humans for a while yet. Most games are decided by the number of own goals each team scores!

key words

- artificial intelligence (AI)
- controller
- effector
- sensor
- software

Smart and smarter

A robot making things in a factory can be 'trained' by a human operator. It learns by copying the movements the human makes. But robots of this type are limited to doing only a handful of tasks.

Artificial intelligence (AI) researchers are now trying to make robots more clever, so that they can do a wider range of jobs. A major aim is to build robots that can work out for themselves how to do things. Experimental robots have been made that can learn and 'evolve' new ways of doing tasks.

Soon, robots will be in our living rooms. A vacuum cleaner that can wander around a room on its own, sucking up dust and dirt, is being developed. But because trailing a power cord might trip people up, it is battery powered.

▼ The basic parts of a robot arm. Most robots will have pressure sensors – a sense of 'touch'. They might also have camera 'eyes', and microphone 'ears', or other non-human sensors like infrared vision. Most robots have an arm that can be fitted with several different effectors.

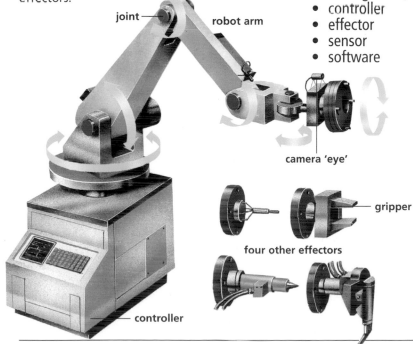

joint — robot arm

camera 'eye'

gripper

four other effectors

controller

Light
and
Sound

Light

We are bathed in light. From a distance of 150 million kilometres the Sun sends light streaming down on us. Our eyes have evolved to make use of this light. Light also helps to keep us warm.

Light is a form of energy that travels very quickly. Burning sticks, hot coals and light bulbs all give off light. The Sun gives us most of the light that we use.

Seeing is the main way humans use light. The eye collects light heading

▲ Light travels in straight lines. You can see that beams of light are straight when dust or mist in the air reflects some of the light, as in this forest scene.

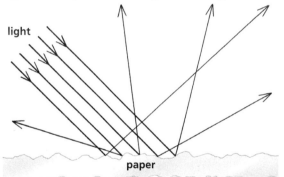

towards it. Special cells inside the eye sense the light and send signals to the brain. Somehow the brain turns these signals into pictures.

Dull, shiny or see-through?

When light hits an object, some of the energy is taken in (absorbed). The rest either bounces back (reflects) or travels straight through the object. Glass and water are transparent (see-through) as they let light travel straight through them without absorbing much energy. Objects that you cannot see through reflect and absorb light.

Shiny objects with a smooth surface reflect light very well. Dark, rough objects do not reflect very well, so they absorb most of the light hitting them. The energy absorbed from light warms the object up. This is partly why we get hot on a sunny day in summer.

▲ Most smooth surfaces, such as paper, are actually quite uneven, and reflect light in all directions. Very smooth and shiny surfaces, such as mirrors, reflect light in a more orderly way.

▶ Very still water is smooth enough to act as an excellent mirror. These mountains in South America are reflected in the still lake.

WAVE BASICS

The British physicist Thomas Young (1773–1829) proved that light consists of waves.

Wave motion consists of a series of peaks and troughs (a). Every wave has a wavelength: the distance the wave travels between two peaks (one complete cycle). The height of each peak or trough is the amplitude of a wave.

The frequency of a wave is the number of cycles the wave goes through every second. The bottom wave (b) is twice the frequency of the top one. Higher frequency waves have shorter wavelengths.

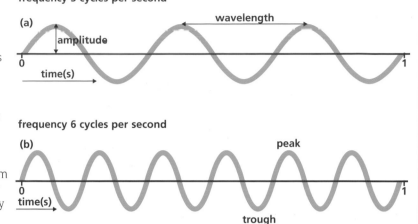

frequency 3 cycles per second

(a) amplitude wavelength time(s)

frequency 6 cycles per second

(b) peak time(s) trough

Light waves

Light travels as a series of tiny waves. When a lamp makes light, the energy streams out like ripples crossing a pond. The distance between two peaks in a series of ripples is called the wavelength. Light waves also have a wavelength. The wavelength of light is very small – you could fit 2500 of the smallest light waves in just one millimetre.

Colours

When we see white light, we are actually looking at many colours mixed together.

▲ In this puppet theatre from Indonesia, the puppets are held between the light source and a semi-transparent screen. The puppets block the light, making dark shadows on the bright screen.

These colours can be split up so we can see them. A rainbow is made when drops of water separate the colours in sunlight. The same thing can be done using a prism (a triangular piece of glass). The pattern of colours is called a spectrum.

Most objects are coloured because of the way they reflect light. White objects reflect all the colours. Black objects hardly reflect any light at all. Coloured objects reflect back some of the colours, but absorb others.

Each colour is light of a different wavelength. Red light has the longest wavelength, while violet light has the shortest. Waves with a longer wavelength than red light are invisible: they are called infrared (IR) waves. At the other end of the spectrum, invisible ultraviolet (UV) waves have wavelengths shorter than violet light.

Bending light

If you hold a straight stick so that it has one end under water, you will see that the stick does not look straight. Light coming from the end of the stick is bent as it comes out of the water.

If you stand on top of a cliff above a beach and watch the waves angling in, you may notice that they sometimes bend as they reach the shore. Waves slow down as the water gets shallower, and because the waves are coming in at an angle, one end is slowed down first. This makes the waves bend.

Light can be bent in the same way: this is called refraction. Light travels more slowly in glass than in air, so when light rays hit a piece of glass at an angle, they bend. The lenses and prisms we use in spectacles, cameras and binoculars all bend light in this way.

Light travels 9461 million million kilometres in a year. Astronomers call this distance a light year. They use it to measure the distances to stars and galaxies.

key words

- absorb
- light year
- reflection
- refraction
- transparent
- wavelength

▶ If you put one end of a straight stick in water, it appears to bend where it enters the water (a). This is because light rays from the underwater end of the stick bend as they move from water into air (b). This fools the eye into seeing the end of the stick nearer to the surface than it actually is.

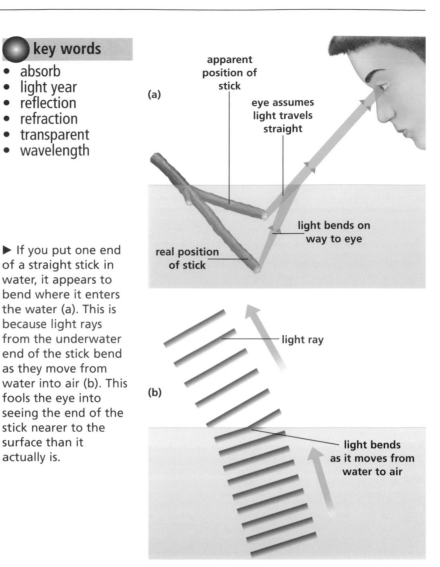

(a) apparent position of stick

eye assumes light travels straight

light bends on way to eye

real position of stick

light ray

(b)

light bends as it moves from water to air

THE FASTEST THING WE KNOW OF

When you switch on a torch, you don't have to wait for it to light something up. This is because light travels very quickly – 300,000 kilometres in a second. At that speed you could travel round the world seven times every second.

When light comes from a very long way away, it takes some time to get to us. Light from the Sun takes over 8 minutes to reach the Earth. But light from the most distant galaxies takes billions of years to reach us.

▶ Light from the Trifid Nebula takes about 4500 years to reach the Earth.

Spectrum

The storm is over. After the crashing violence of the thunder and lightning, the graceful arc of a rainbow extends across the sky. The band of colours a rainbow produces is called a spectrum.

When we see white light, we are actually looking at lots of different colours mixed together. White light can be split up so that the separate colours can be seen. A triangular piece of glass (a prism) is very good at doing this as it bends (refracts) light. The different colours bend by different amounts, so they spread out and form a rainbow pattern. Each colour is a different wavelength of light.

Rainbows

Rainbows are made when there are lots of raindrops in the air. The drops reflect light that is coming from behind you. This is why you never see the Sun in the same direction as a rainbow.

When the light enters a raindrop, it splits into colours. The different colours reflect off the back of the raindrop and split up even further as they come out again. Only one colour from each raindrop will reach your eye. However, you see the whole rainbow, because there are millions of drops reflecting light towards you.

▶ A Brocken spectre is a ghostly figure surrounded by a rainbow, sometimes seen by mountaineers. The 'spectre' is actually the viewer's shadow falling on mist or cloud. The halo around it is produced when sunlight is split into tiny rainbows by water drops in the mist or cloud.

prism

white light

▼ A prism is a triangular-shaped piece of glass that can be used to split white light into a spectrum. White light is partly split as it enters the prism. The colours then travel across the prism in straight lines to be spread even further apart as they leave the glass on the other side.

spectrum

key words

- prism
- rainbow
- reflection
- spectrum

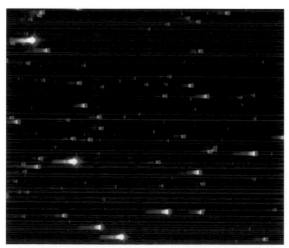

◀ The tiny spectra in this picture are made by stars. The light from the stars was split up by a prism inserted into the telescope used to take the picture. The spectrum for each star is different in detail, as each star produces slightly different light.

If you are looking down on a rainbow from high up (from a mountain, for example), you can sometimes see it as a complete circle, not just an arc.

Extending the spectrum

Sunlight contains other waves besides the ones in the visible spectrum. Just beyond the red end of the spectrum is infrared (IR) radiation, with wavelengths longer than red light. We cannot see IR, but it is given off by warm objects. The remote control on a TV uses infrared.

At the other end of the spectrum is ultraviolet (UV) radiation, which has wavelengths shorter than violet light. UV from the Sun gives us a suntan.

Colour

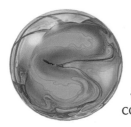

Caught in the light, a soap bubble shimmers with a beautiful and complex pattern of colours. This is an example of the gift evolution has given us – a marvellous colour-sensitive eye.

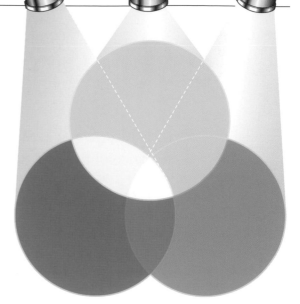

All colours come from light. White light is really a mixture of different colours. There are several ways to separate these colours so that we can see them. The surface of a bubble does this, and so do drops of rainwater, which hang in the air and make a rainbow.

▼ If a disc is painted with the three primary colours and then spun very fast, we see the disc as white.

▲ The three primary colours of light are red, green and blue. By mixing these three colours in different combinations, it is possible to make any other colour.

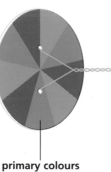

primary colours
repeated 3 times

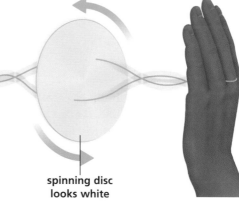

spinning disc
looks white

The colours of light

The pattern of colours in a rainbow is the same as that made by a prism (red to violet) and is called a spectrum. Light travels in the form of waves. The different colours of the spectrum have different wavelengths. If you think of light as being like ripples on the surface of a pond, the wavelength is the distance between the wave peaks. The wavelength of visible light is very small: between 1350 and 2500 light waves would fit in a millimetre, depending on the colour of the light.

Some objects, such as lamps, produce their own light. If they are producing all of the colours, they look white. If they only

◄ A rainbow over Victoria Falls in Zimbabwe. Rainbows are made when sunlight is split into a spectrum of colours by tiny water droplets in the air.

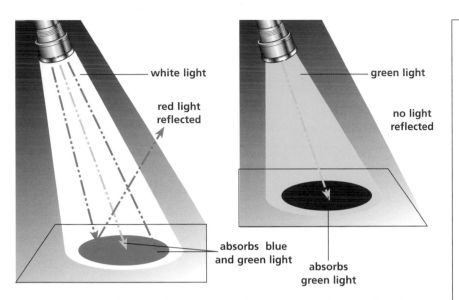

red light reflected

white light

absorbs blue and green light

green light

no light reflected

absorbs green light

produce some of the colours, they will be a colour of the spectrum. Yellow street lamps are yellow simply because they are only making yellow light.

The colours of things

Most of the objects we see reflect light to our eyes. An object that reflects all of the colours equally well (such as a snowman) will look white. A tarmac road looks black because it is hardly reflecting any light at all. Other colours are produced if the object is reflecting some of the light hitting it and absorbing the rest. For example, a red car reflects red light, and absorbs the other colours of the spectrum.

▲ The spot in this picture absorbs blue and green light, but reflects red. In white light the spot looks red, but in green light, no light is reflected, and it looks black.

🔵 key words

- absorb
- colour
- primary colour
- prism
- rainbow
- reflect
- spectrum
- wavelength

COLOUR VISION

Surprisingly, the eye contains only three types of colour-sensitive cell. These cells (called cones) are at the back of the eye (the retina). The cones respond to red, green and blue light. The brain makes out all the other colours by combining the signals from these cells. Yellow light stimulates the red and green cells, but not the blue cells. The brain has learnt to recognize this combined signal as being due to yellow light.

Some of the colours that we see are not part of the spectrum at all. For example, there is no wavelength of light for the colour brown. Such colours are invented by the brain using some combination of signals from the eye.

We can use the way the brain recognizes colours to fool it into seeing colours that are not really there. A colour picture on a conventional CRT TV is made up of tiny red, green and blue strips close together. We see a whole variety of colours because these strips are made to shine at different brightnesses. A yellow shirt is shown on the screen by making the red and green strips shine much more brightly than the blue ones. This produces exactly the same signal to the brain as yellow light. In this way the eye is 'tricked' into seeing a yellow shirt.

▼ If you look closely enough at the screen of a CRT colour TV, you will see that the picture is made up of tiny strips of just three colours: red, green and blue.

◄ The primary colours of pigments (paints, dyes and inks) are red, blue and yellow. You can mix them to make all other colours except white. Mixing all these pigment colours makes black.

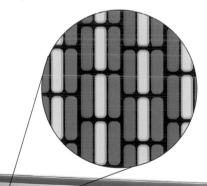

Mirrors and lenses

You are the captain of a ship on a foggy night. You know there are rocks about, so you are glad to see the bright light from a lighthouse. Lighthouses don't just use a big light bulb. There is also a curved mirror to reflect the light forwards and a curved lens to bend it into a powerful beam.

Mirrors reflect light well because they are smooth and shiny. The earliest mirrors were probably polished metal, but now we use coated glass.

Flat mirrors have a shiny aluminium coating on the back of a piece of glass. When you look in a flat mirror, your image seems to be behind the mirror. It is also the wrong way round. Ambulances have words written backwards on them so they can be read the right way round in a car's mirror.

Curved mirrors

Behind the bulb in a torch there is a shiny curved surface. It reflects light from the bulb forwards in a beam. Shapes that curve inwards like this are called concave. This is the sort of mirror used in lighthouses. Concave mirrors are also used in some

▶ Polishing the main mirror for the Hubble Space Telescope. This huge mirror is used to gather light from distant galaxies. To get a sharp image the mirror has to be very, very smooth. The engineers making it wear masks and special suits to keep off every speck of dust.

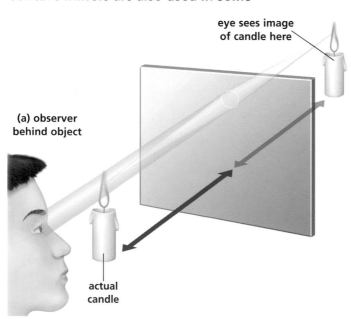

(a) observer behind object

eye sees image of candle here

actual candle

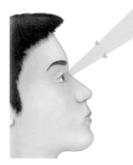

real bird

(a) observer to side of object

image of bird

◀ The image in a mirror seems to be behind the mirror. The eye cannot tell the difference between the light reflected off the mirror and that coming from a real object the same distance away as the image.

telescopes, because they are very good at collecting light.

Convex mirrors curve outwards. They let you see a very wide picture. You sometimes see them placed at difficult road junctions so drivers can see what is coming round the corner.

Lenses

If you look at a flower under a magnifying glass, it seems much bigger. The same lens can also be used to make a picture. If you were to hold it up in front of a window, you could make a picture of the window on a piece of paper. The picture would be smaller than the window and upside-down. A camera uses a lens in just this way to make a picture on a film. The picture does not have to be smaller. A projector uses a lens to throw a very large picture on a screen. Cameras, magnifying glasses and projectors all use lenses that are fat in the middle and thin at the edges. This shape is called convex. Convex lenses bend light so

▶ A camera 'lens' is actually made up of many different lenses. These help to make the image sharp and stop objects from having a halo of colours around the edges.

multiple convex and concave lenses

that it comes together. They are also sometimes called converging lenses.

Some lenses are shaped so they are thin in the middle and fat at the edges. These are concave lenses, and they make light spread out. Such lenses are also known as diverging lenses. Concave lenses are used in spectacles for short-sighted people, who cannot see things that are a long way away.

Special lenses

The lens in our eye is the one we use most often. It has the wonderful ability to get fatter and thinner. Without this, we would have trouble focusing on objects.

A single lens makes pictures that are slightly blurry. Sometimes the colours are not quite right either. To get round this problem, camera and projector 'lenses' are actually made up of several lenses.

key words
- concave
- converging lens
- convex
- diverging lens
- magnifying glass

focal point

light

convex lens

concave lens

light

▲ A convex (converging) lens bends light so that it narrows to a point. A concave (diverging) lens spreads light out.

Eyes

We get 80 per cent of our information about the world around us through a small pair of sense organs – our eyes. For animals such as birds of prey, sight is even more important. Nearly all animals have eyes of some sort. Even plants and very simple creatures have ways of sensing light.

The eyes are our organs of sight, just as our ears are our organs of hearing. The eye is a means of turning light into electrical signals. The brain takes these signals and uses them to make the colourful, moving world we see about us.

The parts of the eye

At the front of the eye is a clear, curved cornea, which bends light as it passes into the eyeball. It is covered by a thin membrane called the conjunctiva. A lens inside the eye bends the light further. Together the lens and cornea focus light onto a sheet of light-sensitive cells at the back of the eye called the retina. When these cells are stimulated by light, they send electrical signals to the brain. The image that the eye makes on the retina is actually upside down, but our brain turns the image the right way up.

▶ The parts of the human eye.

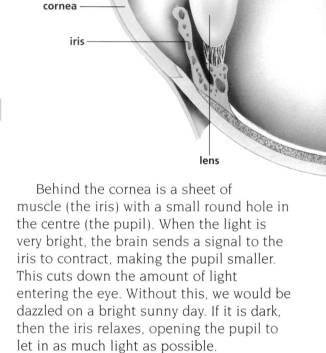

clear jelly

pupil

watery liquid

conjunctiva

cornea

iris

lens

key words
- compound eye
- cone
- iris
- lens
- pupil
- retina
- rod

Behind the cornea is a sheet of muscle (the iris) with a small round hole in the centre (the pupil). When the light is very bright, the brain sends a signal to the iris to contract, making the pupil smaller. This cuts down the amount of light entering the eye. Without this, we would be dazzled on a bright sunny day. If it is dark, then the iris relaxes, opening the pupil to let in as much light as possible.

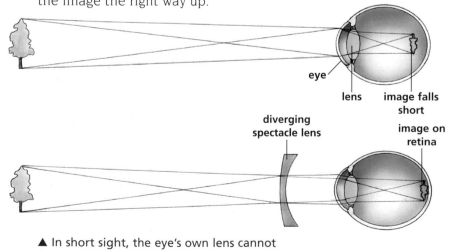

eye

lens

image falls short

diverging spectacle lens

image on retina

▲ In short sight, the eye's own lens cannot focus the image on the retina at back of the eye (top). This is corrected by wearing diverging (concave) lenses.

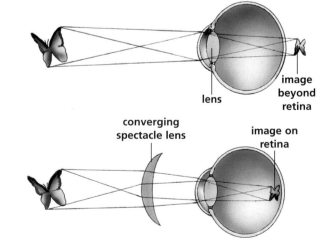

lens

image beyond retina

converging spectacle lens

image on retina

▲ In long sight, the eye's own lens focuses the image beyond the retina (top). This is corrected by wearing converging (convex) lenses.

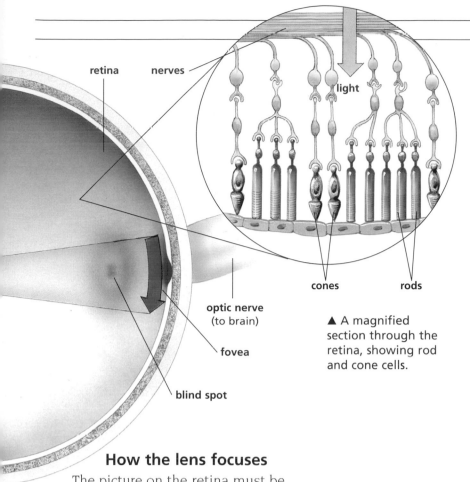

retina   nerves

light

optic nerve
(to brain)

fovea

blind spot

cones   rods

▲ A magnified
section through the
retina, showing rod
and cone cells.

The retina

The retina contains cone-shaped cells that can detect colours. There are also rod-shaped cells that can see in dim light. Rods are not sensitive to colour. This is why things look rather grey at night.

In the centre of the retina is a small yellow area (the fovea) where each cell has its own connection to the brain. In other parts of the retina, many cells have to share a connection. The fovea lets us see in detail, but this only happens at the centre of the image. (Notice that you can make out only a few words on this page at a time). To make up for this, the brain continually moves the eyes back and forth to scan the whole image.

Other eyes

The structure of an animal's eye is often a good clue to how it lives. Owls, cats and other creatures that are mostly active at night have very large pupils so that they can gather in as much light as possible. Dolphins have 7000 times more rods in their eyes than humans do, which helps them to see in the dim light underwater.

How the lens focuses

The picture on the retina must be sharp if we are going to see clearly. Light is partly focused by the curved cornea, but it cannot focus objects that are close and distant things at the same time. To cope with this problem, the eye has a lens that can change shape. Muscles attached to the lens (the ciliary muscles) can contract to make the lens thin, for looking at distant objects. When the ciliary muscles relax, the lens becomes more curved, for close focus.

▶ You can prove that your eyes have a blind spot using this picture. Cover your right eye, and focus on the blue dot with your left one. Keep concentrating on the blue dot, and move the page towards you until the red cross disappears. It has vanished because the image of it is focused on your blind spot.

+   ●

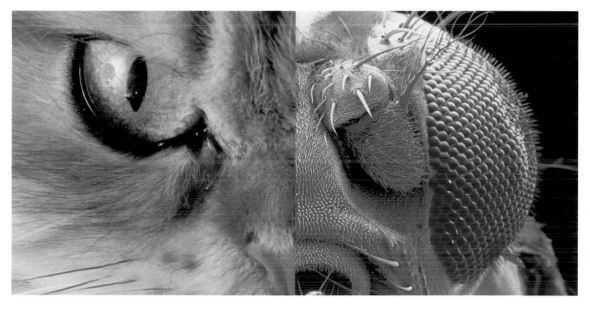

◀ A cat's eye and a fly's compound eye. A cat's pupil is a slit because it is a night hunter. At night, a slit can open much wider than a round pupil, so the cat's eye can take in as much light as possible. A fly's compound eye has 4000 individual tubes, with a lens at one end and light-sensitive cells at the other. The fly's brain puts together the tiny images from each tube to get an image of the world.

Cameras

Cameras are not just used for taking holiday snaps. They can reveal a world that we would not normally see. High-speed cameras can freeze very fast motion so we can see what is happening. They can even photograph a bullet in flight!

Cameras use a lens (a specially curved piece of glass) to make a small, upside-down picture on a film. The film is made from special chemicals that react to light. The film 'remembers' the picture as a pattern of chemicals that have been changed by the light. The film can then be developed using other chemicals to make the picture visible.

When you take a photograph, a metal blind called the shutter slides to one side. This lets light fall on the film. The shutter closes again after a short time. To get to the film, the light has to pass through an adjustable hole called the iris. If you are taking a photograph in dim light, the iris needs to be wide open to let as much light as possible fall on the film.

The right exposure

A picture will only come out correctly if the right amount of light is used. This can be done either by using a lot of light (big iris opening) for a very short time, or not much

▶ A high-speed camera was used to take this photo of a bullet frozen in flight as it cuts through a playing card.

▼ Just the right amount of light needs to fall on a film to get a good photograph. Too little light will make the photo very dark and murky (left). Too much light will make the photograph too bright and wash out the colours (right).

light (small iris opening) for longer. The combination of light and time is called the exposure.

Simple cameras used to have two or three exposure settings. These were labelled as bright, slightly cloudy or overcast. Most cameras today have light-sensitive circuits that set the exposure automatically.

Stay sharp

The picture formed by the lens will only be sharp if the lens is the right distance from the film. When the object you are taking a picture of is close, the lens needs to be moved away from the film. When the object is distant, the lens needs to be moved

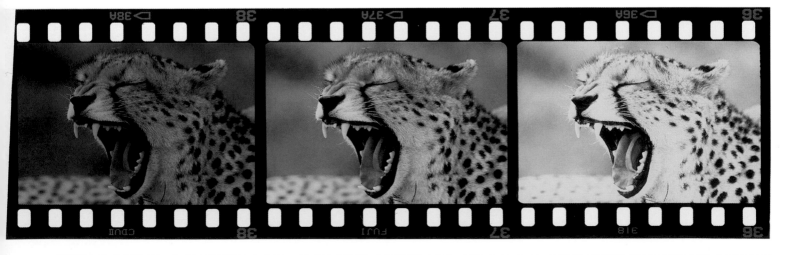

key words

- exposure
- film
- focusing
- iris
- lens
- shutter

▼ Press photographers at the Wimbledon tennis tournament. Professional photographers today use very sophisticated camera equipment.

Special types of camera

High-speed cameras use very sensitive films that can capture an image in a tiny instant. The shutter can also open and close very quickly. This helps to freeze the picture of a rapidly moving object (such as a bullet).

The lens in a digital camera makes its picture on a light-sensitive electronic plate called a charge-coupled device (CCD). Instead of recording the picture onto film, the CCD records information about colour and light levels as a pattern of electric charge. The information is then digitized and stored on something similar to a computer disk. You can look at the picture you have just taken on a screen, so that you can decide if you want to keep it or not.

Movie cameras work rather like ordinary cameras, except that they take lots of separate pictures (usually 24) every second. Each picture holds a frozen image of motion. When the pictures on the developed film are projected onto a screen at the right speed, the eye is fooled into seeing people and things moving about.

closer to the film. Changing the position of the lens like this is called focusing. Many cameras today can focus themselves. A tiny computer in the camera looks at how fuzzy the picture is. The computer controls a motor that moves the lens back and forth until the picture is sharp.

THE SLR CAMERA

Single-lens reflex (SLR) cameras are often used by professionals and other keen photographers.

There is a mirror behind the lens that reflects light to the viewfinder. The photographer can then see exactly what is coming through the lens. An electronic circuit measures the light coming through the lens to set the exposure.

The mirror prevents the light from reaching the shutter, so just before the picture is taken it flips up out of the way, so that light falls on the film when the shutter opens.

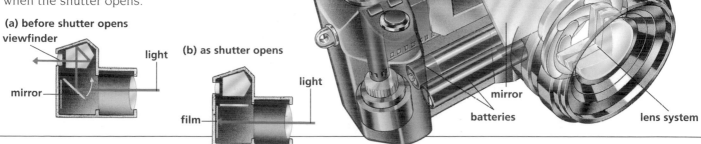

(a) before shutter opens
viewfinder
light
mirror

(b) as shutter opens
light
film

viewfinder
shutter
film
mirror
batteries
prism
iris
lens system

Photography

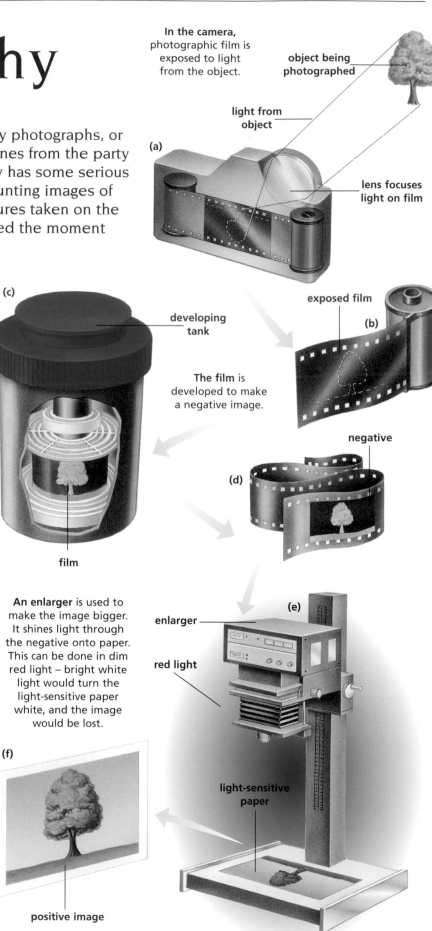

We all enjoy our holiday photographs, or those embarrassing ones from the party we went to, but photography has some serious uses as well. There have been haunting images of starvation in Africa as well as pictures taken on the Moon. We have even photographed the moment when a human life begins.

Photographs are made in three steps. First light is allowed to fall on a film. Next the film is turned into a negative (a picture in which the dark parts of an object look light, and the light bits look dark). Finally a print is made from the negative. The print is the photograph that we look at.

Taking a photograph

A black-and-white film is made from thin plastic coated with a light-sensitive chemical containing silver.

To take a picture, light is let into the camera by opening a shutter. This is called exposing the film. Where a lot of light hits the film, the light changes the chemical on those parts of the film. On other parts of the film not as much light falls, so there is less change in the chemical.

Making a negative

The process of turning an exposed film into a negative is called development. There are three stages.

First of all, the film is dipped in a liquid called the developer. The developer reacts with the exposed chemicals in the film, making them release tiny pieces of silver.

▶ When you press the shutter button on a camera, the shutter opens and light falls briefly on the film (a). There is now an image of the scene on the film, but it can't be seen (b). Developing the film (c) produces a negative version of the scene on the film (d). The negative is put in an enlarger (e), and printed onto photographic paper. Now the light and dark areas on the photo correspond to the light and dark areas in the original scene (f).

In the camera, photographic film is exposed to light from the object.

object being photographed

light from object

(a)

lens focuses light on film

exposed film

(b)

The film is developed to make a negative image.

(c)

developing tank

film

negative

(d)

An enlarger is used to make the image bigger. It shines light through the negative onto paper. This can be done in dim red light – bright white light would turn the light-sensitive paper white, and the image would be lost.

(e)

enlarger

red light

light-sensitive paper

(f)

positive image

Where lots of the film chemical has been exposed, there will be many spots of silver.

Next the film is dipped in another chemical called fixer. The fixer reacts with the chemicals on the film, making them easy to wash off. It also sticks the pieces of silver firmly on the film. Finally the film is washed in water to rinse away all the unused chemicals.

The film is now transparent in some places, and dark in others where the silver has built up. The dark places are where the most light fell when the film was exposed, so the result is a negative image (black where the scene was bright, light where the scene was dark).

Printing

Pictures are printed on special paper with a light-sensitive coating. To do this, you shine light through the negative onto the paper. Where the negative is black, not much light gets through and the paper is not exposed. The transparent parts of the negative let a lot of light onto the paper, exposing the light-sensitive coating.

The paper is then developed by a three-stage process, just like the negative was. At the end of this, the paper has black areas (where silver has built up) and white parts (no silver and the paper shows through) in the right places. It is now a positive image.

▲ A photograph taken in about 1843 by the Englishman William Fox Talbot (1800–1877). The first ever photograph was taken in 1826 by the Frenchman Nicéphore Niepce, but it was Talbot who invented the modern method of making a negative from which many prints can be made.

COLOUR PHOTOGRAPHY

Developing and printing colour photographs is a bit like doing black-and-white ones – three times over.

The colour film has three layers: one is sensitive to red, one to green and one to blue. These are the three primary colours of light – our eyes and brains can be given the sensation of any colour just by mixing red, green and blue light in different amounts.

The negative made from the exposed colour film is called a colour-reversed negative. Colour prints are made by passing first red, then green, then blue light through the negative onto special paper that also has three sensitive layers. The print ends up with the right combination of colours.

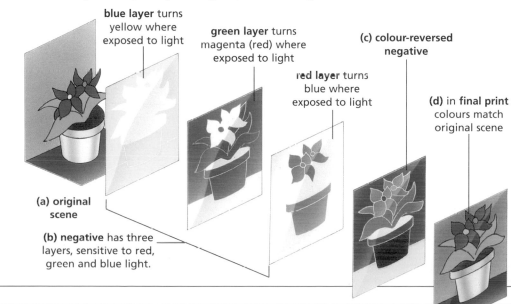

blue layer turns yellow where exposed to light

green layer turns magenta (red) where exposed to light

red layer turns blue where exposed to light

(c) colour-reversed negative

(d) in final print colours match original scene

(a) original scene

(b) negative has three layers, sensitive to red, green and blue light.

key words
- camera
- development
- exposure
- film
- negative
- primary colours
- print
- shutter

Movies

A good film takes us out of ourselves into a world of action, adventure and romance – simply using flickering pictures on a screen.

A movie is a series of still images projected onto a screen very quickly. You see it as a smoothly changing picture because the images are timed to trick your eye. Your eye will continue to see an image for about a twentieth of a second after it has disappeared (this is called persistence of vision). So the eye is still 'holding' the last image when the next one appears.

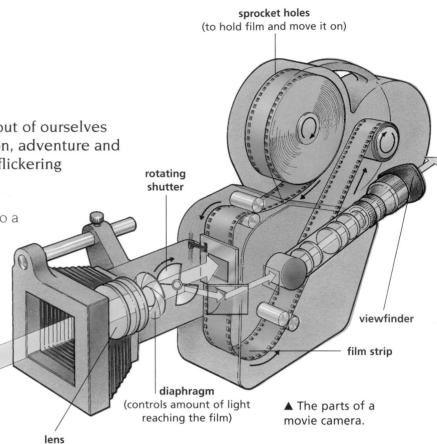

sprocket holes
(to hold film and move it on)

rotating shutter

viewfinder

film strip

diaphragm
(controls amount of light reaching the film)

lens

▲ The parts of a movie camera.

Filming a movie

Movie cameras capture the light coming from moving objects and use it to freeze an image – quickly, so the images are not blurred by the object's movement. The lens captures the light and directs it onto a film. (Movie film is light-sensitive, like ordinary

▼ These photographs of a cat falling were taken by photography pioneer Etienne-Jules Marey in the 1890s. He wanted to try to capture the illusion of movement in still images.

camera film.) The rotating shutter cuts off the light at regular intervals, to break the action up into a series of images.

Projecting the movie

The projector at the cinema contains a lamp and a lens to direct light through the film and onto a screen.

With 24 frames being projected each second, a movie uses a lot of film. This is cut into lengths called reels. Cinemas use two projectors. As soon as one completes its reel, the other starts up.

▼ A thaumatrope is a cardboard disc with an image on each side. If you spin the disc, the two images merge to make a single picture. The thaumatrope shows how your eye can be fooled by fast-moving pictures.

TIME-LAPSE PHOTOGRAPHY

A movie camera takes 24 frames every second. If you take one frame every hour, but project the film back at the normal speed, you can see a day's worth of frames every second! This means you can film something changing extremely slowly, such as a flower unfurling.

Cinema shows 24 frames a second, but TV shows 25. So, when you watch 25 minutes' worth of movie on television, you see it slightly fast – in only 24 minutes.

🔵 **key words**

- camera
- frame
- projector
- reel

▼ The 1933 movie *King Kong* had some of the best special effects of its time. King Kong himself was a model, and in this scene he is set against a 'futuristic' background.

Sound

The movie soundtrack is on the same film as the pictures, sometimes as a patterned strip of light and dark down the edge. The projector shines light through this strip onto a light-sensitive circuit. This converts the pattern into an electrical signal, which is then turned into sound by an amplifier and loudspeaker.

Cartoons that move

Traditional-style cartoons and animations use models, puppets or lots of drawings, but modern animation is usually made using powerful computers. Feature-length cartoons can take years to produce.

As with an ordinary film, a series of images, each one slightly different from the one before, creates the illusion of movement. Puppeteers spend hours patiently moving the bodies of their puppets between each frame. Cartoonists create lots of drawings, each with a tiny change.

Traditional animation can be speeded up by using transparent plastic sheets called cells. The background artwork can remain the same while cells with drawings of the moving characters are placed on top.

Telescopes

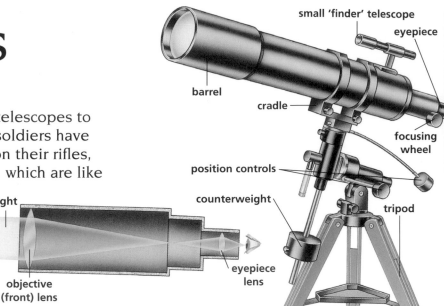

Astronomers use telescopes to study the stars, soldiers have small versions mounted on their rifles, and birdwatchers use binoculars, which are like a double telescope.

Telescopes do two jobs. They make things that are far away seem nearer (they magnify them) and they help us to look at things that are too dim to see just with our eyes.

▲ A modern refracting (lens) telescope, and a cutaway view showing how it magnifies a distant image.

Refracting telescopes

Lens telescopes are called refracting telescopes because they use a lens to refract (bend) light. A Dutch spectacle-maker called Hans Lippershey probably made the first telescope in 1608. We can imagine that one day he held two lenses up, looked through both of them – and was surprised at what he saw!

Word of Lippershey's discovery soon reached the great Italian scientist Galileo Galilei. In 1609 he made an improved telescope. It had a convex (outward-curving) lens at the front and a concave (inward-curving) eyepiece lens.

The big lens at the front of the telescope is called the objective lens. It gathers as much light as possible and produces an image inside the tube of the telescope. The second, smaller lens (the eyepiece) acts like a magnifying glass, producing a bigger version of the image.

Wrong way up

Unfortunately the final image through Galileo's telescope was upside-down. Modern telescopes for use on Earth have a different lens system, so that the final image is the right way up. A similar system is used for binoculars. However, using this lens system blurs the image very slightly. Astronomers looking at very small, dim objects prefer to have a clearer image, even if it is upside-down.

Gathering light

Being able to see things that are very faint is more important to astronomers than magnification, because even a magnified star still looks like a dot. For this reason, astronomical lens telescopes have to have very big objective lenses. The bigger their lens, the more light they can collect.

The problem with this is that large glass lenses are very heavy. The lens has to be held round the edge, otherwise the support

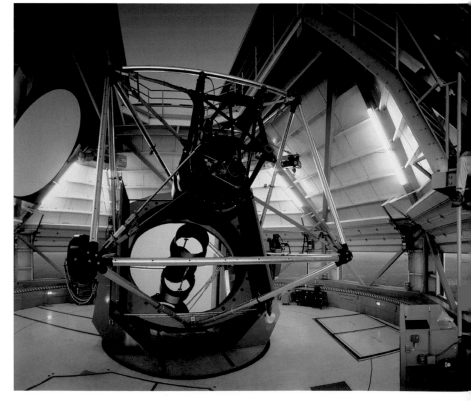

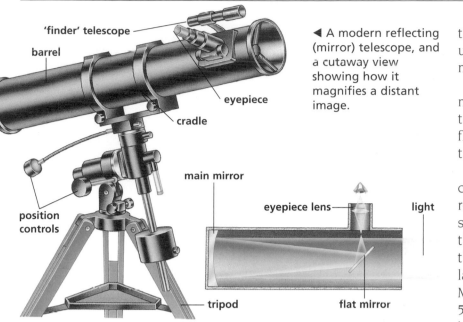

'finder' telescope

barrel

eyepiece

cradle

position controls

main mirror

eyepiece lens

light

tripod

flat mirror

◀ A modern reflecting (mirror) telescope, and a cutaway view showing how it magnifies a distant image.

would block the view, and this limits how big a lens telescope can be (the biggest has a lens about 100 centimetres across). To see even fainter objects, a bigger surface to gather the light is needed. Since a lens will not do, a curved mirror is used to gather the light instead.

Reflecting telescopes

One of the most common ways of making a reflecting telescope, or reflector, was first

thought up by Isaac Newton in 1672. He used a curved mirror, together with a flat mirror and an eyepiece.

In a Newtonian reflector, the concave main mirror gathers the light and brings it to a focus inside the tube. There, a small flat mirror sends the light to the side of the tube, where it is magnified by an eyepiece.

Mirrors have two advantages when it comes to telescopes. First, as the mirror's reflecting surface is at the front, it can be supported from the back. This is easier than trying to hold a lens by its edge, so the mirror can be much bigger. One of the largest single-piece mirror telescopes is at Mount Palomar in California. Its mirror is 5 metres across – five times bigger than the largest lens telescope.

▶ The Antenna galaxy is actually two galaxies colliding together. An image from the Hubble Space Telescope (right) shows in incredible detail new stars being made in the central area. The best ground-based image (left) does not compare.

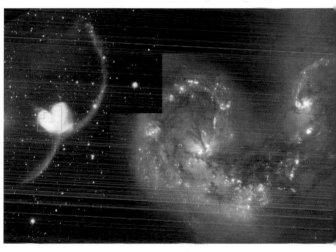

The second advantage is that a mirror reflects all the colours of light in the same way. A lens will not bend all colours by the same amount, so the image in a lens telescope always suffers from some blurring of colours.

Top telescopes

The Keck I Telescope in Hawaii has a huge main mirror 10 metres across. It is made up of 36 hexagonal pieces 2 metres across. The images from a nearby second telescope (Keck II) are combined with those from Keck I to make an even better image. But ground telescopes will always produce slightly blurred images because of Earth's atmosphere. Being in orbit gives space telescopes such as Hubble a great advantage.

key words

- concave
- convex
- lens
- reflector
- refractor

◀ The highly advanced WIYN telescope is one of several telescopes on Kitt Peak mountain in Arizona, USA. A computer controls the shape of the main mirror and its surface temperature, to ensure the sharpest possible pictures.

Microscopes

Imagine being the first person to look at bacteria and tiny insects through a microscope. You would have seen creatures to rival the scariest horror-movie monsters!

An ordinary (light) microscope makes very small things appear larger than life. It uses two lenses fixed at either end of a metal tube. The lens at the far end (the objective lens) collects light from the object and focuses it to make an image inside the tube. You look through the other lens (the eyepiece), which acts like a magnifying glass to enlarge the image made by the objective. Together, these two lenses can magnify the object by as much as 2000 times.

▼ A compound (many-lensed) microscope.

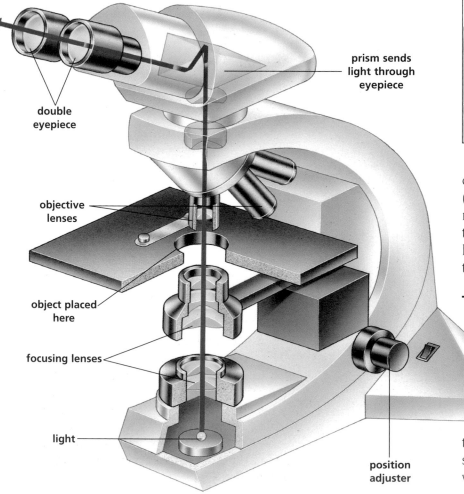

double eyepiece

prism sends light through eyepiece

objective lenses

object placed here

focusing lenses

light

position adjuster

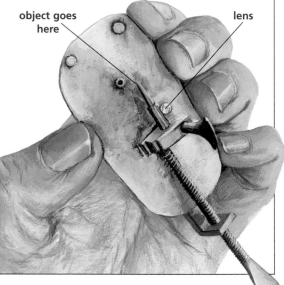

object goes here

lens

Compound microscopes have several objective lenses of different curvature (degrees of being curved). These are mounted on a disc at the far end of the tube, which is turned to bring a selected lens in line with the eyepiece. This changes the magnification of the microscope.

The see-through object

Microscopes are generally used to look at things that are so tiny that they could never reflect enough light into the objective lens to be seen. The object to be viewed has to be transparent and have light shining through it. This is fine for things like bacteria and cells, but objects such as rock samples have to be sliced wafer-thin for the light to get through.

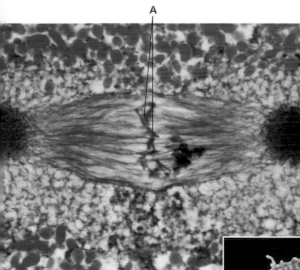

◀ ▼ Three photographs showing a cell's genetic material.

(a) A photograph of a dividing cell, magnified about 200 times. The genetic material is in the chromosomes (A).

the way they move. An electron microscope uses a beam of electrons instead of light, and uses magnets to focus the electron beams instead of the lenses used in a light microscope.

Some electron microscopes send electrons through a transparent object. These are called transmission electron microscopes. Others (scanning electron microscopes) bounce electrons off the object's surface while sweeping the beam back and forth. A computer examines how electrons bounce off the surface and build up a detailed picture. Electron microscopes can magnify objects by up to a million times.

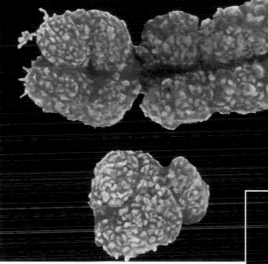

(b) Electron micrograph of a single chromosome pair, magnified over 10,000 times. These are X and Y chromosomes (sex chromosomes). Females have two X chromosomes; males have an X (top) and a Y chromosome, as shown here.

The object is placed on a strip of glass (the slide) and positioned so that light passes through it. If the object is in a liquid, a tiny puddle is trapped between the slide and a small glass square (the cover slip).

Simple microscopes may have a mirror that is tilted to direct light onto the object, but larger ones usually have built-in lamps. They might also have a camera instead of an eyepiece, so that the object can be photographed.

(c) A scanning tunnelling microscope image of a section of DNA, the material chromosomes are made from. The image is magnified over 1½ million times. DNA has a double-helix (spiral) structure. The row of orange/yellow peaks in the centre are the individual turns of the helix.

The limits of light

There is a limit on how much a microscope that uses light can magnify an object, and how small an object can be seen through it. This is because light travels as a wave. Have you ever noticed that water waves will bend round rocks if the rocks are small enough? The same thing can happen with light. If the object is very tiny, the light waves bend round it, so it cannot be seen. To achieve really high magnifications and see minute objects, you have to use an electron microscope.

Electron microscopes

Electrons are tiny particles of matter that come from atoms. They have an electrical charge, so magnets can be used to change

State of the art

Scanning tunnelling microscopes (STMs) are the newest kind of microscope. An STM has a tiny, ultra-fine probe that is moved across the surface of an object. Electrons from the atoms on this surface jump onto the probe tip as it passes. By counting these electrons, it is possible to make an image of the surface capable of showing individual atoms.

🔵 key words

- electron microscope
- eyepiece
- light microscope
- objective lens
- scanning tunnelling microscope

Lights and lamps

The Sun is a huge nuclear furnace that constantly pours out light and heat energy. Without this energy the Earth would freeze and living things would die. But modern life does not stop when the Sun goes down. We have lights in our homes, headlamps on our cars and torches to carry around.

Burning materials such as coal or wood produce a fairly poor light, and once they are burnt, they cannot be used again. Electricity works much better. It tends to heat up any material it passes through. Once the material gets hot enough, it gets rid of excess energy by producing light.

The simplest electric lights contain a coil of thin wire called a filament. It is made of tungsten, a metal with a very high melting point. The filament is placed in a glass bulb filled with a small amount of gas – either argon or nitrogen. The gas stops the filament catching fire.

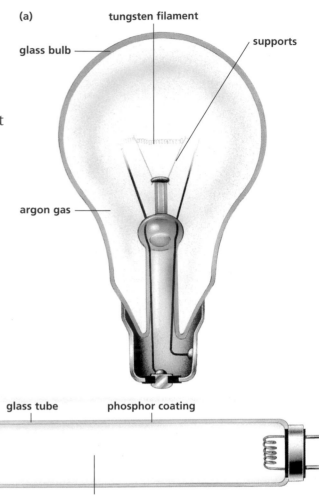

(a)
tungsten filament
glass bulb
supports
argon gas

electrode   glass tube   phosphor coating
(b)
mercury vapour

▲ An incandescent (ordinary) light bulb (a) has a filament made of tungsten. An electric current heats the filament to about 3000 °C, making it glow. Electrodes at either end of a fluorescent tube (b) produce a current through the small amount of gas in the tube. The gas gives off UV light, which makes the phosphor coating glow brightly.

The filament glows brightly when a current passes through it. Over time, the filament gets gradually thinner until eventually it snaps. Then the light bulb must be replaced.

Special bulbs

Quartz-halogen bulbs are used in overhead projectors and spotlights. They produce more light and use less power than ordinary bulbs because they work at a

◀ Glow-worms make their own light from chemical reactions. Scientists are studying them – and using the chemicals they produce – to make new light sources.

much higher temperature. The type of gas used in these bulbs (usually iodine or bromine vapour) gives the filament a longer life. The bulbs are made from quartz rather than glass to survive the high temperature.

A fluorescent light is a glass tube containing a small amount of mercury vapour. When an electric current passes through the gas, it produces ultraviolet (UV) light. As we cannot see UV light, the inside of the tube is coated with phosphor, a material that glows when UV light hits it. It is this glow that we see. A fluorescent tube produces four times the light of an ordinary light bulb of the same power.

Discharge lamps contain a gas that produces visible light when you pass a

key words

- bulb
- filament
- fluorescent light
- laser
- LED

▼ The bright lights of the big city. In Las Vegas, USA, the many casinos and hotels compete for attention with brilliant neon signs.

FATHER OF LIGHT

Thomas Edison (1847–1931) was one of the greatest inventors that ever lived. In 1879 he demonstrated his electric light bulb to the public. It worked by passing an electric current through a thin filament made of carbon, which then glowed brightly. Other inventors also made light bulbs, but Edison went further. In 1885 he opened a power station that supplied electricity to power his bulbs.

Thomas Edison and (above) his light bulb.

current through it. Sodium street lamps use a thin vapour of sodium and glow a bright yellow colour. The many different coloured lamps used to make advertising signs are made the same way. They use the gas neon, mixed with other gases chosen to make different colours.

LEDs and lasers

Light-emitting diodes (LEDs) are small electronic lamps. They come in different colours and are used in hi-fis and radios to show when the power has been turned on. Infrared LEDs are used in TV remote controls. Some modern LEDs are bright enough to be used for car brake lights.

Lasers produce very concentrated light – usually in a tiny beam that is less than a millimetre across. This makes lasers unsuitable for lighting a room, but ideal for some very special uses – such as reading data off compact discs, welding things together or carrying out delicate surgery.

Lasers and holograms

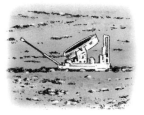

On the Moon is a mirror the size of a tea tray. It was left there by the first astronauts on the Moon. This tiny target is used to reflect back a laser beam sent from Earth – a distance of nearly 400,000 kilometres!

Lasers are useful for all sorts of jobs, because they are so controllable. Doctors direct their heat to weld (fix) retinas in place at the back of the eye, reshape the cornea and seal leaking blood vessels.

Lasers are also used to drop bombs with great accuracy – a laser-guided missile can demolish a target leaving neighbouring buildings untouched.

Surveyors and builders sometimes need to line things up very accurately – for example, if they want to measure heights or mark where a wall should be. A laser is the ideal tool for this, too.

key words

- atom
- coherent light
- hologram
- laser

◄ Lasers have a variety of uses in eye surgery, including re-attaching the retina (the layer of light-sensitive cells inside the eye) if it comes loose. Patients do not need an anaesthetic for this treatment.

Straight lines

Lasers are a special source of light called coherent light. This means that all the light waves they produce are in step with each other and travel in the same direction. This is different from a light bulb, which produces light travelling in all directions.

▼ The ruby laser was the first laser invented, in 1960. A high-intensity light produces a bright flash to start the laser. Atoms of chromium within a rod of artificial ruby are excited by this light flash, and emit red light.

bright light
starts laser

mirror

ruby rod

mirror

light given out by
excited atoms

laser beam

◄ This green laser beam is used to create an artificial 'star' high in the atmosphere. Astronomers can measure changes in the shape of this 'star' caused by the atmosphere, then use this information to improve their images of real stars.

How lasers work

A laser works by making an atom produce light, and forcing the atom next to it to make the same light. It's rather like having a row of dominoes standing up – if you knock one over, the rest fall in sequence.

Lasers have either a crystal inside them or a tube containing a gas or liquid. There is a mirror at either end. Electricity (or a flash of bright light) is used to give energy to the atoms in the laser material. They get rid of this energy by sending out light waves. This triggers other atoms to send out the same waves. The light builds up inside the crystal and reflects from a mirror back down the crystal again, triggering more atoms as it goes. The light carries on again, back and forth, getting steadily stronger. One of the mirrors is not perfectly reflecting, and the laser beam eventually escapes at this end of the tube.

'Laser' stands for 'light amplification by stimulated emission of radiation.' In other words, a light source is made stronger (amplified) by rays (radiation) that are given off (emitted) by atoms that have been given extra energy (stimulated).

Another difference is that a light bulb will seem dimmer if you stand a long way from it. This is because the light spreads out – the further away you are, the less light enters your eye. Laser light hardly spreads out at all. It can be sent a very long way – to the Moon and back – without becoming much dimmer.

Heat and colour

Concentrated light from the Sun can set fire to a piece of paper. A powerful laser can do the same, because all the energy in the light is concentrated into one small spot. Very powerful lasers can even cut through metal. Laser cutters guided by computers are used by manufacturers to carve pieces of metal very precisely into complicated shapes.

Light is a kind of wave. The white light from a light bulb is a mixture of light of many different colours, each of which is a different wavelength. Laser light, however, is a single, pure colour. Each type of laser produces light of one particular wavelength.

THE MAGIC OF HOLOGRAMS

In 1947, the British physicist Dennis Gabor (1900–1979) worked out how it would be possible to record a three-dimensional image on photographic film. No one was able to try out his ideas until the 1960s, when the laser was invented. The first hologram was made in 1962, but a laser had to be shone through the film to make the picture visible. Advances since then have made it possible to make holograms that can be seen in normal light. Holographic images are used on credit cards to make them less easy to copy.

Fibre optics

The journey starts at the touch of a button. Into the tunnel they dive, bouncing one way then the other. They crash against the walls, but keep moving at the fastest possible speed. A hundred kilometres later, the light waves emerge from the tiny glass wire.

Optical fibres are thin strands made from glass or plastic. They are usually about one-eighth of a millimetre in diameter. These amazing fibres play a vital role in science, medicine and communications.

Fibre optics in medicine

Doctors use endoscopes, which have optical fibres to carry light into the body and bring a picture back. They can be used to see inside a person's stomach to find ulcers and other problems. It is not very comfortable having a tube pushed down your throat, but better than being cut open.

For keyhole surgery (operations performed through a small hole), surgeons use endoscopes fitted with little tools. A small hole is cut in the skin and the endoscope is pushed in. The optical fibres allow the surgeons to see what they are doing.

Getting the message

Optical fibres are also used in communications. They carry TV and radio signals, telephone messages and other information. A device sends the information as pulses of infrared light. Fibres can carry far more information than electrical wires.

▶ The inner and outer cores of an optical fibre are designed so that nearly all of the light bounces back when it tries to escape. The light can travel up to 100 km without getting much dimmer.

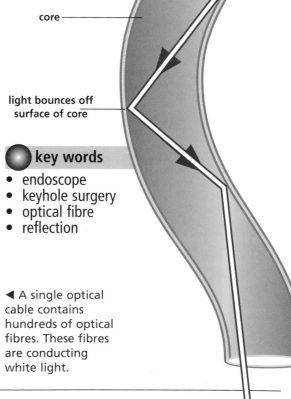

cladding

core

light bounces off surface of core

key words
- endoscope
- keyhole surgery
- optical fibre
- reflection

◀ A single optical cable contains hundreds of optical fibres. These fibres are conducting white light.

Photocopiers

Long ago, the only way to make copies of books was to write them out by hand. This was a job that monks were specialists in. Their work was beautiful – but took years to do. With modern photocopiers we can make hundreds of copies in minutes.

A photocopier 'reads' a piece of paper that you put onto it and prints a new copy. It uses light to read the paper, and static electricity and ink to make the copy. The process is called xerography, a word meaning 'dry writing'.

To use a photocopier, you place a page upside-down on a glass screen. The photocopier moves a light across the page from beneath. The light is reflected off the white parts of the page, but not off the black parts (the writing or image). A lens directs the reflected light onto a flexible belt, which has already been given a positive electric charge. Where light falls on the plate, the charge leaks away.

key words
- photocopier
- toner
- xerography

There is now a 'copy' of the image on the belt, written in electrical charge.

Toning up

A black powder called toner is sprinkled onto the belt. The toner has a negative electric charge. It sticks to the positively charged parts of the belt, but does not stick to the rest.

Next, a piece of paper is pressed against the belt, on top of the toner. Another electric charge transfers the toner onto the paper. At this stage, the toner is on the paper in the pattern of the original writing, but it is not fixed. It can easily be smudged or blown away.

Finally the paper is warmed by heated rollers. This melts the toner particles, forming a sticky ink which quickly dries on the paper. The copy is now ready to be pushed out of the machine.

▼ A modern photocopier is a complex device. Light from the page being copied is reflected onto a belt charged with electricity. Where the page was light, it causes the electrical charge to leak away. The dark areas of the page keep their charge, and black toner powder sticks to these areas. The toner is transferred to a sheet of paper, then fixed by heat.

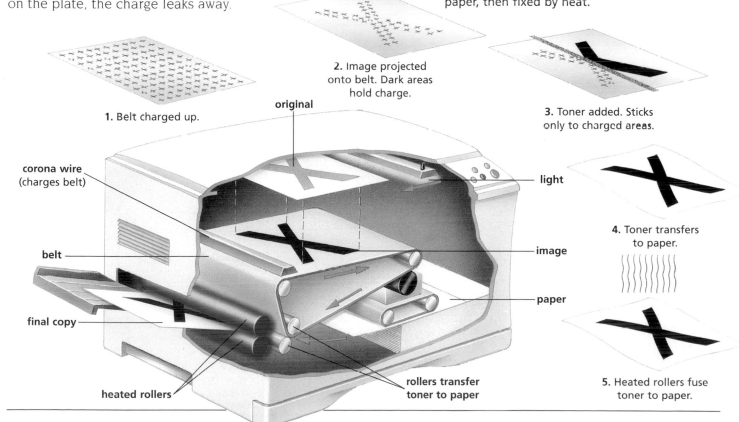

1. Belt charged up.

2. Image projected onto belt. Dark areas hold charge.

3. Toner added. Sticks only to charged areas.

4. Toner transfers to paper.

5. Heated rollers fuse toner to paper.

original

corona wire (charges belt)

light

belt

image

final copy

paper

heated rollers

rollers transfer toner to paper

Electromagnetic spectrum

Imagine it's a sunny day and you're listening to the radio. The ultraviolet rays from the Sun are giving you a tan, and you are very warm, so you are giving off infrared rays. Radio waves, ultraviolet and infrared rays are just some of the invisible waves that belong to the electromagnetic spectrum (range).

Colours are part of this spectrum, too. Since we can see them, we say they are part of the visible spectrum. Blue and red are at opposite ends of the visible spectrum.

Waves of light

Light travels as a series of very tiny waves, rather like ripples spreading out over a lake. The waves are tiny electrical and magnetic disturbances. That is why they are sometimes called electromagnetic waves.

All waves have their own wavelength and frequency. The wavelength is the

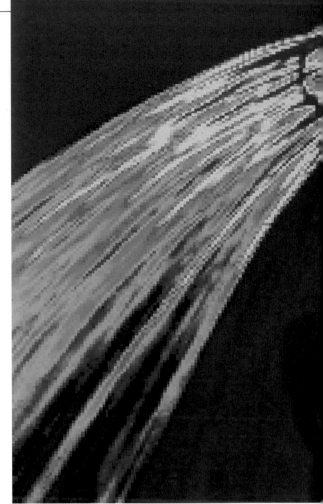

▶ A photograph of a shower taken by a camera which detects infrared (heat) radiation. The different temperatures are shown in the picture as different colours, ranging from red (hot) to blue (cold).

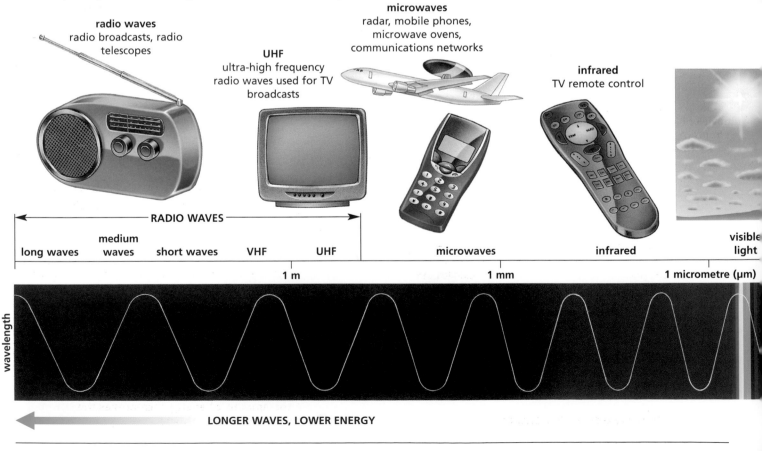

radio waves
radio broadcasts, radio telescopes

UHF
ultra-high frequency radio waves used for TV broadcasts

microwaves
radar, mobile phones, microwave ovens, communications networks

infrared
TV remote control

RADIO WAVES

| long waves | medium waves | short waves | VHF | UHF | microwaves | infrared | visible light |

1 m   1 mm   1 micrometre (µm)

wavelength

LONGER WAVES, LOWER ENERGY

distance between peaks on the wave – for visible light, this is very small. The frequency is how many times the wave vibrates (shakes) each second.

'White' light is really a mixture of all the colours in the rainbow. Each colour has its own wavelength, blue having the shortest wavelength and red the longest. But light is only a small part of the full range of electromagnetic waves. There are similar, invisible waves, some with wavelengths much longer than red light, others with shorter wavelengths than blue light. The complete range is known as the electromagnetic spectrum. Like light, all these kinds of wave can travel through the vacuum of space, and they move at the speed of light (300,000 km/s).

Radio waves

There are radio waves everywhere. We use them to send messages to each other and to broadcast music and television programmes. This is possible because we have found a way to alter radio waves, so that their pattern carries all the information needed for radios, TVs and telephones to recreate sounds and pictures. Each programme or channel has a specific frequency that the radio or TV can tune to.

Radio waves also come from the Sun and outer space. Astronomers use special radio receivers (called radio telescopes) to listen to them. The radio signals tell them about fantastic things going on in deep space, such as fast-spinning pulsars and dying galaxies.

Not just for cooking

Microwaves are a broad band of electromagnetic waves with a shorter wavelength than radio waves. Mobile phones use microwaves to send words and information to a receiver. Recently, people have become quite worried about this. It is possible that the waves from these phones are harmful to the brain.

Radar uses microwaves, too. A radar aerial sends out pulses of microwaves in all directions and then sweeps round to pick up any reflections coming back. Ships use radar to detect other craft at sea.

Microwave ovens use microwaves to heat food. The wavelength is carefully chosen so that it is easily absorbed by water molecules. The energy transferred in this way warms the water up. Most food has a lot of water in it, so this is an effective way to cook it.

Heat waves

Anything that is warm produces infrared (IR) waves – including you. The hotter a thing is, the more IR it produces. Night-vision goggles and cameras work by detecting the IR given out by people and animals and displaying it as visible light.

Some electronic components (parts) in machines produce IR. These are used in TV remote controls to beam IR signals to the television. Many computers have IR transmitters and receivers which they use to send information to other computers.

X-rays
medical X-rays, baggage
checking, X-ray telescopes

gamma rays
given off by radioactive
materials, cosmic rays
from space

**visible light,
ultraviolet (UV)**
both from Sun, but
most UV blocked
by atmosphere

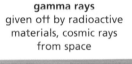

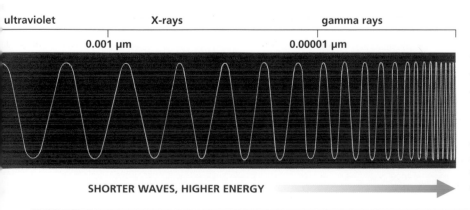

ultraviolet	X-rays	gamma rays
0.001 μm		0.00001 μm

SHORTER WAVES, HIGHER ENERGY →

◀ The full electromagnetic spectrum. All the waves in this spectrum travel at the same speed – the speed of light. They all carry energy, but the amount of energy increases as the wavelength gets shorter.

Waves we can see

Visible light includes a very small range of wavelengths compared to the whole spectrum, but it is important because it is the only range of waves that we can see. When white light passes through a prism (a triangular piece of glass), the different colours in it are bent by different amounts because they have different wavelengths.

Burning waves

Ultraviolet (UV) waves can be harmful. Too much exposure to them can cause sunburn, blindness and skin cancer. The Sun produces a lot of UV. This would wipe out life on Earth if it all reached the planet's surface. Fortunately, we are protected by a layer of gas in the atmosphere (ozone), which absorbs most of the UV. Scientists are becoming concerned that some of the gases that industry produces are removing ozone from the atmosphere. As this could be very dangerous, people are working to cut down on the emission of these gases.

Some ultraviolet still gets through, so it is important to protect yourself in bright sunlight or at high altitudes, where the atmosphere is thin. Sun creams and sunglasses help to block UV. We all need some exposure to ultraviolet, though. Without it, our bodies would not be able to make vitamin D, which is important for keeping us healthy.

Amazing rays

X-rays have a shorter wavelength and more energy than ultraviolet rays. They have many uses. Doctors and dentists use

key words

- gamma ray
- infrared
- microwaves
- radiation
- radio waves
- spectrum
- ultraviolet
- X-ray

▲ A research scientist working on the Gammasphere, a sensitive instrument for detecting gamma radiation. The Gammasphere has been used to study collisions between the centres (nuclei) of certain heavy atoms, which briefly join to form a very large nucleus and then break up, releasing gamma radiation.

X-rays to make shadow pictures of the body so they can see broken bones or damaged teeth.

At airports, X-rays are used to check passengers' luggage. The X-rays pass straight through clothes but are stopped by metal objects, such as guns. X-rays also allow manufacturers to see inside a product, such as a television, and check that it has been put together correctly – without taking the whole machine apart.

Danger rays

Gamma rays come from radioactive materials. They can be very harmful and they can pass through nearly all materials quite easily.

Gamma rays are used to kill cancers, but they have to be carefully controlled to prevent damage to healthy tissues.

Satellites have detected bursts of gamma rays striking the Earth from outer space. No one knows what causes them, but they are too weak to harm us.

JAMES CLERK MAXWELL

The Scot James Clerk Maxwell (1831–1879) was one of the greatest physicists that has ever lived. He made huge contributions to many areas of physics, but he will be most remembered for his work on the theory of electromagnetism. This built on the ideas of earlier pioneers such as Michael Faraday and led to the idea that light was an electromagnetic wave. Later, the German Heinrich Hertz used Maxwell's theory in his discovery of radio waves.

X-rays

A priceless work of art is placed in an X-ray machine, while anxious dealers look on. Without damaging the precious surface paint at all, the machine might reveal previous sketches by the artist – or even a forgery!

X-rays are similar to light waves, but have a much shorter wavelength and a lot more energy. This makes them useful, as they can pass through most materials. It also makes them dangerous, as they can damage living tissues.

X-rays in medicine

X-rays will pass through most materials, but some X-rays are stopped by bones, which is why they are useful in medicine. Bones cast shadows when X-rays are shone on them. A photographic film can be exposed by X-rays that pass straight through the body. However, it will not be exposed in the bone's shadow. The developed picture clearly shows where the bones are. This is very helpful for doctors, especially if they want to see if a patient has broken any bones.

X-rays pass through soft body parts such as the stomach and intestines. Doctors can

▲ An X-ray machine fires a beam of tiny particles called electrons at a piece of metal. When the electrons crash into the metal, X-rays are given off.

X-rays
electron beam
vacuum tube
metal target
electrode

key words
• CAT scanner
• energy
• X-ray telescope

look at these parts by feeding the patient a 'barium meal' – a mix of barium sulphate and water that absorbs X-rays.

A modern type of X-ray machine is the CAT scanner. This uses a computer to build a detailed picture of the patient's body by passing weak X-ray beams through it from lots of different directions.

The problem with using X-rays is that they can damage the body. There are strict rules about how many shadow pictures can be taken of a patient each year and the people who operate X-ray machines every day stand behind lead screens for protection while the picture is being made.

X-rays of high enough energy can also be used to kill cancers. This must be done carefully so no other parts of the body are damaged. One way is to use three weak beams that meet at the cancer to deliver enough energy.

Space rays

The ability to see through things has all sorts of uses. In astronomy, for example, satellites carrying X-ray telescopes are mapping the Milky Way and looking for the strong X-ray sources that may be caused by black holes.

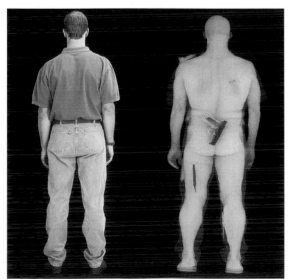

◄ An X-ray detector can discover hidden weapons. The X-rays pass through clothes and the body but are stopped by dense materials like metals.

ACCIDENTAL DISCOVERY
Wilhelm Röntgen (1845–1923) discovered X-rays while experimenting with electron beams. He noticed that material on the bench glowed while the beam was on. X-rays produced by the electrons were making the material fluoresce.

Sound

Hummingbirds hover by flapping their wings very quickly, and their wings shake up the air as they move. The result is a beautiful humming sound.

When someone strums a guitar, you hear a sound. Strumming makes the strings on the guitar vibrate (shake) very quickly. The air carries these vibrations into your ear. Inside the ear, the vibrations are turned into electrical signals that are sent to your brain.

If you twang a ruler, it will wobble up and down. As it does this, it shakes the air particles around it. The shaking particles then make the air particles next to it vibrate as well – the vibrations pass from one set of particles to the next. All of these vibrations are sound waves.

▶ The loudness of a sound is measured in decibels (dB). This scale shows approximate decibel levels for familiar sounds.

▼ The violent vibrations of this pneumatic drill produce very loud sounds. Workers wear ear defenders to protect their hearing.

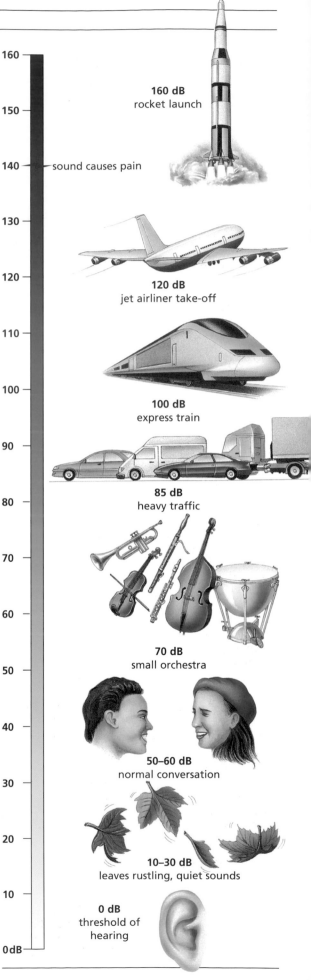

sound causes pain

160 dB
rocket launch

120 dB
jet airliner take-off

100 dB
express train

85 dB
heavy traffic

70 dB
small orchestra

50–60 dB
normal conversation

10–30 dB
leaves rustling, quiet sounds

0 dB
threshold of hearing

Humans make sounds with their voices. To do this, we blow air from the lungs past some tightly stretched cords in the throat (the vocal cords). These cords vibrate and set the air vibrating as well. To be useful, the vibrations must be made louder (amplified). Fortunately, the vibrations make the chest, mouth and throat vibrate as well. All these vibrations together make a sound loud enough to be heard.

High and low, soft and loud

A whistle makes a very high-pitched sound. The vibrations are very fast. A bass guitar makes a very low-pitched sound. Its vibrations are rather slow compared to those made by the whistle.

Every sound has a frequency. This is the number of vibrations made in a second. High-pitched sounds have a high frequency. Low-pitched sounds have a low one.

Humans can hear a range of different frequencies. The lowest sound we can hear has 20 vibrations in a second. The highest sound has 20,000 vibrations in a second. As you get older, you become less sensitive to high-pitched sounds. Some animals, such

▲ An ambulance speeds towards you, siren wailing. As it passes, the siren note changes, becoming lower. But for the ambulance driver, the sound stays the same. This change in the pitch of a sound as it moves towards or away from the listener is known as the Doppler effect.

as bats, can hear much higher-pitched sounds than we can.

Some sounds are very loud, for example when a big truck rumbles past. Other sounds are very soft, such as the rustling of a field mouse. Loud sounds are made by big vibrations. Small vibrations make soft sounds. Listening to very loud sounds for a long time can damage your hearing. For instance, regularly listening to loud music through headphones can be bad for your ears.

Fast and faster

Sound waves travel through the air very quickly – 330 metres per second, or more than 1000 kilometres per hour. At that speed, you could travel the length of three football pitches every second.

Standing at a railway station, you can often tell when a train is coming because the tracks start to buzz. A little time later, you hear the train itself. This is because vibrations made by the train travel through the tracks as well as through the air and the sound travels more quickly through the tracks than through air.

Sound can travel through many different materials, which is why you can sometimes hear your neighbours through the walls! The denser the material, the more quickly sound can travel through it. Submarines

BREAKING THE SOUND BARRIER

Many military aircraft can travel faster than the speed of sound: they are 'supersonic'. The jet-powered car *Thrust* SSC travelled at supersonic speeds on land. The scientific term for the speed of sound is Mach 1. The fastest aircraft can fly at Mach 3 – about 3000 kilometres per hour.

People on the ground hear a 'sonic boom' when a supersonic aircraft flies over. This is caused by the aircraft squashing up air in front of it, creating a 'shock wave' that makes a loud sound.

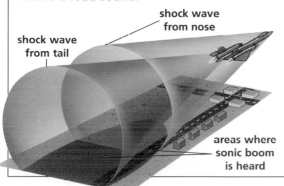

shock wave from nose

shock wave from tail

areas where sonic boom is heard

🔵 key words

- amplify
- decibel
- echo
- frequency
- Mach
- pitch
- supersonic
- vibration

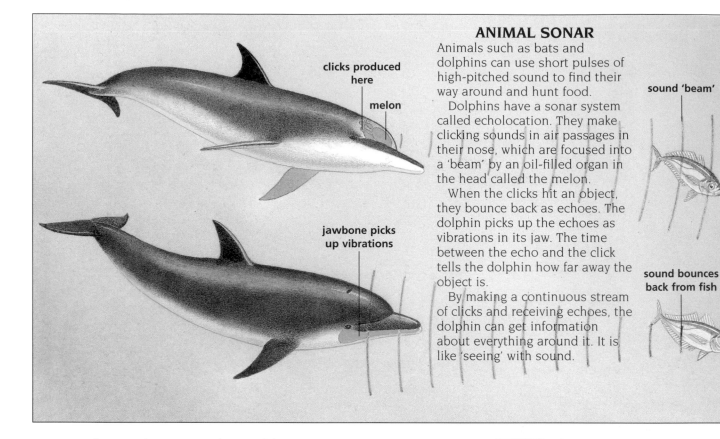

ANIMAL SONAR

Animals such as bats and dolphins can use short pulses of high-pitched sound to find their way around and hunt food.

Dolphins have a sonar system called echolocation. They make clicking sounds in air passages in their nose, which are focused into a 'beam' by an oil-filled organ in the head called the melon.

When the clicks hit an object, they bounce back as echoes. The dolphin picks up the echoes as vibrations in its jaw. The time between the echo and the click tells the dolphin how far away the object is.

By making a continuous stream of clicks and receiving echoes, the dolphin can get information about everything around it. It is like 'seeing' with sound.

use sound waves in water to detect ships. Water is denser than air, and sound travels five times faster through it. Sound can travel 15 times faster in steel than in air.

Echoes

If you make a loud noise in a large, empty room, you sometimes hear the noise repeated a few times. These repeated noises are echoes. Echoes are made when sound waves bounce off things. The echo arrives back a moment after the original sound.

When a sound wave hits an object, some of it will bounce off or be reflected. But some of the vibrations will be swallowed up (absorbed) by the object.

Soft objects tend to absorb sound, while hard objects reflect sound. That's why a room with no furniture is ideal for making echoes. The hard walls and floor reflect sound, and there are no soft sofas or carpets to absorb it.

▶ An echo-free chamber. The floor, ceiling and walls are made of glass-fibre wedges designed to absorb noise, so that no sounds are reflected.

Ears

Hearing is very important in the natural world. Many animals have a highly developed sense of hearing. It is often easier to hear something that is trying to eat you than to see it – especially if it is hiding from you!

The ear is the organ we use to detect sounds. Sounds are made when objects shake (vibrate). These vibrations shake up the air to make sound waves.

Any organ that senses sounds needs three things. It has to have a way of collecting sound waves. It needs a way of making them stronger (amplifying them). And it needs to turn the amplified waves into electrical signals. Somehow, the brain turns these signals into the rich world of sound that we hear.

▲ A bat's ears are a vital part of its echolocation system. The bat compares the tiny differences between the echoes reaching each ear to help build up a picture of its environment.

The human ear

In humans the outer ear is funnel-shaped to help collect sound waves. The waves then strike a thin membrane called the eardrum, making it vibrate.

The other side of the eardrum is linked to a set of tiny bones (ossicles). As the drum vibrates back and forth, it pushes and pulls on these bones. Working together, the ossicles make the vibrations stronger. This is the amplifying part of the ear.

The bones strike a tiny membrane (the oval window), making it vibrate. On the other side of the oval window is the inner ear. This snail-shaped container (cochlea) is filled with liquid. The vibrations of the oval window make the liquid move about. Tiny hairs line the inner ear and wave about in this sloshing liquid. The hairs are rooted in sensitive cells. Triggered by the waving hairs, these cells send electrical signals to the brain.

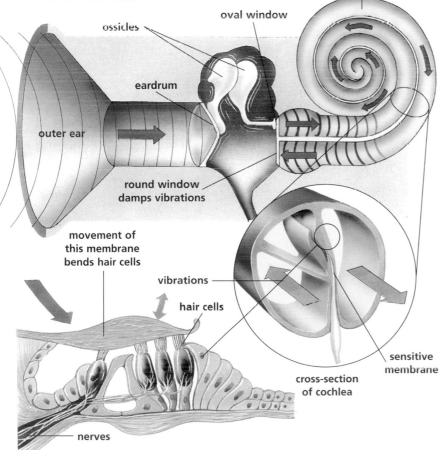

◄ How the ear works. Sounds cause the eardrum to vibrate; the ossicles amplify these vibrations and pass them to the cochlea. Movement of the liquid inside the cochlea affects tiny hair cells, which send nerve signals to the brain.

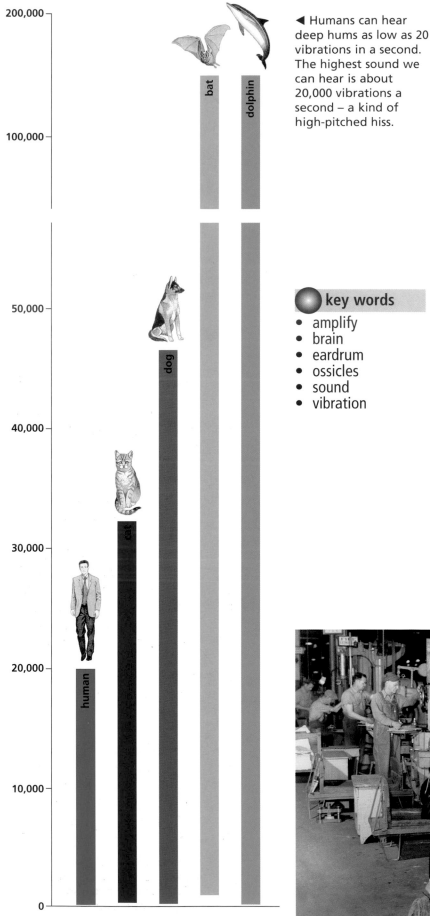

◀ Humans can hear deep hums as low as 20 vibrations in a second. The highest sound we can hear is about 20,000 vibrations a second – a kind of high-pitched hiss.

🔵 **key words**
- amplify
- brain
- eardrum
- ossicles
- sound
- vibration

Another part of the inner ear, called the semicircular canals, is not involved in hearing but is important for balance.

Other ears

All mammals have ears. Some of them, such as rabbits and the fennec fox, have huge ears in relation to their size. Large ears are very sensitive as they collect a lot of sound waves. Big-eared animals can often pick up sounds that are too quiet for humans to hear.

Bats are mammals that rely a great deal on their sense of hearing. Most bats live in the dark, so sight is not much use to them. They 'see' using an echolocation system. They make bursts of short, high-pitched sounds (too high for humans to hear), then listen for any echoes coming back. The pattern of echoes tells them about their surroundings. They can also track things they like to eat by bouncing sound waves off them.

Many insects that live on land hear with a small membrane on their legs. Spiders sense vibrations through their legs, often transmitted through the large webs that they weave. Fish have a 'sixth sense' – they have an organ (called the lateral line) down each side that can detect waves and gives them a form of hearing.

▼ Constantly being exposed to loud noises can damage your hearing. In the 1930s industrial workers like these did not wear ear protection, and many of them developed hearing problems.

Music

People have been making music since the dawn of time, and it has evolved into an incredibly varied collection of styles. One 20th-century composer wrote a symphony for full orchestra, accompanied by a washing machine and vacuum cleaner!

Music is a collection of noises that have been arranged to sound interesting. It can make you happy, sad, relaxed or excited. Some people enjoy singing or playing musical instruments. Others just like to listen to recordings or live musicians.

Sounds are made by objects that are shaking back and forth (vibrating). These vibrations can be very quick, or rather slow.

Fast vibrations make sounds that have a high pitch. Slow vibrations make low-pitched sounds.

Each vibration has a certain frequency. This is the number of vibrations that occur every

▶ A singer with the flamenco group Los Activos. The human voice is the simplest musical instrument. The air in the throat is set vibrating by tiny strings called vocal cords.

key words

- frequency
- harmony
- note
- octave
- pitch
- scale
- vibration

second. The frequencies of sounds that go well together form a pattern. A sound of one frequency always goes very well with a sound of twice that frequency. Patterns like this make music.

Musical notes

Musical sounds are organized into notes. The pitch of every note is a certain frequency. A scale is a sequence of notes. Most scales used in Western music start with a note of one frequency and end with the note of twice that frequency. These two notes are an octave (eight notes) apart.

Harmony is created when two or more notes with different pitches are sounded together. The length of a note can vary too. The mix of long and short sounds adds rhythm, which is a very important element in all music.

Musical instruments

All musical instruments make vibrations. They are designed so the vibrations produce musical notes. There are three main types of instrument. String instruments make notes from vibrating

◀ Each key on a piano plays a different note. Several notes played at the same time produce a chord.

strings. Wind instruments have to be blown in some way. Percussion instruments have to be struck by something.

Sounds different

A guitar and a violin sound very different, even if they are playing the same note.

When an instrument makes a note, lots of different vibrations are produced. One of these vibrations will make the pitch of the note. It will be the loudest. Any other vibrations will be much quieter. The sound that we hear is made up of all these vibrations.

A violin will make one collection of vibrations. A guitar will make a slightly different collection. This is why they sound different.

▶ Electronic instruments make electric wave patterns similar to the sound waves produced by other instruments. These are then turned into sounds by loudspeakers. They can also take recorded samples of real sounds and change them in many different ways.

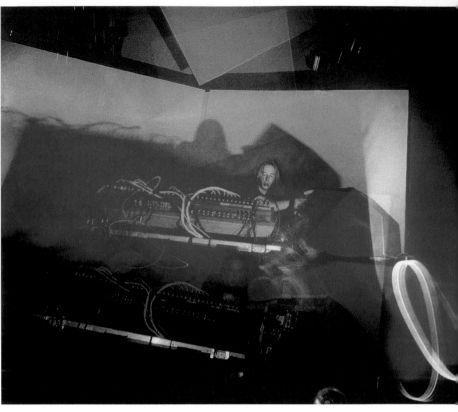

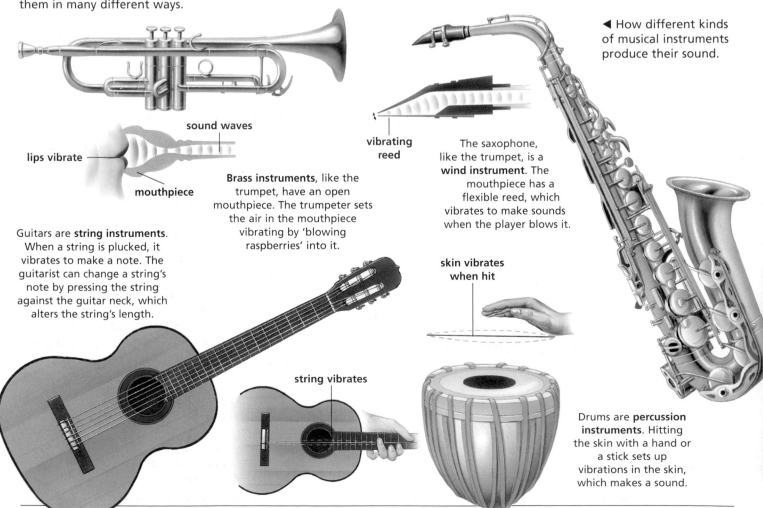

◀ How different kinds of musical instruments produce their sound.

sound waves

lips vibrate

mouthpiece

Brass instruments, like the trumpet, have an open mouthpiece. The trumpeter sets the air in the mouthpiece vibrating by 'blowing raspberries' into it.

vibrating reed

The saxophone, like the trumpet, is a **wind instrument**. The mouthpiece has a flexible reed, which vibrates to make sounds when the player blows it.

Guitars are **string instruments**. When a string is plucked, it vibrates to make a note. The guitarist can change a string's note by pressing the string against the guitar neck, which alters the string's length.

string vibrates

skin vibrates when hit

Drums are **percussion instruments**. Hitting the skin with a hand or a stick sets up vibrations in the skin, which makes a sound.

Sound recording

O ne of the strangest recordings ever made is winging its way through space. A long way from Earth, two *Voyager* space probes are heading for the stars. They carry recordings of sounds from Earth. Perhaps some day one of them will be found by aliens, who will play it back to hear what our planet is like.

Sounds are made by things that shake (vibrate). These vibrations shake up the air, making a sound wave. If the vibrations stop, the sound dies away. To record a sound, the vibrations have to be caught and changed into something else.

Sounds can be recorded using a microphone. This changes the sound vibrations into an electrical copy of the sound called a signal.

▶ This mini hi-fi system can play sounds recorded on cassette, CD or minidisc.

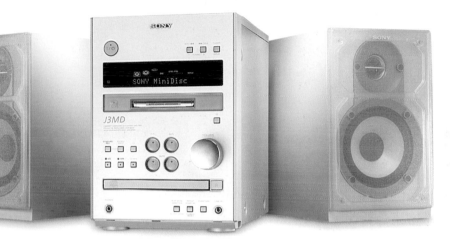

There are many ways of storing signals for a long time. One way is to turn them into patterns of magnetism.

In a recording studio, microphones are used to turn sound waves into electrical signals. These signals are made stronger (amplified) by special electronic circuits. The signals travel down wires to the mixing desk. Electronic instruments make their own electrical signals, which can be sent straight to the desk.

At the mixing desk, a technician controls the signals and mixes them together. Then they are recorded on to a large magnetic tape (the master tape). Copies can be made from the master tape in many different formats, including CD (compact disc), cassette and minidisc. Eventually, music will be sold on computer chips.

Replaying music

Once the music is stored in some form, it can be played back whenever you want. The player reads the stored music and turns it back into a pattern of electricity. This is then made stronger by an amplifier. From the amplifier, the electrical signals are passed to a set of loudspeakers. These turn the signals into vibrations of the loudspeaker cones, which we hear as sounds.

◀ In a modern recording studio, each instrument or voice is recorded separately on its own 'track'. The recording engineer uses a mixing desk to combine the tracks. He can control how loud each track is. He can also add echo or other effects.

▼ In a stereo recording, the sound is recorded as two slightly different 'tracks'. For example, an instrument may be slightly louder on the left-hand track than on the right. This will make the instrument sound as if it is closer to the left-hand loudspeaker.

Analogue and digital

The music on the master tape is recorded as a smoothly changing pattern – an analogue recording. The recording on a cassette tape is analogue too.

Analogue recordings are very fragile. They cannot be copied very often or they lose quality. These days most recordings are made digitally.

The first step in making a digital recording is to turn the music into a pattern of numbers (digits). This is called

'Hi-fi' is short for 'high fidelity'. Fidelity means faithfulness, and so the name refers to systems that reproduce sounds that are faithful to the original recording.

▼ A microphone turns sounds into an analogue (smoothly changing) signal. In a cassette, this signal is copied directly onto tape. In a CD, the signal is digitized and the numbers are recorded as a pattern of bumps.

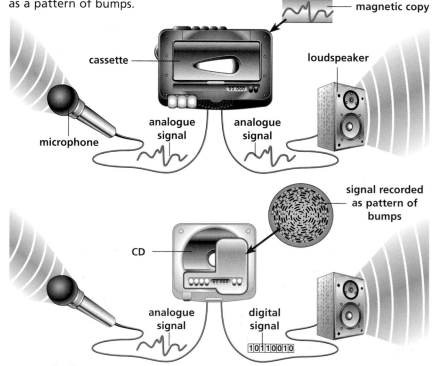

magnetic copy

cassette

loudspeaker

analogue signal

analogue signal

microphone

signal recorded as pattern of bumps

CD

analogue signal

digital signal

10110010

sampling and is done by an electronic circuit. From here, the music can be stored in a variety of ways. On a CD the numbers are stored as a pattern of bumps. On a minidisc, they are stored as spots of magnetism.

The quality of digital recordings is very high. Once the music is in the form of numbers, it can be copied many times without losing any quality.

Stereo

A stereo recording tries to create the illusion that you are listening to real musicians in the room. It does this by tricking your ears. For stereo to work there must be two loudspeakers with some distance between them.

Microphones and speakers

Be careful what you say! Spies use special microphones to hear conversations from a long way away. The same microphones can also record birdsong from a distance. Later, the tape can be played back through a loudspeaker.

Microphones turn sounds into a pattern of electricity (an electric signal). Loudspeakers do the opposite: they turn electric signals into sounds that you can hear.

The need to shake

Sound is made by something shaking (vibrating). These vibrations shake up the air to make a sound wave.

Microphones have a moving part that can be shaken by a sound wave. Often this is a thin disc called a diaphragm. Different types of microphone use different methods for turning the vibrations of the diaphragm into electric signals.

In loudspeakers, electric signals produce vibrations in something that can shake up the air. Most loudspeakers

▶ The shell-shaped Nautilus speaker is designed to give outstanding sound quality, adding nothing and taking nothing away from the pure sound. It stands more than a metre high, and weighs 110 kg.

▶ How a condenser microphone works. Two thin plates carry an electric charge across them, which varies depending on how far apart the plates are. Sound causes one plate to vibrate. This changes the distance between the two plates, causing similar changes in the charge on the plates.

▲ How a loudspeaker works. The loudspeaker coil is attached to the cone. An electric signal passing through the coil causes it to be attracted to or repelled from the magnet. This pushes and pulls the cone, making sound waves.

have cones that vibrate. A telephone's speaker uses a metal diaphragm rather than a cone.

Using microphones and loudspeakers

Microphones and speakers have many uses. Hearing aids use small microphones to collect sound. The sounds are then amplified and played back through a loudspeaker in the earpiece. Microphones and speakers are used for music concerts, and there is a loudspeaker in every TV. Telephones and most computers have built-in microphones and speakers.

cone

coil

magnet

fixed plate

moving plate (diaphragm)

● **key words**
- cone
- diaphragm
- electric signal
- loudspeaker
- microphone
- vibration

Compact discs

The ancient library at Alexandria, in Egypt, contained 500,000 scrolls, filling many rooms. Nowadays we can put the same amount of information on a few hundred CDs, which would fit on a couple of library shelves.

Compact discs (CDs) can store a great deal of information. Often this information is music. A CD-ROM is a compact disc that stores text (words), pictures, sound, computer games or computer software. The 'ROM' stands for 'Read Only Memory'.

The information is held on the disc as a series of bumps on its shiny surface. The bumps follow a spiral track, starting near the middle of the disc and ending at the edge.

The disc is read by shining a laser beam onto it. As the beam sweeps over the bumps, it reflects as a series of flashes which are picked up by a light-sensitive circuit and turned into electrical signals.

Turning sound into bumps

Sound is vibrations in the air. When a CD is recorded, the sound is 'written down' as a series of numbers, each recording the size of the sound vibration at a particular moment. With complex music, the vibrations change quickly, so the sound has to be written down thousands of times per second. On the CD the sound values are coded as binary numbers – numbers written using only 1s and 0s. Each bump is a 1, no bump is a 0.

▲ An electron microscope photo of the surface of a CD. The bumps are just 5 millionths of a metre across and about twice as long. The whole spiral track is over 8 kilometres long!

Other types of disc

Digital videodiscs (DVDs) hold even more information than CDs. They use smaller bumps and have two reflective layers. Recordable CDs (CD-Rs) do not have bumps. They use patches of colour on the disc to change the reflected laser light.

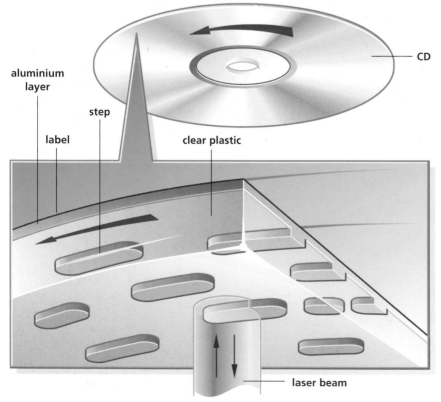

aluminium layer

step

label

clear plastic

CD

laser beam

◀ How a CD player works. The laser reads the spiral track by sweeping across the disc as it spins. A detector picks up the changes in the reflected beam when the laser hits a bump.

key words
- CD-R
- CD-ROM
- DVD
- laser
- spiral track

Ultrasound

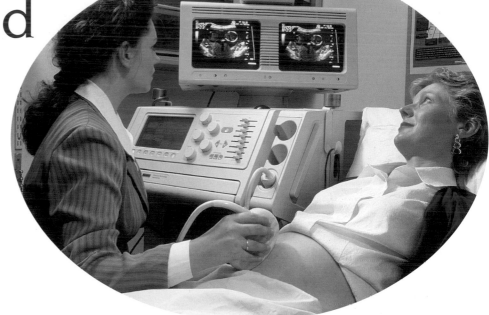

Blow a dog whistle and you might think that it was broken! The whistle's sound is so high-pitched that humans cannot hear it. Sounds that are too high-pitched for humans to hear are called ultrasound.

We cannot hear ultrasound, but we can make machines to produce ultrasound and detectors to measure it. Scientists have found many uses for ultra-high pitched sounds.

Using ultrasound in medicine

Sending waves of ultrasound into the body is a way of making a picture of what is inside. The ultrasound is reflected by organs in the body, and a detector collects the reflections. Computers can use the pattern these make to build up a picture. Pregnant women are often given ultrasound scans, so that doctors can see how their baby is growing.

Ultrasound can also be used to treat some medical problems. Sometimes tiny bits of solid matter can grow in the kidney.

🔵 **key words**
- hearing
- sound
- ultrasound
- welding

▼ An ultrasound scanner uses an electrical signal to make a special crystal vibrate fast enough to produce ultrasound waves. A detector in the scanner head picks up the reflected waves.

▲ Ultrasound scanners are used to check that a baby is growing well. You can see the baby moving about, and even watch its heart beating. Ultrasound is used instead of other types of scanner because it is very safe and will not harm the growing baby.

The result is a kidney stone. A beam of ultrasound can shake up kidney stones so much that they break up and can be passed harmlessly out of the body.

Melting metal

A very strong beam of ultrasound can even melt a piece of metal. Metal shapes can be cut out this way. Two pieces of metal can be joined together by melting them where they touch. They are then allowed to solidify. This is called ultrasonic welding.

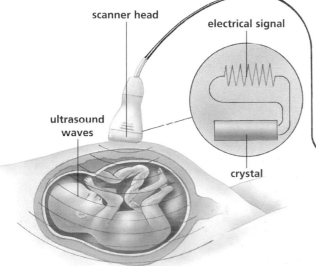

scanner head

electrical signal

ultrasound waves

crystal

computer turns pattern of reflections into a picture

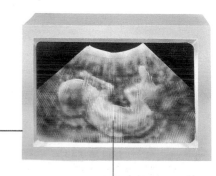

picture displayed on video screen

Materials

Resources

Every hour of every day oilfields around the world pump some 100 million litres of crude oil, or petroleum, out of the ground. Oil is one of the most valuable resources, or substances we need to produce the materials we use in our everyday lives.

Oil is valuable for two reasons. One, it can be made into fuels, such as petrol. In fact, it is one of our main energy resources, along with natural gas and coal. Two, oil can be converted into useful chemicals. From these chemicals, many different products can be made, such as plastics, paints and pesticides.

Minerals are very important resources too. They are the substances that make up the rocks in the Earth's crust. In some places, there are concentrations, or deposits, of useful minerals, which can be obtained by mining.

The vital ores

By far the most valuable of these deposits are materials called ores. These are the minerals that we can process into metals. Our modern civilization could not exist without metals. They enable us to build the

▶ Natural deposits of sulphur are often found around volcanic vents (openings). Sulphur is used to make many things, including gunpowder, insecticides and fertilizers.

▼ This map shows where major deposits of mineral ores are found around the world. Some ores, such as iron, are found widely. Others, such as aluminium, are found only in a few places.

Key
▼ aluminium
■ copper
● gold
■ iron
♦ silver

many machines used in industry, transport and in our homes.

Other useful resources

Many other minerals and mineral mixtures are useful for industry. Limestone is used to make cement and in iron-making furnaces. The sand on the seashore is one of the main ingredients of glass. Clays are used to make bricks and pottery.

Many minerals can form crystals, which have regular shapes and flat surfaces. Some crystals are very beautiful and provide us with sparkling gems – diamonds, sapphires, rubies and emeralds are the most prized.

Sea sources

The oceans are another valuable resource. They are full of minerals, dissolved in the water. The main one is common salt, or sodium chloride. This is extracted from sea water on a large scale.

Sea water also contains magnesium salts. Most of the world's magnesium is extracted from sea water by a process known as electrolysis, which involves passing electricity through it.

Up in the air

Even the air we breathe is a useful source of chemicals for industry. Air is a mixture of many gases, the chief

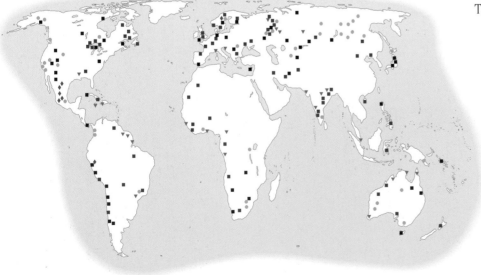

ones being nitrogen and oxygen. Both these gases are widely used in industry. Nitrogen, for example, is used to make fertilizers, while liquid oxygen is used as a propellant in rockets.

The air is also the main source of the noble, or inert, gases. The most common of these gases, argon, is used to fill electric light bulbs. Because argon is inert, or unreactive, it helps to prevent the bulb's white-hot wire filament from burning up.

Living resources

Living things can also be an important resource. Forests provide us with wood. Farms and plantations give us useful crops such as rubber and cotton. Other crops,

▲ Many of the products that we use every day have been made using natural resources.

key words
- minerals
- mining
- oil
- ores
- renewable resources
- salts

such as rape, sunflowers and flax, are grown for the oil contained in their seeds.

Properly managed, forests and farms can continue to produce wood and crops year after year. They are known as renewable resources. Oil, coal, gas and mineral deposits are not renewable. They took hundreds of millions of years to form, and once they have been used up, they will be gone for ever. This is why it is vitally important that we do our best to look after these precious resources.

▼ Rainforests are rich in natural resources, including wood. By means of a process called photosynthesis, they also supply most of the world's oxygen.

Mining

In a tunnel nearly 4000 metres underground, the air is full of dust after an explosion. The temperature is 50°C. Stripped to the waist, miners are loading shattered rock onto wagons. They are risking their lives to dig out one of the most precious metals on Earth – gold.

Many metals are mined, or dug out of the Earth's crust, underground. They include copper, zinc, lead and nickel. These metals are found in minerals, or ores, in the rocks. To mine these ores, shafts are sunk vertically down into the ground. Tunnels are then driven horizontally across to reach the ore deposits. Explosives are used to break up the rocks containing the ores, then the pieces are transported to the surface.

▶ In a silver mine in Mexico, miners drill holes in the rock, into which they will place explosives. The explosives will break up the rock, which contains the silver ore.

key words

- drilling
- opencast mine
- ores
- panning
- placer deposits
- quarrying

In most coal mines, a different method is used. Coal is found in thick layers, or seams, and is much softer than mineral ores. So it can be dug out by coal-cutting machines known as shearers.

Keeping cool

Large mines have hundreds of kilometres of tunnels on many levels, fanning out from many shafts. Some of the mines have lifts and railways to transport the miners to the ore deposits. Some shafts have hoists, or skips, to lift out the ore or coal. Other shafts are used for ventilation to supply fresh, cool air for the miners to breathe.

shaft mining

drift mining

air shaft

seams

hydraulic mining

opencast mining

◀ Different methods of mining are needed to reach mineral or coal deposits. Opencast mining digs out surface deposits. Hydraulic mining breaks up soft deposits with water jets. Underground deposits can be reached from hillsides or through shafts.

On the surface

It is cheaper and safer to mine on the surface of the ground. Fortunately, quite a few ore deposits are found on or near the surface. They include iron and copper ores and also the aluminium ore bauxite. Many coal seams are found near the surface too.

Mining at the surface is called opencast mining. Mining begins by stripping off any soil, or overburden, covering the deposit. This is done by huge excavators, such as drag-lines. If the ore or coal deposit is soft, it can be dug out and loaded into wagons or trucks. If it is hard, it must first be broken up by explosives.

Quarrying is the name given to the surface mining of rock, such as chalk, limestone and marble. Marble is widely used for decoration in building work. It has to be removed carefully by driving wedges into natural cracks in the rock.

Flash in the pan

Gold is found deep underground, and on the surface in 'placer' deposits, in stream and river beds. In the early days of gold mining, miners would 'pan' for gold using a

The Bingham Canyon copper mine in Utah, USA, is the world's largest man-made hole. Covering an area of 7 square kilometres, it is nearly a kilometre deep.

shallow pan. They would swirl material from the river bed around in the pan with some water. The lighter, gravelly material would wash away, leaving the heavier gold behind. Today, mechanical panning methods are used.

Tin ore (cassiterite) is also found in placer deposits, particularly in Malaysia. The ore is dug out by huge dredges. These are floating platforms which use a conveyor belt of buckets to dig up material from the sea or river bed.

▲ Cassiterite (tin ore) is dug out from opencast mines in Malaysia, as well as from placer deposits.

◄ Gold miners use hoses to suck up mud and gravel from the bed of the Madre de Dios river, Peru. The mixture is fed through a device called a sluice box. Heavy specks of gold fall to the bottom, while the lighter mud and gravel flow back into the river.

Out of a hole

Resources can also be taken from the ground by drilling. For example, holes are drilled down to deposits of crude oil, or petroleum, which are then piped back to the surface.

Borehole mining is used to extract underground salt deposits. Water is pumped into a hole bored into the solid salt. It dissolves the salt and is then pumped back to the surface as brine, a mixture of water and salt. Evaporating the brine recovers the salt. Sulphur can be mined in a similar way, using very hot water to melt the deposit.

Iron and steel

Pure iron is quite a weak metal and is not particularly hard. But if you add a tiny amount of carbon to it, it becomes both strong and hard. It turns into the most useful metal we know – steel.

The world uses more iron (in the form of steel) than all the other metals put together. Yearly iron production is around 600 million tonnes, nearly 30 times as much as aluminium, our next most important metal.

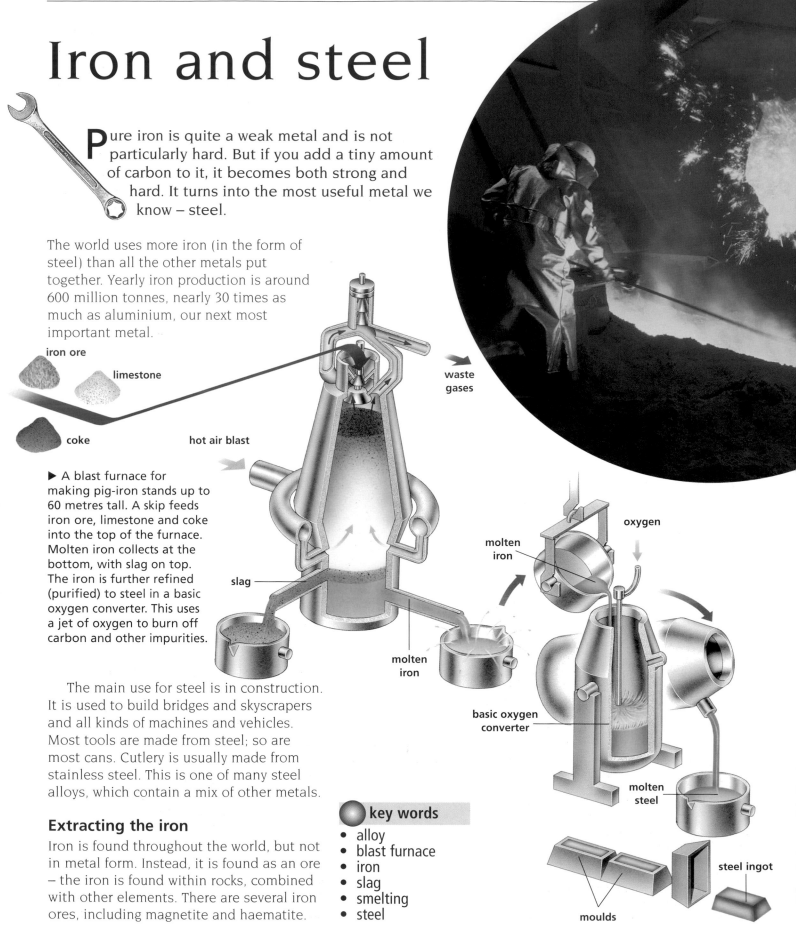

iron ore

limestone

coke

hot air blast

waste gases

▶ A blast furnace for making pig-iron stands up to 60 metres tall. A skip feeds iron ore, limestone and coke into the top of the furnace. Molten iron collects at the bottom, with slag on top. The iron is further refined (purified) to steel in a basic oxygen converter. This uses a jet of oxygen to burn off carbon and other impurities.

slag

molten iron

oxygen

molten iron

basic oxygen converter

molten steel

The main use for steel is in construction. It is used to build bridges and skyscrapers and all kinds of machines and vehicles. Most tools are made from steel; so are most cans. Cutlery is usually made from stainless steel. This is one of many steel alloys, which contain a mix of other metals.

Extracting the iron

Iron is found throughout the world, but not in metal form. Instead, it is found as an ore – the iron is found within rocks, combined with other elements. There are several iron ores, including magnetite and haematite.

key words
- alloy
- blast furnace
- iron
- slag
- smelting
- steel

moulds

steel ingot

◀ Wearing protective clothing and using a long rod, a worker takes a sample of molten iron from a blast furnace.

Iron is extracted from iron ore by smelting – heating it to a high temperature, along with other materials. Smelting is carried out in a blast furnace, so called because hot air is blasted into it. The excess carbon quickly burns off, and the impurities form a slag.

Reducing the ore

Iron ore is fed into the blast furnace together with coke and limestone. The hot air being blasted in makes the coke burn fiercely, and temperatures rise as high as 1600°C. As the coke burns, carbon monoxide gas is produced. This combines with the oxygen in the iron ore, leaving behind iron metal.

At such a high temperature, the iron is molten (liquid) and trickles down to the bottom of the furnace.

Meanwhile, impurities in the ore combine with the limestone to form a molten slag. This is lighter and floats on top of the iron. From time to time, both the iron and the slag are removed In this state, the iron is known as pig-iron.

▼ Red-hot molten steel is poured into a container. The steel has been produced using the basic oxygen process, which changes pig-iron into steel with the help of a blast of oxygen.

When the molten iron leaves the furnace, it flows along a channel into moulds. These moulds are called pigs, because they are clustered round the channel like a group of suckling piglets around their mother.

Refining the iron

Pig-iron still contains many impurities, especially excess carbon (from the coke). They must be removed before the metal can become really useful. Refining, or purifying, the metal, takes place in other furnaces.

Most pig-iron is refined by the basic oxygen process. The iron is poured in its molten state into a conical vessel called a converter. Then a high-speed jet of oxygen is blasted into it. Most of the carbon quickly burns off, while other impurities form a slag. In a typical converter, up to 400 tonnes of pig-iron can be converted to steel in about half an hour.

The best-quality steels, such as stainless steels, are made in electric-arc furnaces. Usually, these steels are made using steel scrap, rather than molten iron. The steel is heated to high temperature by means of an electric arc, a kind of giant electric spark.

HENRY BESSEMER

The Romans were making a kind of steel over 2000 years ago. But steel only began to be easily and cheaply made in 1856. In that year, the English industrialist Henry Bessemer (1813–1898) invented a way of producing steel by blowing air through molten pig-iron to burn out the impurities. Bessemer's process led to the mass-production of cheap, good-quality steel. This made possible new kinds of building and ship, and greatly improved the railways. The basic oxygen converter used in steelmaking today is a refinement of Bessemer's furnace.

The first iron people used was metal that fell to Earth from outer space, in meteorites.

Aluminium

Without aluminium, aircraft would probably still be built of wood, wire and fabric. And we would probably not be living in a space age. But thanks to aluminium we can build planes and spacecraft that are both lightweight and strong.

After iron, aluminium is the second-most important metal to us. About 11 million tonnes of aluminium are produced each year. Its lightness is the main reason why aluminium is so useful. It is less than half as heavy as iron. Unlike iron, it does not corrode, or rust.

Pure aluminium is soft and weak. It is used as thin foil – for cooking, for example. But it becomes much more useful when traces of other metals (such as copper) are mixed with it to form alloys.

Light conductors

Aluminium alloys have many uses. The alloys from which aircraft and spacecraft are made are as strong as steel but very light. Some are used to make cookware for the home. They heat up readily because aluminium is a good conductor of heat, allowing heat to travel through it easily. The metal is also a good conductor of electricity, which is why it is used for the transmission lines that carry electricity from power stations to our homes.

▶ Aluminium is used to make bodies for aircraft and other vehicles like cars and coaches.

key words

- alloy
- bauxite
- conductor
- corrosion
- electrolysis

Making the metal

There is more aluminium in the Earth's crust than any other metal (8 per cent). It is found combined with other elements in many minerals in clays and rocks. But it can only easily be extracted from an ore called bauxite, which contains the mineral alumina, or aluminium oxide. Australia has the largest bauxite deposits.

Aluminium metal is obtained from alumina by electrolysis – passing electricity through it. The process was discovered independently in 1886 by Charles Hall in the USA and Paul Héroult in France.

bauxite

caustic soda

rotary kiln (dryer)

settling tank

dry alumina

aluminium oxide (alumina)

filter

impurities

reaction vessel

pure aluminium

molten alumina and cryolite

electrolysis bath

electrodes

◀ To make aluminium, alumina (aluminium oxide) is first separated from other material in the bauxite ore. Electricity is then passed through a molten (liquid) mixture of alumina and cryolite (another aluminium mineral).

Copper

Over 13 million tonnes of copper are produced worldwide every year. About half of it is used by the electrical industry because copper conducts, or passes on, electricity better than any other metal except silver. And silver is too expensive to use for electrical wiring.

Millions of kilometres of copper wires carry electricity into and around homes throughout the world. Copper is easy to make into wires because it is one of the most ductile of metals. This means that it can be pulled, or drawn out, into long lengths without breaking.

Copper is not only used by itself, but also in alloys, or mixtures with other metals. Common alloys are bronze, brass and cupronickel. Copper and its alloys are very useful to us because they can resist corrosion, or rusting. This means that they last a long time.

▼ Bingham Canyon copper mine in the USA is the largest opencast mine in the world. It is nearly a kilometre deep and 4 kilometres wide. The mine is the richest source of copper in the world, but mining operations have caused a great deal of damage to the environment.

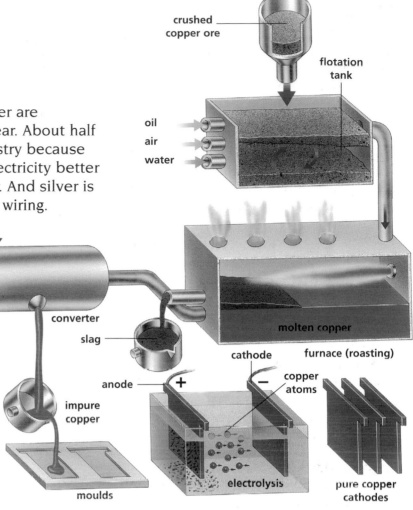

▲ To extract copper from copper ore, the ore is crushed and then fed to flotation tanks. These concentrate the copper minerals. The minerals are roasted in furnaces, where impurities burn off or form a slag. The nearly pure metal is finally refined by electrolysis. Electricity causes pure metal to be deposited on the cathode, or negative electrode, of the electrolysis cell.

Going native

Copper was one of the first metals people used, at least 10,000 years ago. This is because copper is one of the few metals that can be found in metal form in the ground. We call this kind of metal 'native metal'.

But native copper is rare, and most copper is produced from copper ores found in rocks. There are huge deposits of copper ores in the Andes Mountains of South America, the Rocky Mountains of North America, and in Congo and Zambia, sometimes called the copper belt, in central Africa.

key words

- alloy
- conductor
- corrosion
- electrolysis
- native metal
- ore

Gold and silver

In 1939, a horde of treasure was found in the remains of a buried ship at Sutton Hoo in eastern England. It included 41 items made of solid gold, among them a beautiful helmet. When they were washed, they looked as good as they must have done when they were buried 1300 years earlier.

Gold has always been admired for its rich beauty. It remains beautiful because it does not corrode, or rust, in the air or in the ground.

Because gold is so prized, it is called a precious metal. It was once used to make coins, but its main use today is in jewellery. Usually, other metals (such as copper) are added to it to make a harder alloy.

Beat that!

Many metals can be beaten into shape. We say they are malleable. Gold is the most malleable metal of all. It can be beaten into gold leaf so thin that 10,000 sheets stacked together would measure only 1 millimetre thick. Gold is also the most ductile of metals, which means that it can be pulled into very fine wire without breaking.

Silver is another beautiful precious metal that has been used for jewellery since ancient times. But its main use today

◄ This gold necklace, found in a Roman grave, is almost 2000 years old.

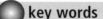

key words
- alloy
- corrode
- native metals
- ores

► This piece of rock, which contains native gold, comes from California, USA.

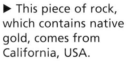

▼ When gold was discovered in Australia in the 19th century, people flocked to the gold-fields from all over the world. This painting shows prospectors hoping to strike it rich.

is in photography, because many silver salts darken when they are exposed to light.

Like gold, silver is ductile and malleable. It is also the best conductor of heat and electricity that we know.

The platinum group

Some metals are even more precious than gold. Platinum, for example, is rarer, harder and melts at a higher temperature. Its main use in industry is as a catalyst, a substance that helps chemical reactions take place. Platinum is one of a group of heavy metals with similar properties.

Rich deposits

All the precious metals are found native, or in metal form in the ground. Native deposits provide most gold and platinum. But most silver comes from silver ores, such as argentite. The ores are treated with chemicals to produce the metal.

Alloys

Copper and tin have many useful properties – for example, they do not easily corrode, or rust. The trouble is that they are quite soft and weak. But the metal you get when you mix them together is hard and strong, and still doesn't rust. It is one of our most useful metal mixtures, or alloys, and it is called bronze.

Like copper and tin, most metals are quite soft and weak in their pure state. But they become much harder and stronger when they are mixed with other metals to form alloys. Most metals used today are alloys, from the coins in our pockets and the cutlery we eat with, to the airframes and engines of aircraft.

▶ Some common alloys, with typical uses.

tool steel
(iron, chromium, tungsten)

dental amalgam
(mercury, silver, tin, zinc, copper)

duralumin
(aluminium, copper, magnesium)

stainless steel
(iron, chromium, nickel)

brass
(copper, zinc)

cupronickel
(copper, nickel)

key words
- alloy
- corrode
- metallurgist

The right recipe

Alloys have been used for thousands of years. Today, metallurgists, the scientists who work with metals, can produce alloys with a wide range of different properties. They do so by carefully selecting the alloying ingredients – choosing the right 'recipe'.

Our most common metal, steel, is an alloy. It is a mixture of iron, a little carbon, and traces of other metals. It is the carbon that makes it so strong.

One drawback with ordinary steel is that it corrodes, or rusts. To stop it rusting, metallurgists add chromium and nickel to it. These metals do not rust and make the steel rust-resistant too. The alloy formed is stainless steel.

Some of the most advanced alloys are found inside jet engines. They have to remain strong at temperatures up to 1000°C. Some of these so-called

▶ Bronze is hard and does not rust. People have used this alloy for thousands of years to make things like sculptures.

superalloys may contain 10 or more different metals, including titanium and tungsten, which melt only at high temperatures.

The value of alloys was discovered in very ancient times. Bronze was made before 3000 BC, and brass (copper and zinc) has been used for nearly as long. Pewter is an ancient alloy made from tin and lead, first used over 2000 years ago. Modern pewter uses other metals instead of lead. This makes it safe to use for plates and mugs.

Memory metals are alloys of titanium and nickel that can 'remember' their shape. If an object made of memory metal becomes twisted, it will return to its original shape if it is gently heated.

Metalworking

The blacksmith is heating a strip of iron on a fierce fire. A horse waits patiently nearby. When the iron is red-hot, the blacksmith places it on an anvil. Then he begins hammering it into the shape of a horseshoe. He is carrying out the earliest method of shaping metal, called forging.

Forging is still one of the main ways in which metal is shaped. But these days, forging is carried out in factories, using mechanical hammers. They have a heavy ram that shapes metal when it drops onto it from a height. This method is called drop forging. Usually, the metal is hammered into a shaped mould, or die. In an alternative method using a forging press, metal is shaped by a squeezing action rather than by sudden blows.

Moulding metal

Another ancient way of shaping metal is by casting. The metal is heated until it is molten (liquid). Then it is poured into a shaped mould. It takes the shape of the mould when it cools and sets hard. Many

▶ A red-hot sheet of metal is rolled in a steel mill. Hot rolling is usually followed by cold rolling, which improves the surface finish.

castings are produced using moulds made from wet sand. Mould-makers can make large and complicated shapes, such as ships' propellers. Sand moulds have to be broken up to release the castings.

Many objects, however, are made in permanent moulds, called dies, which can be used over and over again. This method,

▼ Metal can be shaped in many different ways, including rolling (a, b), drawing (c), forging or pressing (d) and casting (e).

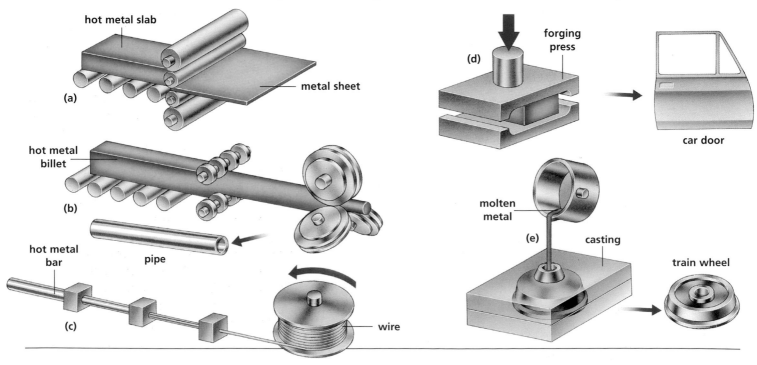

hot metal slab

metal sheet

(a)

hot metal billet

(b)

hot metal bar

pipe

(c)

wire

forging press

(d)

car door

molten metal

(e)

casting

train wheel

known as die-casting, is widely used for mass-producing small castings for toys and domestic appliances.

Rolling along

Huge amounts of metal are used in the form of plate or sheet, to make things like ships' hulls and car bodies. These products start life as thick slabs, which are made thinner and longer by rolling.

This is done in rolling mills. Here, red-hot slabs are passed back and forth through sets of heavy rollers. As the metal passes through each set, it gets thinner and longer. A thick slab originally 10 metres long would typically end up as a sheet 2 millimetres thick and 1.5 kilometres long.

After hot rolling, sheet is often rolled cold. This is done to give it an accurate thickness and a harder finish.

Pressing and stamping

One main use for sheet steel is for car bodies. The sheet is shaped cold on hydraulic presses, similar to but smaller

▼ A welder joins pieces of metal that have been heated and softened using an electric arc.

▶ A huge hydraulic press is used to make a shaft for a steam turbine (a kind of engine used in power stations). The press can exert a force of 4000 tonnes on the hot metal.

Electrical arcs (large sparks) can form underwater as well as in air. This means that electric arc welding can be used to join pieces of metal underwater.

than forging presses. Smaller versions of the drop forge are used to shape small objects, such as coins, from cold metal. They force metal into shape in dies, a process called stamping.

Other methods use dies for shaping. Rods and tubes may be made by extrusion, which involves forcing metal through holes in dies. Wire is made by drawing metal through sets of dies with smaller and smaller holes.

Joining up

Metal pieces often need to be joined together to make large objects, such as ships' hulls and pipelines. Welding is the most common method.

In welding, the edges of the parts to be joined are first softened by heating them to high temperatures. Then molten metal from a filler rod is added. The added metal bonds with the softened metal. This fills in the gaps and produces a strong joint when it cools. Gas welding uses a burning gas torch to heat the metal. Arc welding uses an electric arc to heat it.

Soldering is another method using molten metal (solder) to form joints. It is used mostly to join wires in electrical circuits. Soldering is carried out at much lower temperatures than welding, and joints are not as strong.

Ceramics

When the space shuttle returns to Earth, it uses the atmosphere to slow it down. Friction of the air against the fast-moving craft produces great heat, which makes the tiles covering the shuttle glow red-hot. But the astronauts inside are safe because the tiles stop the heat from reaching them.

The space shuttle tiles are products we call ceramics. Many ceramics are made by baking earthy materials such as sand and clay at high temperatures. Pottery is the most common ceramic product, and has been around for many thousands of years. So have those other common ceramic materials – bricks and tiles.

Preparing pottery

All pottery is made from clay. Different kinds of pottery are made from different kinds of clay and are fired (baked) at different temperatures. Firing takes place in ovens called kilns.

The ordinary kind of pottery, such as the crockery we use everyday, is known as earthenware. It is fired at about 1000°C.

▼ A potter shapes wet clay with his hands as it spins round on a rotating wheel.

▶ An ancient Greek black-figure vase showing women running. In this kind of vase, the figures were painted in black. Details were added to the black figures by scraping away the paint to reveal the red clay beneath.

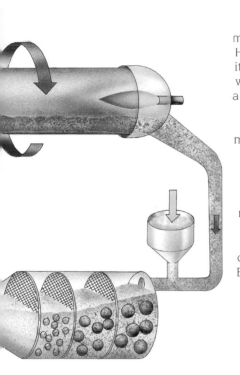

CEMENT AND CONCRETE

Concrete is the most widely used material in engineering construction. Hundreds of thousands of tonnes of it are used every day throughout the world. It is made by adding water to a mixture of cement, sand and gravel or stones, to form a pasty mass. When the mass sets, it forms a material that is very hard – concrete. Cement is a ceramic product, made by fiercely heating earthy materials like limestone and clay. This is usually done in a long, rotating kiln in which temperatures may reach 1500°C (see left). Concrete is strong under compression – when it is squeezed. But it is weak under tension – when it is stretched. To prevent this weakness, construction engineers cast steel rods into the concrete. The result is called reinforced concrete.

By itself it is dull in appearance and porous, which means that it lets water through. To make it look better and make it watertight, it has to be glazed, which involves giving it a glassy coating.

The finest-quality pottery is porcelain. This is made from only the purest white clays, such as kaolin, also called china clay. It is fired at temperatures up to about 1400°C. At these temperatures, the clay vitrifies, or becomes glass-like. This makes it watertight. Bone china is an imitation porcelain made using clay mixed with bone ash.

Brickmaking

The first bricks were shaped blocks of mud that were dried in the sun. Houses are still built of mud bricks, called adobe, in some sunny countries.

Ordinary house bricks are now made of a mixture of clay, shale and iron ore. The mixture is first crushed fine and then kneaded with water into a doughy mass. This is forced through an opening to form a long ribbon, rather like toothpaste being squeezed out of a tube. Rotating wires cut the ribbon into individual bricks. The bricks

key words
- ceramics
- clay
- firing
- kiln
- refractory

▶ A technologist removes a sample of cermet from a furnace. This cermet (<u>cer</u>amic <u>met</u>al) is made by heating and mixing together the ceramic material boron carbide and aluminium. It is lighter than aluminium and stronger than steel.

The wheel was first used for making pottery around 3500 BC, probably before it was used to make the first vehicles.

then pass through a tunnel-like kiln, which slowly heats them, then cools them again.

Remarkable refractories

Special bricks are made to line the inside of industrial furnaces, like those used to make iron and steel. They are made from naturally occurring minerals such as silica (sand), dolomite and alumina, which melt only at high temperatures.

Materials that resist high temperatures are known as refractories. They include the space shuttle tiles already mentioned, which are made out of silica fibres. Some of the best refractory materials contain tungsten, the metal with the highest melting-point (3380°C). They include tungsten carbide, which is used to make cutting tools that remain sharp even when they get red-hot. Tungsten and titanium carbides are mixed with ceramics to form cermets, which are used in the high-temperature parts of jet and rocket engines.

Glass

Take some sand and some limestone, two of the most common materials in the ground. Add some soda ash, and heat the mixture to about 1500°C, until it becomes a red-hot, molten mass. Let it cool, and the mass becomes transparent. It has turned into glass.

Glass is one of the most remarkable materials there is. Not only is it transparent, but it is also waterproof and does not rot or rust. It is resistant to all common chemicals and is easy to clean. It can easily be shaped into blocks, sheets and fibres. Glass fibres are widely used for reinforcing (strengthening) plastics. In fibre optics, very fine glass fibres are used to carry data and communications, such as telephone calls.

The main ingredient in glass-making is sand, the mineral silica. If this is melted, then cooled, it forms glass. But other ingredients must be added to it to make it melt at a reasonable temperature. The ordinary glass used for bottles and windows is known as soda-lime glass because it is made using soda ash and limestone.

► A magnificent stained-glass window in Canterbury cathedral, UK. Coloured glasses are made by including compounds of certain metals (copper, chromium, nickel, cobalt) in the glass-making recipe.

key words
- borosilicate glass
- float glass
- lead glass
- silica

Special glasses

Other ingredients are added to the glass-making recipe to produce glasses with special properties. Adding lead oxide, for example, makes lead, or crystal, glass. This has extra brilliance and, when expertly cut, gleams and sparkles like diamond. Glass with a very high lead content is made for the nuclear industry, because it blocks harmful radiation.

Ordinary glass expands rapidly when it is heated. When you pour boiling water into a cold glass bottle, for example, the sudden expansion will make it crack and shatter. But when you add boron to the glass-making recipe, you produce a glass that hardly expands at all. This borosilicate glass is used to make heat-resistant cookware and laboratory equipment.

▼ To make sheet glass, a thin layer of molten (liquid) glass from the furnace is floated on a bath of molten tin. Because the surface of the liquid tin is perfectly flat, the glass layer is perfectly flat too.

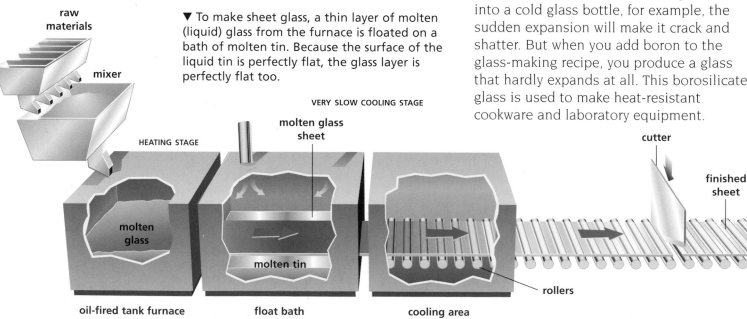

raw materials

mixer

HEATING STAGE

molten glass sheet

VERY SLOW COOLING STAGE

molten glass

molten tin

rollers

cutter

finished sheet

oil-fired tank furnace

float bath

cooling area

Wood and timber

In a forest in North America, the trees have been growing for more than a century – many are over 60 metres tall. Now the buzzing of chainsaws signals that the lumberjacks have moved in. The chainsaws cut through thick trunks in minutes, and the mighty trees start crashing down.

Timber – the wood from cut-down, or felled trees – has always been one of the most useful materials to people. It is used in house-building, for making furniture, building boats, and much more besides.

Timber is also used to make such products as plywood (thin layers of wood glued together to make boards) and chipboard (a material made from wood chippings pressed and glued together). Wood is also a useful raw material for making such products as paper, textile fibres and even explosives. However, the biggest use of wood by far throughout the world is for burning on fires.

▼ Violins and many other musical instruments are usually crafted from the finest-quality hardwood.

Key

- coniferous forest
- deciduous forest
- tropical forest

Softwoods and hardwoods

The common timber used in building is called softwood, because it is relatively soft and easy to cut and work with. Most softwood trees have narrow, needle-like leaves and bear their seeds in cones. They keep their leaves all year round. Known as evergreen conifers, they include firs, pines, cedars and spruces. Large areas of natural conifer forests are found in the cool, northern regions of the world, and they are planted in warmer climates too.

▲ The forest regions of the world. The largest region of natural forest is in the north of North America, Europe and Asia. Evergreen conifers grow there. The other main area is around the Equator. In these tropical forests, broad-leaved evergreens grow. In the temperate climates between these main forest regions, the native trees are broad-leaved and deciduous.

However, in warmer regions the natural forest trees yield a harder wood, so they are called hardwoods. They include oak, beech, chestnut and maple. These trees are deciduous, which means that they shed their broad leaves every autumn. Hardwood trees grow in the natural forests around the Equator. These broad-leaved trees are evergreen. The most valuable hardwoods include mahogany, ebony and teak.

Managing the forests

At one time about two-thirds of the Earth's surface was covered by forests. But for

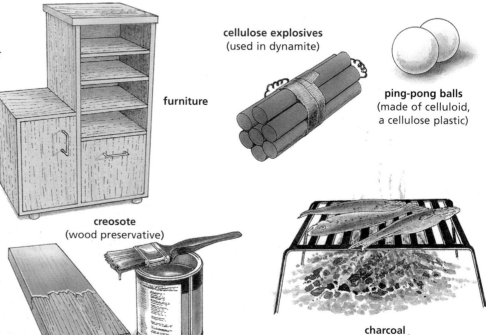

▲ In a tropical forest in Cameroon in central Africa, two men saw a massive tree trunk into logs.

thousands of years people have been felling trees for timber, for firewood, and to clear land for agriculture. Only a fraction of the original forest land remains. And destruction of the natural forest continues, especially the tropical rainforests of South-east Asia.

Elsewhere, more and more timber is coming from managed forests. In these forests, the trees are cultivated as a crop, with new trees being planted as mature ones are cut down. Forestry workers raise tree seedlings, plant them out, and look after them while they grow, protecting them from pests and diseases.

From forest to sawmill

To fell a tree, a lumberjack first cuts a wedge out of the trunk low down. Then he makes a slice above it. Because of the undercut, the tree loses balance and topples over. After trees are felled, they are cut into logs.

The logs may be taken out of the forest by tractors, animals (such as elephants), cables, or water slides. They travel to sawmills on trucks or railway wagons, or are towed on huge rafts across lakes.

At the sawmill, the logs are de-barked and then sawn into pieces of standard sizes. Afterwards, the cut timber has to be stacked so that the air can dry it out. This is called seasoning. Sometimes the wood is seasoned artificially in heated kilns.

Chemical products

Wood is made up mainly of fibres of cellulose, which are held together by a substance called lignin. Cellulose is the starting-point for making rayon fibres, cellulose plastics and explosives.

Useful oils and solvents can be obtained by distilling wood, which involves heating it in enclosed vessels. These products include creosote, used to preserve timber, and turpentine, used in paints. Partly burning wood produces charcoal, a valuable fuel.

key words

- conifers
- deciduous
- evergreen
- felling
- seasoning
- timber

▼ Many things that we use every day are made from wood or wood products.

furniture

cellulose explosives
(used in dynamite)

ping-pong balls
(made of celluloid,
a cellulose plastic)

creosote
(wood preservative)

charcoal

Paper

As you read these words, you are looking at a material that started life in a forest in the wilds of Canada or Scandinavia. You are looking at paper, which is made from the wood of trees.

Paper is one of the greatest inventions of all time. It has allowed ideas and knowledge to be written down and passed on from generation to generation. Even in this electronic age, we are using more paper than ever before. Each year an area of forest the size of Sweden has to be cut down for papermaking.

▶ A worker in a paper-mill takes a sample of wood pulp from a roller. The sample will be tested for quality.

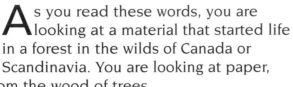

logs — de-barking — chipping — digester turns chips to pulp — wood pulp washed and bleached — beater frays wood fibres — water added — pulp — pressing rollers — wire mesh belt — heated rollers — dryer — heavy rollers give smooth finish (calendaring) — paper roll

Pulping

The first stage of papermaking is to turn the wood from logs into a mass of fibres, called pulp. The cheapest pulp is made by shredding the wood using a rotating grindstone. It is used to make newsprint, the paper newspapers are printed on. Better-quality pulp is made by treating wood chips with chemicals. The chemicals release the wood fibres (cellulose) by dissolving the substance that binds them together (lignin).

◀ In the paper mill, logs are first chipped, then mixed with chemicals to make pulp. The pulp then goes to the paper-making machine. Excess water drains away, then the damp paper is pressed, dried and further rolled to smooth the surface.

🔵 key words
- cellulose
- fibres
- lignin
- newsprint
- pulp
- wood

Papermaking

At the paper-mill, the wood pulp first goes to a machine that beats the fibres and makes them frayed and flexible. The beaten pulp then goes into a mixer, where certain materials are added. They may include china clay to give the paper more weight; a glue-like material to make the paper easier to write on, and pigments to add colour. The thoroughly mixed pulp is then fed to the papermaking machine.

Rubber

The dare-devil girl dives off the high bridge and plunges towards the river far below. Down she goes until she is only a few feet above the water. But she doesn't plunge in because she is bungee-jumping. An elastic rope attached to her feet pulls her back up.

The elastic rope is made of rubber. Being elastic is only one of rubber's useful properties. It is also airtight and waterproof, and absorbs shock well. These properties make it suited to two of its main uses – for motor tyres and footwear.

Rubber can be natural or synthetic. Both natural and synthetic rubber are made up of long molecules, which are folded back on themselves rather like a spring. They unfold when the rubber stretches, then spring back when released.

Making rubber

Natural rubber is prepared from the white milky sap, or latex, of rubber trees. Synthetic rubber is made from chemicals

key words
- elastic
- latex
- polymers
- synthetic rubber
- vulcanization

▲ Once the different parts of a tyre have been assembled, they are fused together, and the rubber is hardened, in a tyre press. Here, a tyre press releases a new tyre, still steaming, from its mould.

obtained from petroleum, or crude oil. These chemicals form long chains, or polymers, when they react together, producing a substance similar to natural latex.

Some latex is made into products such as rubber gloves, but most is processed further. One of the most important processes is called vulcanization. This involves adding sulphur and heating the rubber. This makes it harder and tougher.

▼ Making natural rubber, and its use in manufacturing car tyres.

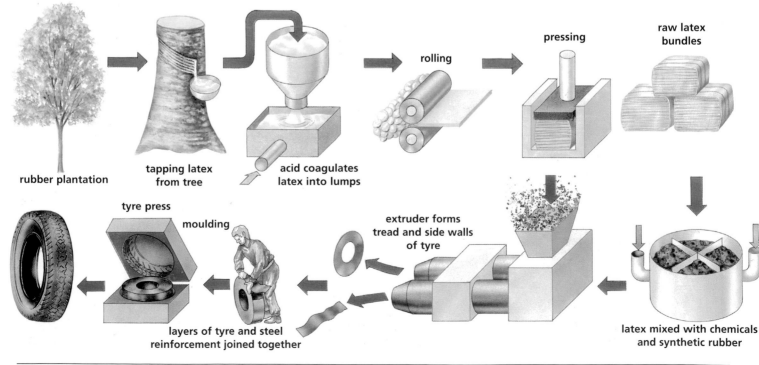

rubber plantation

tapping latex from tree

acid coagulates latex into lumps

rolling

pressing

raw latex bundles

latex mixed with chemicals and synthetic rubber

extruder forms tread and side walls of tyre

layers of tyre and steel reinforcement joined together

moulding

tyre press

Fibres and textiles

The little worm has been gorging itself on mulberry leaves for five weeks. Now it is starting to spin its cocoon. Two streams of liquid coming from its spinning glands harden into fine threads as they hit the air. These threads are one of our most prized textile fibres – silk.

Silk is just one of several natural fibres we use to make fabrics, or textiles. Others include cotton, wool and linen. Equally important these days are man-made fibres. Some, such as rayon, are made by processing natural materials. Others, called synthetic fibres, are made from chemicals.

Most textiles are made in two stages. First, bundles of fibres are drawn out and twisted into long threads, or yarns. This process is called spinning. Then the yarns are interlaced together, in a process called weaving.

▶ The thick fleeces being shorn from these sheep will be spun into woollen yarn to make clothing.

Animal fibres

Silk is one of two main fibres we get from animals. It is the only one that is produced in the form of a continuous thread, or filament. Several threads are twisted together to make a silk yarn strong enough for weaving.

The wool from sheep is the other main animal fibre. Australia is the world's biggest producer, and the global output is about 1.5 million tonnes a year. Goats, camels and llamas also produce useful fibres.

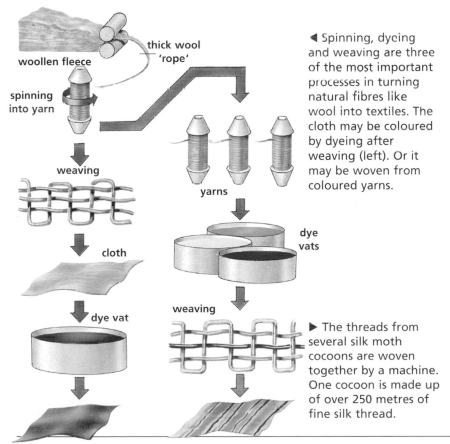

woollen fleece

thick wool 'rope'

spinning into yarn

weaving

cloth

dye vat

yarns

dye vats

weaving

◀ Spinning, dyeing and weaving are three of the most important processes in turning natural fibres like wool into textiles. The cloth may be coloured by dyeing after weaving (left). Or it may be woven from coloured yarns.

▶ The threads from several silk moth cocoons are woven together by a machine. One cocoon is made up of over 250 metres of fine silk thread.

Plant fibres

Cotton is by far the most important plant fibre. Cotton plants produce fibres in the seed pod, or boll. They grow only in tropical and subtropical regions, with China and the southern states of the USA being leading producers. World output is about 20 million tonnes a year.

Linen is another plant fibre, made from the flax plant. These plants grow in cooler climates and are cultivated in much the same way as cereal crops. The fibres are found inside the stalks.

Rayon

Cotton is used as a raw material to make rayon, the most widely used man-made fibre. Wood pulp is also used to make rayon. Cotton and wood pulp both contain cellulose.

The most common form of rayon is called viscose. It is made by dissolving the cellulose with chemicals. This makes a syrupy solution, which is then pumped through tiny holes in a device called a spinneret, into a bath of acid. In contact with the acid, the streams of solution turn into continuous threads, or filaments, of pure cellulose.

key words

- cellulose
- fibres
- spinneret
- spinning
- synthetic
- weaving

▶ Nylon is produced by melt-spinning. Molten (liquid) nylon is forced through the holes of a spinneret. The liquid is then cooled to form fibres. Bundles of fibres are gathered to form a strong yarn.

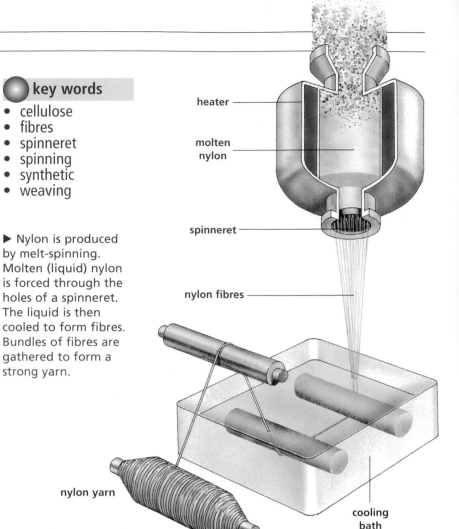

heater

molten nylon

spinneret

nylon fibres

nylon yarn

cooling bath

▼ A worker in a textile factory carries out one of the early stages in the weaving process.

Synthetic fibres

Synthetic fibres are kinds of plastics that can be pulled, or drawn out, into fine threads. They are made mainly from petroleum chemicals. The best-known synthetic fibre is nylon. Nylon was first made in 1935 by a team led by the US chemist Wallace Carothers.

Synthetic fibres are formed by so-called spinning processes. The plastic material is pumped through the holes of a spinneret and comes out as long continuous threads. The threads are usually chopped into shorter fibres, often mixed with natural fibres, and then spun into yarn for weaving.

Drip dry

Synthetic fibres have many advantages over natural fibres. They are usually much stronger, resist insect attack and do not rot. They do not absorb water, which means that they dry quickly. They resist creasing too, so fabrics keep their shape well.

Chemicals

Salt is a very useful substance. In the home, we use it to make our food taste better. In industry, it is a valuable raw material. From salt, a wide range of chemicals is produced, including sodium carbonate (used in making glass) and caustic soda (used in making soap).

The chemical industry makes millions of tonnes of sodium carbonate and caustic soda every year. They are produced in such large quantities that they are known as heavy chemicals. Other heavy chemicals include sulphuric and nitric acids, ammonia and benzene.

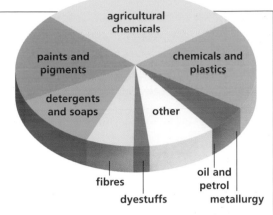

▲ The main uses of sulphuric acid.

● **key words**

- catalyst
- chemical engineering
- molecules
- reactions
- sulphuric acid
- synthetic

▼ Froth flotation tanks like this are used to concentrate silver and zinc ores. Froth flotation is a process that separates the minerals from earthy impurities. The ore is ground to a fine powder and mixed with water and chemicals to make a froth liquid. The mineral particles cling to the froth bubbles at the surface, while waste earthy material sinks to the bottom.

SULPHURIC ACID

The world produces almost twice as much sulphuric acid as any other chemical. It is so important in manufacturing that it is often called the 'lifeblood of industry'. Sulphuric acid is made from sulphur by the contact process. The sulphur (S) is first burned in air (containing oxygen, O_2) in a furnace, which produces sulphur dioxide (SO_2) gas. The gas then passes with more air into a converter containing a catalyst, such as platinum.

In contact with the catalyst, the sulphur dioxide combines with more oxygen from the air to form sulphur trioxide (SO_3). Sulphur trioxide can then be combined with water (H_2O) to form sulphuric acid (H_2SO_4).

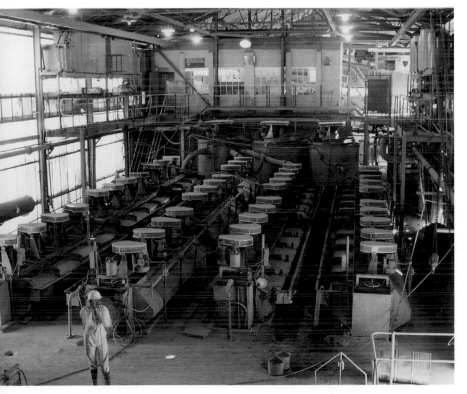

Benzene is what is known as an organic chemical (organic chemicals are ones with carbon in them). The other heavy chemicals are classed as inorganic. Most inorganic chemicals are produced from minerals (chemicals extracted from rocks). Organic chemicals are mainly produced from crude oil, or petroleum, which is a mixture of hydrocarbons (compounds made from hydrogen and carbon). The different hydrocarbons provide chemical starting points for a huge variety of products.

Chemical operations

The chemical industry uses all kinds of processes, or reactions, to make chemicals. A common one is oxidation, which means adding oxygen to a substance. Oxidation is involved in the manufacture of sulphuric acid, for example. Hydrogenation is another common reaction, which means adding hydrogen. It is used in making margarine and other spreads.

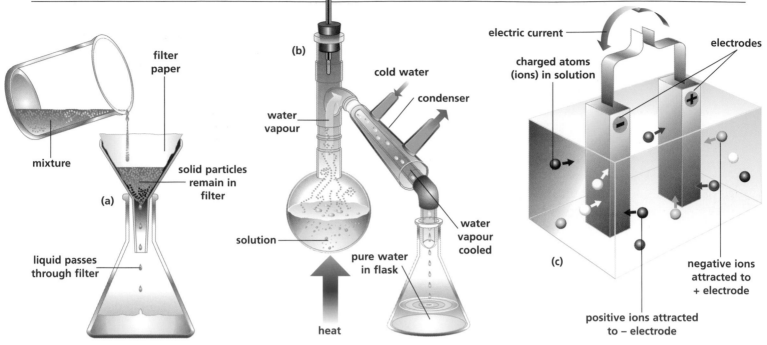

filter paper

mixture

(a)

solid particles remain in filter

liquid passes through filter

(b)

cold water

condenser

water vapour

solution

water vapour cooled

pure water in flask

heat

electric current

charged atoms (ions) in solution

electrodes

(c)

negative ions attracted to + electrode

positive ions attracted to – electrode

Polymerization is the reaction by which plastics are produced. It involves the linking together of small molecules (monomers) to form large ones (polymers). Cracking is an operation in which the opposite happens – large molecules are broken down into smaller ones. It is an important reaction in refining petroleum.

▼ A chemical engineer inspects a small pilot plant to find out how a large chemical plant might work.

▲ Common processes used in chemical plants include mixing, dissolving, filtering (a) and distilling (b shows distilling water). Electrolysis (c) is a process in which electricity is used to separate chemicals.

Many reactions have to take place at high temperatures or high pressures: the common plastic polyethylene is produced at pressures of up to 2000 times normal atmospheric pressure. Other reactions will not take place properly unless a catalyst is present. A catalyst is a substance that can make a reaction go faster, but is not itself changed in the process.

Chemical engineering

The people who design the chemical plants (factories) in which the reactions are carried out are called chemical engineers. They have to take a chemical process that works in the laboratory and make it work on a large scale.

Chemical engineers have to design the vessels (containers) in which reactions take place. They must also design the equipment that ensures that the chemicals involved are in the right state and in the right place at the right time. This includes pumps, heaters, pipes, valves, and so on.

When designing a new chemical plant, the engineers first build a small-scale one, called a pilot plant. If this works, they can go ahead with the full-size one.

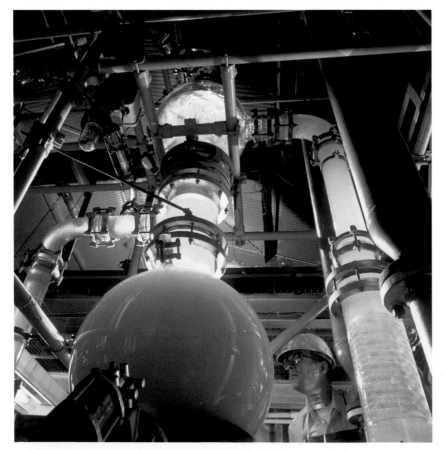

Detergents

At the bird sanctuary, a team of workers has brought in a flock of sea birds. They have been covered in oil leaking from a wrecked ship. The team sets to work cleaning the birds with detergent. This breaks up the oil into droplets, which are then washed away with water. The birds look bedraggled, but they will survive.

Detergents are powerful cleaning agents that will get rid of oil on sea birds, as well as grease and dirt on dishes, clothes, and so on. Detergents are synthetic products made from petroleum chemicals. Before people had detergents, the main cleaning agent was soap. Today we use soap mainly for cleaning ourselves.

key words
- detergent
- molecule
- soap

▼ Following an oil spill off the South African coast, teams of workers clean penguins by scrubbing them with detergent.

▼ Soaps and detergents are made up of a similar type of molecule (basic unit). These molecules have a head and a tail. The head 'likes' water, while the tail 'likes' grease and dirt. When soap or detergent is used to wash clothes, the tail ends of the molecules attach themselves to the bits of dirt. Soon the bits are surrounded, leaving only the heads in contact with the water. When the clothes move about, the water washes the bits away.

head

tail

greasy dirt particles

detergent molecules in water

greasy dirt

clothing fibres

Soap has been made for thousands of years. It is produced by heating fat or oil with a substance that is an alkali, like caustic soda. In the past, animal fats were used, but now soaps are made using vegetable oils such as palm oil. Another product we get from making soap is glycerine, which can be used to make plastics and explosives.

Beating the scum

The problem with soap is that it sometimes forms a messy scum. Detergents do not. They also have a more efficient cleaning action than soap. Different detergents are made for different purposes. Washing-up liquid, laundry detergents for washing clothes, and shampoos all contain different ingredients. Laundry detergents, for example, can contain brighteners to make fabrics look extra bright, and enzymes, which can dissolve stains such as sweat and blood.

Oil products

The bar of the pole vault is set at 6 metres. The athlete sprints towards it, long pole in hand. He digs the pole into the ground and launches himself into the air. The pole bends right over, looking as though it will break, but then straightens. It helps throw the vaulter over the bar, with millimetres to spare.

No natural material, like wood or metal, could be used for such a vaulting pole. It would not be light enough, flexible enough or strong enough. The pole is made of fibreglass, a plastic material that is reinforced (strengthened) by having long glass fibres running through it. Such a material is called a composite. Another type of composite uses carbon fibres to strengthen the plastic. It is used, for example, to make tennis rackets.

Composites and plastics are examples of synthetic materials. These are manufactured from chemicals made in factories, not from natural materials. Thousands of different products are synthesized from chemicals these days – not only plastics, but also dyes, drugs, detergents, explosives, fibres, pesticides, and so on.

Sources of synthetics

Most synthetic materials are manufactured from organic chemicals, which are carbon compounds. These compounds are called 'organic' because it was once thought that they could only be produced by living things (we now know this is not true).

▲ Oil refineries are run mainly from the control room, where workers can monitor the various processes. Everything works automatically, under computer control.

◄ In an oil refinery, crude oil is processed into many different products, including petrol, kerosene and diesel oil.

key words

- cracking
- distillation
- fraction
- hydrocarbon
- molecule
- plastics
- refining

▶ Crude oil is separated into fractions in a fractionating tower up to 80 metres tall. It is heated into a vapour, which enters the tower. In the tower, the vapour rises through trays at different levels. Each tray is kept at a different temperature – high at the bottom, low at the top. The oil fractions condense back to liquids in the trays according to their boiling points.

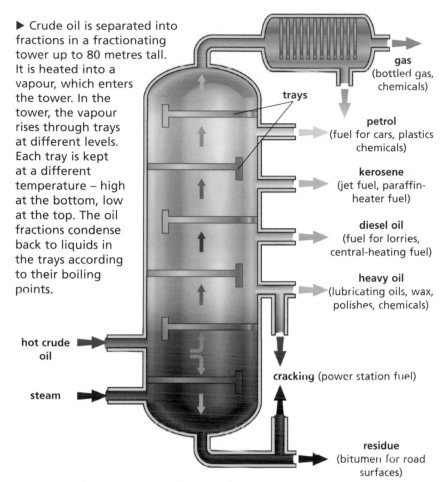

trays

hot crude oil

steam

gas
(bottled gas, chemicals)

petrol
(fuel for cars, plastics chemicals)

kerosene
(jet fuel, paraffin-heater fuel)

diesel oil
(fuel for lorries, central-heating fuel)

heavy oil
(lubricating oils, wax, polishes, chemicals)

cracking (power station fuel)

residue
(bitumen for road surfaces)

Distillation is just the first stage in processing, or refining, the oil. It separates the oil into various parts (fractions). Some of these fractions can be used directly as fuels. Other fractions and gases provide the starting-point for making a wide range of chemicals, often called petrochemicals.

Get cracking

Heavy oil fractions can be made into more useful products by cracking. This is a process by which the large molecules in the heavy oil are broken down into smaller ones. This produces lighter oils, fuels and gases. In turn, the gases can be converted into fuels and chemicals. This is done by polymerization, a process of building up larger molecules from smaller ones. Together, these and the many other processes that take place in an oil refinery, make it possible to use every part of the crude oil.

Living things contain thousands of different carbon compounds, and it is from the remains of living things that we get our organic chemicals. We get them mostly from crude oil (petroleum), which scientists believe is the remains of tiny creatures that died and decayed millions of years ago.

Crude oil is a mixture of hundreds of different carbon compounds. They are called hydrocarbons because they are made up of carbon and hydrogen. Their molecules (basic units) have a backbone of carbon atoms joined together in chains or rings.

Sorting out

The hydrocarbon mixture that is crude oil is of little use as it is. The hydrocarbons have to be sorted out before they become useful. Fortunately, this is quite easy because they all have different boiling-points. This means that they can be separated by distillation. In this process, a substance is heated so that it evaporates (turns to vapour). Then the vapour is allowed to cool and condense (turn back into liquid).

▼ Crude oil is such a valuable source of chemicals that it seems almost a waste to burn it as fuel. A tank of petrol takes an average family car about 500 kilometres. But we could convert that fuel into chemicals, which could be used to make any of the products shown here.

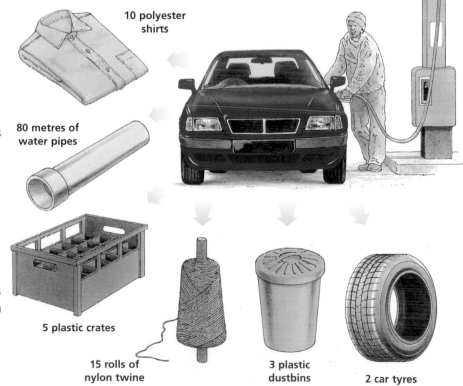

10 polyester shirts

80 metres of water pipes

5 plastic crates

15 rolls of nylon twine

3 plastic dustbins

2 car tyres

Plastics

Chemists make plastics in much the same way as we make daisy-chains. They link together chemicals with short molecules (basic units) in chains to make long molecules. If a short molecule was the length of a daisy stalk, a plastics molecule would be up to 3000 metres long.

All the materials we call plastics are made up of long molecules. It is these long molecules that make plastics so special. Most other materials have short molecules, made up of just a few atoms joined together. In a plastics molecule, tens of thousands of atoms may be joined together.

(a)

(b)

▲ Kevlar is a tough plastic that is closely related to nylon. It is used for making bullet-proof vests. Kevlar molecules are long polymer chains (a), made up of individual units (b) that contain two carbon rings.

key words

- molecule
- moulding
- polymer
- polymerization
- synthetic
- thermoplastic
- thermoset

◄ A technician in a plastics factory checks the production of plastic tubing. Wide tubing like this is used to make dustbin bags and plastic sheets.

There are substances in nature that have long molecules, including rubber and wood. But we don't call them plastics. Plastics are synthetic substances, manufactured from chemicals. An important property of many plastics is that they are easy to shape by heating.

We find plastics everywhere. We drink from plastic cups, fry food in non-stick plastic-coated pans, wrap goods in plastic bags, and wear plastics in the form of synthetic fibres. Drainpipes, squeeze bottles, heat-proof surfaces, floor coverings, tyres and superglues are just a few of the many other products made from plastics that we come across every day.

Many parts

Another general name for plastics is 'polymers'. The word means 'many parts'. This tells us that plastics are made by stringing many small parts (short molecules) together. The chemical process of making plastics is called polymerization.

◀ This tailplane for the Bombardier Global Express jet aircraft is made from a light, strong composite material. A composite has fibres of a very strong material such as carbon fibre or Kevlar embedded in plastic.

In almost all plastics, the long chains that form the molecules are linked together by carbon atoms. Carbon is the only chemical element that can link together in this way.

Thermoplastics and thermosets

All plastics are shaped by heating, but react differently to heat afterwards. If you place a hot saucepan on the plastic worktop in the kitchen, nothing happens. But place it in an empty polythene washing-up bowl, and the plastic will melt. This happens because the two plastics are different types.

Polythene softens and melts when heated. It is a type of plastic called a thermoplastic. Many other common plastics are thermoplastics, including PVC (polyvinyl chloride), polystyrene and nylon.

The worktop plastic does not soften or melt when heated, although it will burn eventually. It is a type of plastic called a thermoset. The worktop is made from a thermoset called melamine-formaldehyde, after the substances it is made from. The first synthetic plastic, Bakelite, was made from phenol and formaldehyde.

SHAPING PLASTICS

Plastic is usually shaped by a process of moulding. Warm plastic may be blown into shape in a mould (a), or molten (liquid) plastic may be injected into a mould (b). Plastic packaging material is often formed from a sheet of plastic, sucked into a mould using a vacuum (c). To produce rods and tubes, molten plastic is forced through a hole, or die, in a process called extrusion (d). Plastic sheet used for kitchen worktops is made by laminating. This involves pressing sheets of plastic and filler material together and heating them.

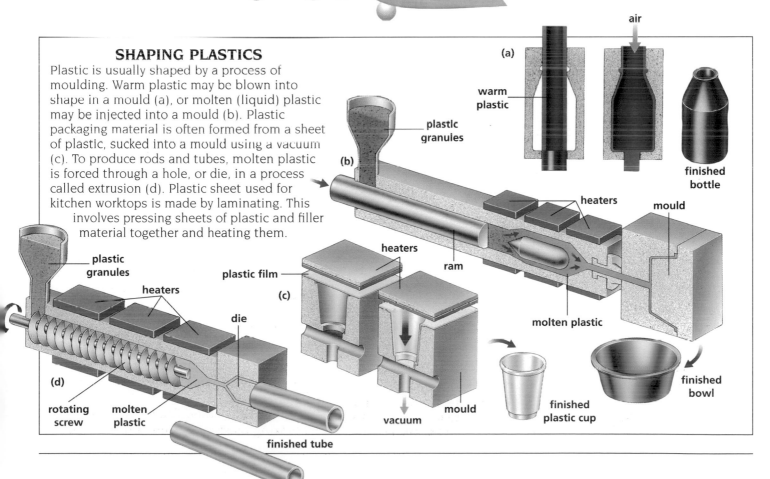

Dyes and pigments

Buddhist priests the world over wear bright-orange robes, which get their colour from the dye saffron. This dye is obtained from the stigmas (pollen-collecting organs) of crocus flowers. The stigmas of over 150,000 blooms are needed to make just 1 kilogram of saffron dye.

Saffron is one of several natural dyes that have been used to colour fabrics since ancient times. Other plant dyes include madder (red) and indigo (blue), which come from the madder and indigo plants. Natural dyes can also come from animals. Cochineal red, for example, is a dye extracted from insects.

Most dyes used today, however, are synthetic. They are usually made from chemicals obtained from crude oil. Aniline, for instance, is a compound from oil that is the starting point for making many dyes.

The molecules that make up most dyes, whether natural or synthetic, contain rings of carbon atoms. These carbon rings are important in giving a dye its colour.

▶ Newly dyed cloth hangs out to dry in the streets of Marrakesh, Morocco.

key words

- dye
- mordant
- pigment
- ring compound
- synthetic

Fast colours

In general, synthetic dyes have more brilliant colours than natural dyes. They bond well with fabric fibres so that they do not readily wash out. Also, they are colour-fast, which means they do not fade easily.

Natural dyes do not bond well with natural fibres such as cotton. These fibres first have to be treated with a substance called a mordant. The mordant clings to the fibres and then bonds with the dye.

Pigments

Dyes are colouring substances that dissolve in water. Pigments are colouring substances that do not dissolve in water or other solvents (dissolving liquids). They are used to colour materials such as inks, paints and cosmetics. Traditional pigments include coloured earths such as ochre, and metal compounds such as iron and titanium oxides. Most pigments are now synthetic.

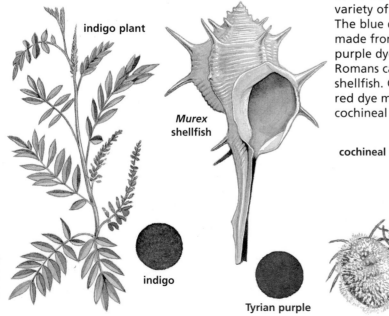

indigo plant

Murex shellfish

indigo

Tyrian purple

▼ Traditional dyes come from a wide variety of sources. The blue dye indigo is made from a plant; a purple dye used by the Romans came from a shellfish. Cochineal is a red dye made from cochineal insects.

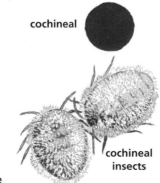

cochineal

cochineal insects

WILLIAM PERKIN
The English chemist William Perkin (1838–1907) discovered the first synthetic dye, mauvein, in 1856, and set up a factory to produce it. He made it from aniline, a chemical now extracted from oil.

Paints and varnishes

Left to themselves, wood rots and iron rusts when exposed to the weather. But give them a thin coat of paint, and they can last for centuries.

Paint is a liquid mixture containing colouring matter, which dries to form a thin, tough film. This film decorates the surface underneath and protects it from attack by water, air and insects.

The substance that forms the film is called the vehicle, or binder. The colouring is provided by pigments. To make the mixture flow easily when applied, it is dissolved in a solvent, often called thinners.

▼ Many coatings are needed to build up the shiny paintwork on a car body. First, the body is dipped in phosphate solution to help it resist corrosion. Then it is given one or two coats of primer, followed by a base coat, an undercoat and one or more top coats. The final coats are baked, or stoved. (Colours shown are not actual colours of different coatings.)

▶ Wearing a mask as protection against poisonous fumes, a worker spray-paints the side of a car.

Early paints used natural oils like linseed oil as a vehicle. Modern paints use synthetic resins, which are kinds of plastics. In the oil paints generally used for painting outside, the usual solvent is white spirit, a product we get from oil refining.

A strong bond

After the paint has been applied, two processes take place. The solvent evaporates, and the binder reacts with the oxygen in the air. As a result, the molecules of the binder join up to form a rigid polymer, or plastic material – the paint film

Many paints these days use water as a solvent, and so are cleaner to use and cause no air pollution – unlike some oil-based paints. One kind of water-based paint is an emulsion. In an emulsion, the vehicle particles do not dissolve, but are spread out in the water as very fine droplets.

● **key words**
- emulsion
- evaporation
- pigment
- solvent
- vehicle

A clear, hard varnish called shellac is made from the secretions of the tiny red lac insect from Thailand. At certain times of year, lac insects swarm in huge numbers on trees, literally feeding themselves to death. But before she dies, each female lays her eggs on the tree, protecting them with a clear material called lac. This is later harvested and made into shellac.

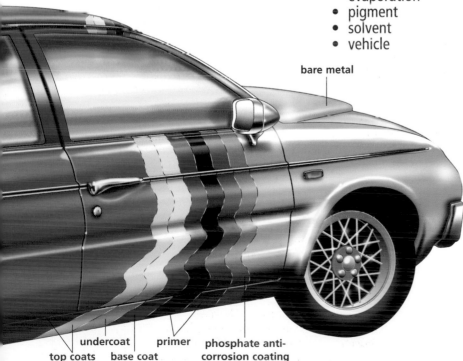

bare metal

top coats · undercoat · base coat · primer · phosphate anti-corrosion coating

Drugs

When the native peoples who live in the Amazon jungle get a fever, they chew the bark of the cinchona tree. The fever is brought on by malaria. Cinchona bark contains a drug, quinine, that fights the disease.

Malaria is one of the most widespread diseases in the world, affecting as many as 500 million people. Quinine is still one of the main drugs used to treat it. But nowadays quinine is a synthetic product, manufactured from chemicals.

Most drugs, also called pharmaceuticals, are now synthetic. But quite a few natural drugs are still used. One long-used plant drug, digitalis, is extracted from foxglove. It is used to treat heart conditions.

Another natural drug is morphine, extracted from the seeds of the opium poppy. It is a powerful painkiller. Heroin comes from the same plant. Both morphine and heroin are highly addictive, or habit-forming. The use of heroin is one of the major causes of drug addiction.

▲ This enlarged picture shows the effect of an antibiotic on bacteria. The bacterium on the right has not yet been damaged, but that on the left has been attacked and destroyed.

key words
- antibiotic
- bacteria
- drug addiction
- vaccination
- virus

◄ Certain drugs are illegal and people try to smuggle them from country to country in their luggage. Police use specially trained dogs to sniff out these hidden drugs.

PENICILLIN PIONEERS
Alexander Fleming (1881–1955) discovered penicillin in 1928 while working at St Mary's Hospital, London. But it was not produced in a pure form until 1940, when it was shown to have amazing antibiotic properties. This latter work was carried out at Oxford by a team led by Ernst Chain (1906–1979) and Howard Florey (1898–1968). The three pioneering scientists shared the 1945 Nobel prize for medicine.

Ernst Chain

Howard Florey

Beating bacteria

Tiny, microscopic organisms called bacteria are the cause of most dangerous diseases, including blood poisoning, cholera, typhoid and tuberculosis. Bacterial infection can be treated by synthetic drugs such as the sulphonamides, but these days it is usually treated by antibiotics.

Antibiotics are substances produced naturally by certain moulds and bacteria. Penicillin was the original antibiotic and is still the most widely used. Others include streptomycin, terramycin and tetracycline. Each of these antibiotics is suited to treating certain diseases.

The use of antibiotics over the years has dramatically reduced the death rate from disease. But antibiotics have been used so much that some bacteria are becoming resistant to them – which means that the antibiotic cannot destroy the bacteria. So scientists are always looking for new antibiotics.

Viruses and vaccines

Antibiotics cannot cure all diseases. In particular, they cannot treat diseases caused by viruses, such as influenza, measles, mumps, hepatitis and polio.

But doctors can prevent some virus diseases by vaccination. This involves injecting a vaccine into the patient's body. A vaccine is made up of a dead or weakened form of the same virus. The body produces antibodies to fight the invading virus. Later, if the body is exposed to the real virus, the antibodies are already there to attack it before it multiplies.

The English doctor Edward Jenner pioneered vaccination to treat smallpox in 1796. A worldwide mass vaccination programme 200 years later wiped the disease from the face of the Earth.

Designer drugs

Some synthetic drugs, such as quinine, are exact copies of natural substances.

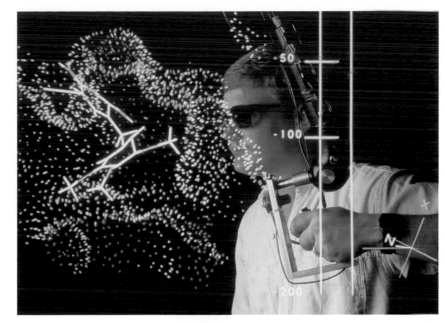

▲ This chemist is using a virtual reality program to look at the action of a drug molecule.

▶ Different ways of administering (giving) drugs.

inhaler (used for asthma)

syringe (injection)

cream or ointment

spray

medicine

powdered drug

capsules

COMMON TYPES OF DRUG	
Type	Effects
Anaesthetic	Prevents patients feeling pain; local anaesthetic acts locally; general anaesthetic creates unconsciousness
Analgesic	Prevents or reduces pain
Antibiotic	Kills the bacteria that cause disease
Antihistamine	Relieves symptoms of asthma, hay fever and other allergies
Hormone	Used to overcome a hormone deficiency in the body
Narcotic	Helps prevents pain by deadening the whole nervous system
Sedative	Helps induce sleep
Tranquillizer	Helps calm a person
Vaccine	Helps the body fight a virus disease by triggering its natural defences in advance

Increasingly, though, new drugs are being created to target diseases. Biochemists, who design drugs, can test a drug using a process called molecular modelling. This involves drawing models of the molecules (basic units) that make up the drug and the disease, on a very powerful computer. They then see how the different molecules behave together. This tells them whether or not the drug will be able to fight the disease.

Fertilizers

In farming country, autumn can be a smelly time of year because many farmers pump sewage sludge onto their land. This sludge contains nitrogen compounds, which get washed into the soil and will help the next crop of plants to grow well.

Sewage sludge is one of several materials farmers spread on their land to help make the soil more productive, or more fertile. It is a fertilizer.

As plants grow, they take in certain essential elements from the soil. Fertilizers are designed to put back these elements so that future crops can also grow well. The most important elements are nitrogen, phosphorus and potassium.

Nitrogen fertilizers

Sewage sludge is just one way of replacing nitrogen. Farmyard manure is another. But most fertilizers are synthetic, produced from chemicals. These fertilizers include ammonia, and two chemicals made from ammonia – ammonium nitrate and urea. Ammonia production is a big part of the chemical industry.

Some plants make their own fertilizer. They are the legumes, and include crops such as beans and clover. Sometimes farmers grow these crops and then

▶ Manure is scattered over a field by a mechanical spreader.

key words

- calcium
- manure
- nitrogen
- phosphorus
- potassium

▼ The effects of growing plants with different amounts of nitrogen fertilizer ('N' on the labels). The plant on the left has added sulphur (S) but no fertilizer.

plough them into the soil as fertilizer. This process is called green manuring.

From rocks and bones

The chemical industry makes huge quantities of fertilizer that contains phosphorus. Called superphosphate, it is manufactured by treating phosphate rock with sulphuric acid.

Bone-meal is a phosphorus fertilizer used widely by gardeners. It is made from animal bones, which consist mainly of calcium phosphate. The phosphorus is released from the bone-meal slowly.

Potassium fertilizers come mainly from mineral deposits. Often they are mixed with nitrogen and phosphorus compounds to form a compound fertilizer.

+S No N   0·1g N   0·2g N   0·3g N   0·4g N

Glues and adhesives

When you lick a stamp, join the parts of a model together, or stick a Post-it note in a book, you are using adhesives. Adhesives are sticky substances that bond surfaces together.

Glues and gums are adhesives made from natural materials. Glues come from animals. They are made by boiling up such things as the bones and skin of cattle, and fish bones. Gums come from the sticky resins made by certain plants.

However, most adhesives used these days are synthetic, and are usually made from petroleum chemicals. These adhesives are plastic materials, or polymers, which set after they have been applied.

Making contact

There are hundreds of different kinds of synthetic adhesives. For example, contact adhesives are made from synthetic rubber dissolved in a solvent. You coat each of the surfaces to be joined with adhesive, let them dry for a while, and then press the surfaces together.

Model-makers use an adhesive containing the plastic polystyrene in a solvent. After it has set, it can be softened by warming, which makes it easy to reshape joints. It is called a thermoplastic adhesive, because it softens when heated.

key words

- adhesive
- glue
- resin
- synthetic
- superglue
- thermoplastic

▶ How superglue works.

(a) In the tube, a substance in the superglue called a stabilizer stops the molecules from linking together.

(b) When the glue is spread on a surface, minute traces of water stop the stabilizer from working.

(c) The molecules of resin immediately link up with one another to form a solid adhesive.

Big sticks

Among the strongest adhesives are the epoxy resins. They have even been used to stick cars to advertising hoardings. Epoxy resins come in two parts that have to be mixed together. One part is the resin, the other is a hardener. Adding the hardener makes the resin set into a rigid plastic material, or thermoset polymer. This process takes about half an hour. The adhesives called superglues, however, set in seconds. They are made from acrylic resins.

▼ High-tech aircraft like this B-2 Spirit stealth bomber are made from a number of different extra-light materials. Super-strong adhesives are often used to join these materials together.

Explosives

'Whoosh!' goes the firework rocket as it shoots high into the sky. The coloured stars it releases explode with bangs like pistol shots. The substance that propels the rockets and makes the bangs is gunpowder, an explosive the Chinese first made over 1000 years ago.

Gunpowder got its name because it was once used to fire bullets from guns. It is a mixture of chemicals – carbon (in the form of charcoal), sulphur and potassium nitrate. When ignited (set alight), these substances burn rapidly and produce large amounts of gases. These gases expand suddenly, in a violent explosion. The explosion creates shock waves, which we hear as a bang.

ALFRED NOBEL

The Swedish chemist Alfred Nobel (1833–1896) invented dynamite in 1867. Feeling guilty that his invention caused so much death and destruction, he set up a fund to award the annual Nobel prizes, one of which was to be a peace prize.

▲ High explosives blast open a hillside in Arizona, USA, to make way for copper miners.

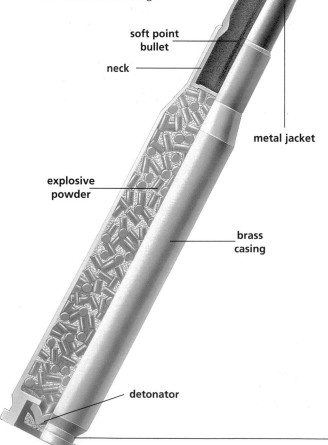

- soft point bullet
- neck
- metal jacket
- explosive powder
- brass casing
- detonator

◄ The ammunition used in rifles is called a cartridge. When the rifle's firing pin strikes a detonator in the base of the cartridge, it ignites a low-explosive powder. This fires a metal bullet from the gun.

key words
- detonator
- high explosive
- low explosive
- nitrogen

All explosives work in this way. Some, called high explosives, burn many thousands of times faster than gunpowder. They are used in mining and tunnelling to blast rocks apart, and in weapons such as shells and bombs.

The nitrogen connection

Almost all explosives contain nitrogen. The nitrogen compound ammonia is the starting point for several explosives.

Two of the most powerful high explosives are nitroglycerine and TNT (trinitrotoluene). Nitroglycerine is an oily liquid that is very dangerous to handle, because it explodes easily. In dynamite, nitroglycerine is mixed with an earthy material to make it safer to use.

All explosives need something to set them off. Low explosives can be set off by a burning fuse or by a sharp blow. High explosives have to be set off by a detonator.

Pesticides

The stem of the beautiful rose is covered with greenfly feeding on the sap, while ladybirds and lacewings feed on them. The gardener sprays the rose with insecticide and soon the greenfly die. But the ladybirds and lacewings fly off – they are not affected.

Insecticides are one kind of pesticide, a chemical that kills harmful organisms on farms and in homes and gardens. The other main types of pesticide are herbicides, designed to kill weeds, and fungicides, which kill fungus diseases.

Some minerals and plant extracts are used as pesticides. Sulphur and copper sulphate, for example, are used to treat fungus diseases.

Most pesticides are synthetic, made mainly from petroleum chemicals. They are often compounds containing chlorine and phosphorus. The trouble is that they may kill not only harmful pests but also useful ones. They may also build up in the environment. This happened widely in the 1950s and 1960s, when a pesticide called DDT was used on a large scale. It was later found to be poisonous to birds and other animals.

Being selective

DDT and similar substances have now been banned in many countries to protect the environment and wildlife. New pesticides have been developed that break down rapidly after they have been used and so are not a long-term danger.

Pesticides have also been developed that are selective in their action, like the

▲ A crop-sprayer flies low to spray insecticide over a field of rape.

key words
- environment
- fungicide
- herbicide
- pesticide

insecticide that kills aphids but not ladybirds. Selective lawn herbicides kill broadleaf weeds but leave the thin blades of grass untouched.

Sometimes pests can be controlled without using chemicals. Parasites or other organisms that naturally prey on the pests are used. This method is known as biological control.

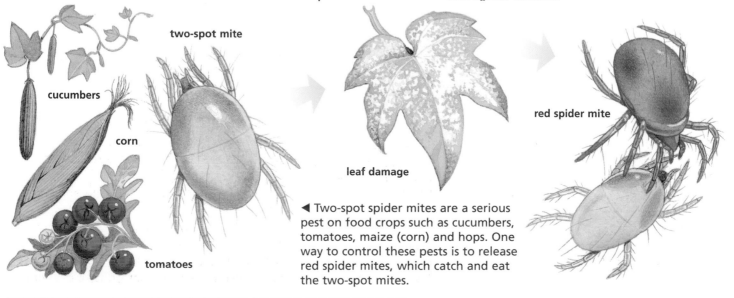

two-spot mite

cucumbers

corn

tomatoes

leaf damage

red spider mite

◀ Two-spot spider mites are a serious pest on food crops such as cucumbers, tomatoes, maize (corn) and hops. One way to control these pests is to release red spider mites, which catch and eat the two-spot mites.

Pollution

The year 2000 began badly for the environment. In January, oil smothered and killed over 150,000 sea birds on the north-west coast of France. In February, cyanide poisoned hundreds of tonnes of freshwater fish in Hungary's Tisa River. In March, raw sewage killed thousands of sea fish in a lagoon near Rio de Janeiro, Brazil.

Oil, deadly chemicals and sewage are three of the things that can pollute or poison our environment and our water.

The oil that smothered the birds in France came from a wrecked oil tanker. At any time, hundreds of oil tankers are sailing the world's seas, together carrying millions of tonnes of oil. When tankers get holed in collisions, or run aground on rocks, vast amounts of oil can pour into the sea and drift ashore. All kinds of sea- and shore-life are affected, from shellfish to seals. Some animals may be saved by washing them with detergent, but most perish.

► This cormorant was just one of the many victims of a huge oil spill that took place off the Shetland Islands in 1993.

DISASTER AT BHOPAL

The world's worst chemical disaster happened in the Indian city of Bhopal in 1984. An explosion at a chemical plant making insecticides (below) released a cloud of deadly gas into the air. Because the gas was twice as heavy as air, it did not drift away, but formed a 'blanket' over the surrounding area. It attacked people's lungs and affected their breathing. Eventually, as many as 3000 people died and many thousands more had their health ruined.

▼ The environment is under attack from all directions.

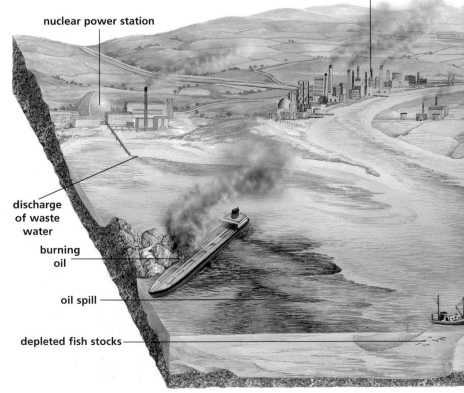

chemical works

nuclear power station

discharge of waste water

burning oil

oil spill

depleted fish stocks

Chemical attack

The cyanide that slaughtered the fish in Hungary came from a gold mine, where it was used to extract gold. Many industries produce poisonous waste products. Usually they are treated to make them harmless before they are released back into the environment.

Chemicals from farming also affect the environment. Farmers apply chemical fertilizers such as nitrates to the land. Sometimes they apply too much, and the surplus chemicals get washed by rain into rivers. Eventually, they can get into our drinking water.

More deadly than nitrates are the pesticides farmers use to protect their crops from insect and weeds. Many pesticides are persistent, which means that they remain active for a long time, and can be poisonous to other animals.

Polluting the air

The air can become polluted too. One of the main causes of air pollution is the car. When car engines burn their fuel, they give

▲ The sun sets behind a blanket of smog hanging over Mexico City. Smog, a mixture of smoke and fog or chemical fumes, pollutes many of the world's big cities.

off fumes, such as nitrogen oxides, carbon dioxide and soot. These fumes may cause breathing problems.

Raining acid

Power stations and factories burn fuels such as coal and oil to produce energy. They too give off fumes that pollute the air, including sulphur and nitrogen oxides. These oxides combine with oxygen and moisture in the air to form sulphuric and nitric acids. When it rains, the rain is acidic.

Acid rain falls into lakes and rivers, and can make them too acid to support plant and animal life. Acid rain also kills trees. Lifeless lakes and dying forests are already found in parts of northern North America and northern Europe.

In a greenhouse

The carbon dioxide that factories and cars produce when they burn their fuels builds up in the Earth's atmosphere. It makes the atmosphere act rather like a greenhouse and trap more of the Sun's heat. This is causing world temperatures to rise, or global warming.

Chemicals called chlorofluorocarbons (CFCs), found in sprays and refrigerators, increase the greenhouse effect. They also attack the layer of ozone in the Earth's upper atmosphere, which protects us from much harmful radiation from the Sun. If the ozone layer thins too much, it will let through more of this dangerous radiation.

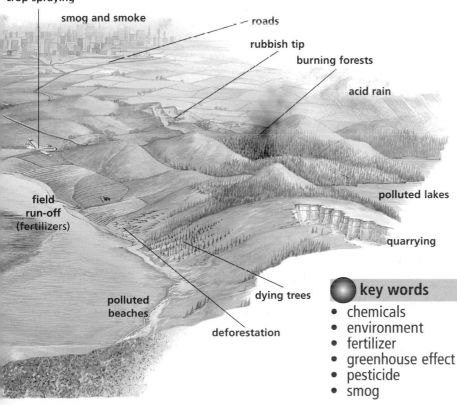

crop spraying

smog and smoke

roads

rubbish tip

burning forests

acid rain

field run-off (fertilizers)

polluted lakes

quarrying

polluted beaches

dying trees

deforestation

key words
- chemicals
- environment
- fertilizer
- greenhouse effect
- pesticide
- smog

Waste disposal

Every day the people of New York City throw away up to 25,000 tonnes of waste – newspapers, plastic bags, food scraps, cans, old clothes, bottles, and so on. Twice a week this rubbish is collected and dumped on a site on Staten Island. It is the biggest waste tip in the world.

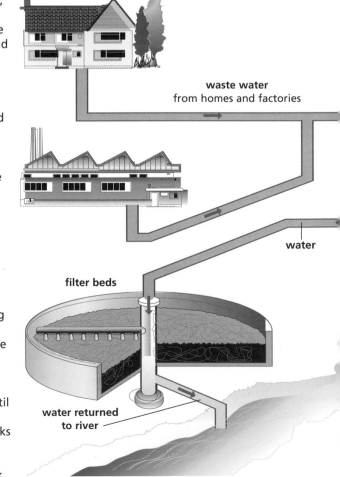

Most household rubbish is disposed of at waste dumps like this. They are called landfill sites. Usually, a great pit is dug in the ground and filled with rubbish. The rubbish is then covered over and replanted with plants and grass.

The problem is that we are producing so much rubbish that we are running out of suitable sites. Also, harmful substances in the buried rubbish can find their way into our water supplies. And the rotting matter in the waste produces the gas methane, which can cause explosions. On many old landfill sites, this gas is piped away and used as fuel – it is the same gas that we use for cooking in our homes.

Up in smoke

Another method of dealing with rubbish is by burning, or incineration. Modern

▶ About 90% of the world's domestic waste goes to landfill sites.

▶ At a sewage works, screens and settling tanks first remove the larger objects, grit and sludge. The sludge is further processed to make fuel gas and fertilizer. The water remaining is sprinkled over filter beds containing microbes that feed on any remaining waste. The water is then clean enough to go back into a river.

waste water
from homes and factories

water

filter beds

water returned
to river

◀ An engraving of the Paris sewers from the 1850s. Paris's sewers were neglected and little known until the early 1800s, when the city's works inspector, Pierre Bruneseau, mapped the 2100-km network.

incinerators not only burn waste, but often use the heat this produces, for heating or generating electricity. Before waste can be used as fuel, materials that will not burn, such as metal and glass, must be separated from those that will burn, like paper.

Increasingly, local authorities are encouraging households to take their waste paper, metals, glass and plastic to recycling centres. The different materials are then processed before being used again.

In the sewers

As well as all the solid rubbish we throw away, we produce a lot of liquid waste. This includes body wastes from toilets, and water from sinks, washing-machines and baths. This liquid waste is called sewage.

In some parts of the world, raw (untreated) sewage is pumped directly into rivers or the sea, polluting the water. But in most communities, a system of pipelines called the sewers carries the sewage to treatment plants. Here, solids and harmful substances are removed so that the water can be returned to the environment. The sludge left over can be treated to make fuel gas and fertilizer.

Wastes at work

Many industries, particularly the chemical industry, use dangerous substances. This produces wastes that can be harmful to our health and the environment. Landfill is often used for the safe disposal of solid wastes. Liquid wastes are treated to make them harmless before they are released. Unfortunately, this doesn't always happen, and pollution can result.

Some of the deadliest waste is produced by the nuclear industry. The waste is radioactive, which means that it gives off harmful radiation. Some waste remains active and dangerous for thousands of years.

For safety, most nuclear waste is stored underground. The surrounding soil and rock stop the radiation from reaching the surface. Liquid wastes are often kept in tanks surrounded by thick concrete. Some waste is made into a kind of glass and stored in sealed containers in deep mines.

key words

- incineration
- landfill
- pollution
- radioactive
- recycling
- sewage

▼ Liquid nuclear waste glass is poured into a steel mould. In glass form, nuclear waste can be disposed of safely.

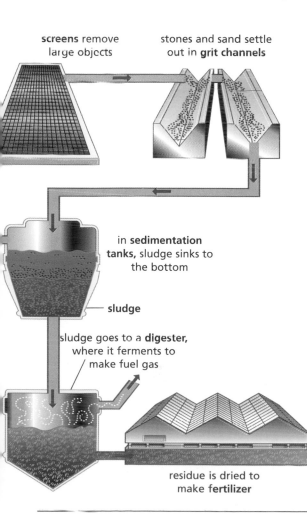

screens remove large objects

stones and sand settle out in **grit channels**

in **sedimentation tanks,** sludge sinks to the bottom

sludge

sludge goes to a **digester,** where it ferments to make fuel gas

residue is dried to make **fertilizer**

Recycling

Next time you drink a can of cola or fizzy lemonade, spare a thought for the can. It is made of aluminium, and the metal has probably been used before. It might once have been cooking foil, milk-bottle tops, or even part of an aircraft wing.

Aluminium is one of the materials that are recycled, or used again, in many countries. Glass, paper and plastics are also widely recycled. Many towns have recycling centres, where people can deposit these materials. Elsewhere, there are scrapyards, which collect metal scrap, from old lead pipes to crashed cars.

There are three main reasons why recycling is a good idea. One, it reduces the amount of waste we produce. Getting rid of waste, from homes and industry, has become one of the world's biggest environmental problems. The American people alone throw away 200 million tonnes of rubbish every year. Most of this could be recycled.

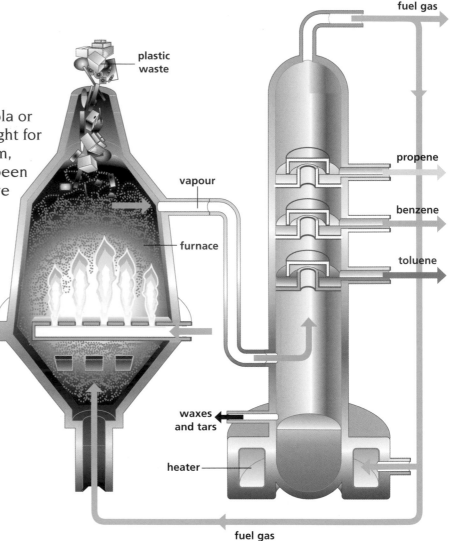

▲ In a recycling plant, plastics waste is heated at temperatures up to 800°C, in the absence of air. The materials turn to vapour, which then goes to a distillation tower. In the tower, the various substances in the vapour separate out at different levels. Some are used as fuels; others are valuable raw materials for the chemical and plastics industries.

Saving energy

Another reason for recycling is to save energy. This is why it pays to recycle aluminium. It takes large amounts of electricity to extract this metal from its ore, bauxite. Re-melting aluminium waste takes much less energy and therefore saves money.

It also pays to recycle glass, for the same reason. Glass is made by melting together a mixture of sand and limestone. The mixture melts more easily when waste glass is added to it.

Thinking of the future

The third main reason for recycling is to save Earth's resources – the raw materials we need to make the goods we use. Paper,

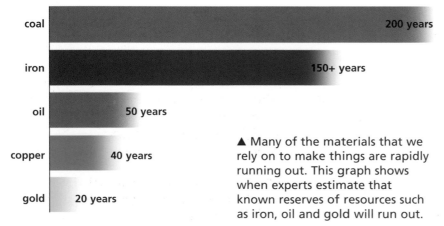

coal	200 years
iron	150+ years
oil	50 years
copper	40 years
gold	20 years

▲ Many of the materials that we rely on to make things are rapidly running out. This graph shows when experts estimate that known reserves of resources such as iron, oil and gold will run out.

for example, is made from wood pulp, which comes from trees. The more paper we recycle, the fewer trees we have to cut down for wood pulp.

Trees are a renewable resource – we can keep growing them. Most of the materials we use, such as oil and minerals, are not. Once we have used them up, they will be gone for ever.

Oil, for example, will almost certainly run out later this century. This is why we need to recycle plastics, which are made from oil. Plastics can be broken down by heat into a range of chemicals, which can be used to make plastics once again. At present, however, recycling plastic is difficult and expensive.

Precious metals

We get most of our metals by processing ores (minerals) that we take from the ground. The ores of some of our most useful metals, such as aluminium and iron, are found in huge quantities in the Earth's crust. They will last us for hundreds of years. But ores of other vital metals could

key words
- biodegradable
- decomposer
- distillation
- oil
- ore
- recycling

▲ A digger lifts a pile of paper that has been shredded in preparation for recycling.

run out later this century. These include lead, tin, zinc, copper, silver and gold.

The loss of copper, silver and gold would be particularly disastrous. Copper is vital to the electrical industry because it is one of the best conductors of electricity. Silver is essential to photography, as light-sensitive chemicals containing silver record the picture on film. Gold is used in jewellery, and increasingly in electronics.

The decomposers

Nature carries out some recycling for us. Organic waste, such as food scraps and vegetable matter, gets eaten by worms, insects, fungi and bacteria. They convert it back into chemicals that enrich the ground and help new growth.

Substances that naturally rot away are biodegradable. Metals, glass and most plastics cannot be broken down in this way. But biodegradable plastics are now being made. Some are designed to break down in the sunlight. Others contain starch, which can be broken down by natural decomposers such as bacteria.

◄ Bales of crushed aluminium drinks cans, ready for recycling. Each bale contains over 1 million cans.

Glossary

This glossary gives simple explanations of difficult or specialist words that readers might be unfamiliar with. Words in *italic* have their own glossary entry.

AC Alternating Current. Electric *current* that flows first one way around a *circuit* and then the other way. The mains electricity in homes is AC.

acceleration The rate at which the speed of an object increases.

alloy A mixture of *metals* or a metal and another substance, such as carbon.

analogue Representing quantities or signals in a physical form. An analogue watch, for example, measures time by the position of hands on a dial. Compare *digital*.

antibiotic A drug, for example penicillin, that destroys bacteria or prevents them from growing.

atom The smallest particle of an *element*. Atoms are made up of a tiny central *nucleus*, surrounded by a cloud of even tinier, fast-moving *electrons*.

battery A device that stores *electricity*, until it is needed, in the form of chemical energy. Also known as a cell.

camera A device that exposes *light* onto a film or electronic plate in order to record a picture.

capacitor Part of a *circuit* that stores *electrons* (charge) between two metal plates. The plates are usually rolled up inside a cylinder.

casting A method of shaping *metal*. Molten metal is poured into a mould and left to cool.

catalyst A chemical used to help bring about or speed up a chemical reaction, but which is not actually changed itself in the process.

ceramic A material made by baking earthy substances such as clay at high temperatures.

circuit A conducting wire loop that allows *electrons* to travel around it.

On the way, the electrons do useful jobs, such as making a light bulb glow.

colour A sensation produced by the eye and brain when *light* of a particular *wavelength* is detected. An object's colour depends on the wavelengths of light it produces or reflects.

compact disc A disk that stores information as a pattern of tiny bumps on a flat surface.

composite A product made from *plastic* containing a strengthening mesh of fibres.

compound A substance that is made up of different kinds of atom bonded together (as opposed to an element, which is made of only one kind of atom).

computer A machine that stores and processes information (data) under the control of a list of instructions called a *program*.

concave Of a *lens* or *mirror*, curved like the inside of a ball or circle.

condensation The process by which a gas turns into a liquid.

conductor A substance, such as a *metal*, that allows an electric current to flow through it.

convex Of a *lens* or *mirror*, curved like the outside of a ball or circle.

corrosion The gradual destruction of a *metal* by chemical action.

cracking A process carried out at an oil refinery in which large oil *molecules* are broken down into smaller ones.

current Measure of the rate at which electric charge (*electrons*) flow around a *circuit*. Measured

in amperes, often shortened to 'amps'.

DC Direct Current. DC flows in only one direction around a circuit. *Batteries* provide DC.

digital Representing quantities or signals by means of precise numbers. A computer is digital and represents data as a series of binary numbers, using 0s and 1s only. Compare *analogue*.

displacement The amount of a liquid or gas pushed aside (displaced) by a solid object floating on or in it. Displacement is used to measure the volume of large objects like ships.

DVD (**D**igital **V**ideo, or **V**ersatile, **D**isk) A device for storing digital information, similar to a *compact disc* but with greater storage capacity.

electricity A form of energy carried by certain particles of matter (*electrons* and protons), used for lighting and heating and for making machines work.

electrolysis A method of extracting and purifying *metals* using electricity.

electromagnetic induction The production of an electric *current* in a *circuit* when the circuit is placed in a changing *magnetic field*. Electricity *generators* use induction to make electricity.

electromagnetic radiation A kind of *radiation*, including *light* and ranging between radio *waves*, which have long waves, and gamma *rays*, which have very short waves.

electron Tiny negatively charged particle that orbits atoms. Some electrons are free to move, creating electric *current*.

element A substance that is made up of only one kind of *atom* (as opposed to a compound, which is made up of different kinds of atom).

email (electronic mail) Messages that are sent and received electronically, between *computers* that are linked over the *internet*.

endoscope A medical instrument that uses *optical fibres* to see inside the body.

energy That which is needed to make all actions happen. Movement, heat, light, sound and electricity are different forms of energy.

engine A machine that uses fuel to create movement.

evaporation The process by which a liquid turns into a gas.

fertilizer A substance used to enrich the soil so that plants can grow well.

force A push or pull that one object or material exerts on another.

forging A method of shaping *metal* by hammering or squeezing.

frequency The number of *vibrations* made each second by a *wave* of sound or light.

friction A *force* that slows a moving object or prevents it from moving.

fuel A material that is burned to produce *energy*. Coal, petrol and gas are all fuels.

furnace A structure in which substances (such as *ores* and *metals*) are heated to very high temperatures.

generator A machine that produces electric *current*. Generators are driven by giant turbines that are powered by steam (in coal, oil and nuclear power stations) or by water (in hydroelectric power stations).

gravity The *force* that attracts two objects. Earth's gravity keeps everything on Earth from floating out into space. It makes things flow downhill and fall to the ground.

hard disk A spinning magnetic disk on which *computers* record (save) and retrieve (open) data files.

hologram A three-dimensional image of an object made by storing the pattern of *light* it reflects.

hydraulic Describing a kind of machine that produces power using the *pressure* of liquid.

hydroelectric power Electricity that is made using the energy of running water.

insulator A substance, such as rubber, that blocks the flow of electric *current*.

internet A global *computer* network connected via satellites, optical fibres and telephone wires.

laser (**L**ight **A**mplification by **S**timulated **E**mission of **R**adiation A device that produces a thin, bright beam of *light* of a single *frequency*.

lens A curved piece of plastic or glass used to bend *light rays*.

lever A rigid bar resting on a fixed point that can be turned in order to lift an object or force an object open.

lift The *force* that holds a flying object, such as an aircraft or bird, up in the air.

light *Radiation* that stimulates the sense of sight and makes things visible.

light year The distance that *light* travels in one year (about 9.5 million million kilometres).

loudspeaker A device for converting patterns of electricity into sound *waves*. Often used to play back recorded music.

magnet A substance in which *electrons* spin in one direction, creating a *magnetic field*. Similar ends (poles) of magnets will push away (repel) each other, while different ends will attract each other.

magnetic field A region around magnets, magnetic materials and current-carrying conductors, where a magnetic force is present.

magnetic tape Material for storing sounds or pictures as patterns of magnetism. Cassette tapes and video tapes are examples.

mass The amount of material (solid, liquid or gas) that something contains.

memory chip A microchip in which digital data is stored until needed.

metal An *element* that is usually shiny and solid at room temperature. Metals are good *conductors* of heat and electricity. Those that are found in the ground in metal form, such as gold and copper, are called native metals.

microchip A chip of silicon containing a complex *circuit* made of thousands of microscopic *transistors*, *capacitors* and *resistors*. They use very little power and work extremely fast as parts are very close together.

microphone A device for converting sound *waves* into patterns of electricity. The electrical patterns can then be stored or transmitted.

microprocessor A *microchip* that performs simple calculations on computer data but at lightning-fast speeds. Microprocessors contain many millions of *transistors*, but are no bigger than a thumbnail.

microscope An instrument that produces a magnified image of a small object.

mineral A natural solid material that has a specific chemical composition and a definite crystalline structure.

mirror A shiny surface that reflects light and forms an image.

molecule A group of two or more *atoms* bonded to each other.

nucleus The central part of an *atom*.

optical fibre A thin wire of plastic or glass along which *light* can travel very easily.

ore A *mineral* from which a *metal* can be extracted.

pesticide A substance that is used, especially by farmers, to destroy insects or other animals that are harmful to plants or to animals.

petroleum Oil as it is extracted from the ground; also called crude oil.

pitch The highness or lowness of a voice or musical note.

plastic A *synthetic* substance with long *molecules* that is easy to shape; also called a *polymer*.

pneumatic Describing a kind of machine that produces power using the *pressure* of gas, such as air.

pollution The poisoning of the environment by such things as oil, chemicals and car exhaust fumes.

polymerization A chemical process that makes large *molecules* out of small ones, producing polymers, or *plastics*.

power The rate at which *energy* is turned from one form into another. For example, the power of an engine is the rate at which it can drive a machine.

pressure The amount of *force* with which a liquid or gas pushes on a surface.

program The list of instructions, or software, followed by a *computer's* hardware. Usually supplied on a floppy disk, CD or DVD, or may be downloaded from the *internet*.

radiation Energy given off as *waves* or tiny particles. Heat, *light*, cosmic *rays*, ultraviolet light and sound are different types of radiation.

ray A thin beam of *light*, heat or other *radiation*.

recording The process of turning sound or *light* into patterns of electricity that can then be stored.

recycling Using the same materials again, for either the same or a different purpose.

refining Purifying or separating materials (such as oil or *metals*) to produce more useful substances.

reflection *Light* or sound bouncing back off an object.

refraction *Light* or sound *waves* changing direction as they pass from one material into an other.

refractory A material that withstands very high temperatures.

relativity A theory developed by the physicist Albert Einstein. The theory of special relativity shows that time does not pass at the same speed for someone moving very fast and someone who is still. The second theory, general relativity, says that matter, such as stars, makes space curve, causing light rays to bend.

renewable resources Materials that, once used, can be replaced naturally, or by careful management. Wood is a renewable resource.

resistance A measure of how hard it is to push a *current* through a substance. Measured in ohms.

resistor Part of a *circuit* that resists the flow of *current*, causing a voltage (electrical pressure) to be raised across it.

retina The layer of light-sensitive cells at the back of the human eye.

smelting The main method of extracting *metals* from their *ores*, by heating them in a *furnace*.

solar power Energy obtained from the Sun, either by storing its heat or by turning its rays into electricity.

solvent A liquid that is used for dissolving other substances.

spectrum The full range of *electromagnetic radiation*. Part of this range, the visible spectrum, can be seen by the human eye. Ultraviolet, X-rays and gamma rays are too short to be seen by the human eye. Infrared, microwaves and radio *waves* are too long to be seen.

switch Part of a *circuit* that opens and closes like a gate, letting *electrons* flow only when you want them to.

synthetic Made from chemicals.

telescope An instrument that produces a magnified image of a distant object.

theory The reasons that a scientist gives to explain why something happens.

transformer Part of a *circuit* that either increases or decreases the size of an AC signal.

transistor Part of a *circuit* that either boosts (amplifies) a signal or turns it on and off to represent digital data in *computers*.

transmitter Equipment used to produce and send signals as electromagnetic waves. Transmitters are used to send radio waves to radio and television aerials.

turbine A machine in which blades rotate to produce *power*.

ultrasound Sound *waves* of a *frequency* too high for humans to hear.

vaccine A substance that is used to immunize a person or animal against a disease.

vacuum Complete emptiness; the total absence of air or any other material.

vibration The shaking movement of an object.

volt Measure of the electrical pressure (potential difference) in a *circuit*. This pressure urges *electrons* to flow.

watt Measure of the power produced or consumed by a *circuit*.

wave The way in which sound, light, heat and electricity travel.

wavelength The distance between two peaks on a *wave*.

weight The *force* with which everything presses down on the ground, water or air beneath it, as a result of *gravity*.

World Wide Web A part of the *internet* that helps users to find information by providing links between documents.

X-ray A type of *wave* that can pass easily through materials that are not very dense. X-rays are often used to inspect the insides of objects, including the human body.

Index

Page numbers in **bold** mean that this is where you will find the most information on that subject. If both a heading and a page number are in bold, there is an article with that title. A page number in *italic* means that there is a picture of that subject. There may also be other information about the subject on the same page.

Acknowledgements

Key
t = top; c = centre; b = bottom; r = right;
l = left; back = background;
fore = foreground

Artwork
Baker, Julian: 22 b; 68 tr; 98 tr; 100 c; 102 b; 134 t; 134 br; 154 b; 163 tr; 165 tl.
Birkett, Georgie: 117 tr.
D'Achille, Gino: 8 t; 11 tr; 22 cl; 25 tr; 45 tr; 52 tr; 57 bl; 59 tr; 61 tr; 71 bl; 72 br; 83 br; 86 bl; 92 br; 97 tl; 124 bc; 145 bl; 166 tr; 168 br; 170 cr; 174 tr.
Franklin, Mark: 14 t; 19 tl, tr; 23 b; 26 br; 28 bc; 31 cr; 33 tr; 38 tr; 40 bl; 43 b; 44 cr; 45 bl; 47 t; 49 c; 66 cr, b; 67 tr; 75 b; 106 br; 109 bl; 114 bl; 112–113 tc; 122–123 b; 144 br; 146 b; 147 tr; 14 b; 167 b; 170 b.
Full Steam Ahead: 71 bc; 80 tr; 86 br; 97 tr; 105 br; 161 tr; 180 bl.
Gecko Ltd.: 63 bl.
Hadler, Terry: 13 tl.
Hawken, Nick: 99 cr; 100 tl; 101 bl; 110 br.
Hinks, Gary: 176–177 bc.
Howatson, Ian: 146 tl.
Jakeway, Rob: 87 tr; 92 bl; 100 tr; 101 br; 120 cl; 135 tr; 135 b; 162 t; 166–167 c; 178–179 bc; 180 tr.
Learoyd, Tracey: 36 bl; 140 b; 155 cr.
Morris, Tony: 117 tr.
Oxford Designers and Illustrators: 17 cr; 23 cl; 46 b; 48 c; 110 tr.
Parsley, Helen: 90 tr; 114 cr; 131 bl.
Saunders, Michael: 20 tr; 21 t; 23 tl; 25 b; 29 b; 34 b; 37 t; 42 cr; 60 tr, c; 64 bl; 69 b; 78 br; 82–83 b; 91 c; 93 bl; 104 b; 129 bl; 104–105 tc; 141 t; 149 tr; 152–153 tc; 157 bl; 158 b; 159 bl; 160 tr; 169 bl.
Smith, Guy: 53 tc; 55c; 56 tr; 57 bc; 58 tr, bl; 61 cr; 72 bl; 74 cr; 76–77 tc; 84–85 c; 96 c; 103 b; 108 cl; 116 tr; 118 br; 121 b; 125 tr; 126 cl; 132 b; 137 b; 173 tr; 174 bl.
Sneddon, James: 32 cl; 56 br; 62 tr; 77 b; 136 bl; 142 b.
Visscher, Peter: 8 tl; 9 main; 10 tr; 11 tl; 13 b; 15 tl; 17 tl; 18 tl; 20 tl; 22 tl; 25 tl; 27 tl; 28 tl; 29 tl; 30 tl, cr; 32 tl; 33 tl; 34 tl; 35 tr; 36 tl; 38 tl; 40 tl; 42 tl; 44 tl; 45 tl; 46 tl; 48 tl; 49 tl; 52 tl; 55 tl; 56 tl; 58 tl; 60 tl; 62 tl; 63 tl; 64 tl; 66 tl; 68 tl; 70 tl, b; 72 tl; 72–73 c; 74 tl, bl; 75 tl; 76 tl; 78 tl; 79 tl; 80–81 b; 82 tl; 84 tl; 86 tl; 90 tl; 91 tl; 93 tl; 96 tl; 99 tl; 102 tl; 104 tl; 108 tl; 112 tl; 114 tl; 116 tl; 118 tl; 120 tl; 121 tl; 122 tl; 125 tl; 126 tl; 131 tl; 133 tl; 135 tl; 136 tl; 137 tl; 140 tl; 142 tl; 144 tl; 147 tl; 148 tl; 149 tl; 150 tl; 152 tl; 154 tl; 155 tl; 156 br; 157 tl; 158 tl; 159 tl; 161 tl; 163 tl; 164 tl; 165 br; 166 tl; 168 tl; 169 tl; 170 tl; 172 tl; 173 tl; 174 tl; 175 tl; 176 tl; 178 tl; 180 bl.
Wood, Michael: 24 t; 128 t; 130 cl; 129 tl; 168 bl; 175 b.

Photos
The publishers would like to thank the following for permission to use their photographs.

3d Systems Europe Ltd.: 89 bl.
Allsport: 8 b (Jon Ferrey); 13 tr (Clive Mason); 15 r (F. Rickard Vandysadt); 17 b (Zoom); 33 bl (Brian Bahr).
Art Archive, The: 148 tr, bl (Archaeological Museum Zara/Dagli Orti); 149 bc (Araldo de Luca); 154 tr (Canterbury Cathedral/Dagli Orti); 178 bl (JFB).
B&W Loudspeakers Ltd.: 135 c.
BAE Systems: 48 tr.
BBC: 77 tr.
Bubbles Photo Library: 53 br (Loisjoy Thurstun).
C Technologies AB: 81 tr.
Canon: 103tr; 106 tl.
Corbis: 11 b (Tony Arruza); 14 br (Adam Woolfitt); 16 bl (Vince Streano); 22 tr (Richard T. Novitz); 32 bl; 36 tr (Sally A. Morgan); 40 tr (Hubert Stadler); 41 bl (Phil Schermeister); 47 b; 60 bl (David Samuel); 65 bl (Bettmann); 86 tr (Jim Sugar Photography); 97 cr (Charles & Josette Lenars); 99 tr (Galen Rowell); 107 c (Ales Fevzer); 126 bl (David Reed); 147 bl (Charles E. Rotkin); 152 br (Araldo de Luca); 155 bl (Adam Woolfitt); 159 tr (James L. Amos); 162 bl (James L. Amos); 164 cl (Roger Wood); 168 tr (Robert Holmes); 170 bl (Galen Rowell); 172 tr (Gehl Company).
David Mellor: 18 tr (Pete Hill).

Digital Vision: 10 b; 39 br; 39 cl; 39 tr; 42–43 t; 44 bl; 130 br; 145 cr; 146 tr; 150 tr; 151 bl; 164 bl; 181 tr.
Eon Productions: 78 cl (Jim Clark/Avid Technology).
Ford: 57 tc.
Google Inc.: 92 tl.
H. J. Banks & Co Ltd.: 20 cl.
Haddon Davies: 12 t; 16; 18 bl, br; 20 br; 26 tl, tr; 27 bl.
Hutchison Picture Library: 75 tr (Christina Dodwell).
Intel Corporation: 82 tr.
ISCOR Ltd.: 161 bl.
Kobal: 88 bl, tl (Disney Enterprises); 111 br (RKO).
Lego: 63 cr.
Levington Agriculture Ltd.: 172 b.
Michel Brigaud: 41 tr.
Michelin: 158 tr.
NASA: 27 tc; 56 bl; 89 tr (NASA/CXC/SAO; NASA/HST (optical); CSIRO/ATNF/ATCA (radio)); 113 cr (Brad Whitmore (STScI)).
Nokia: 73 cr; 91 bl.
Oxford Scientific Films: 21 b (Gerard Soury); 31 t (Mark Jones); 52 b (Warren Faidley); 55 bl (David M. Dennis); 100 bl (John Downer); 106–107 tc (Raj Kamal); 111 cl; 116 bl (Jorge Sierra); 129 tr (Carols Sanchez); 137 bc (Colin Monteath); 143 bl (Peter Ryley); 156 t (Edward Parker); 174 cr (Marty Cordano); 175 cr (Tim Shepherd).
Panos Pictures: 143 cr (Chris Stowers); 176 bl (Roderick Johnson); 177 tr (Liba Taylor).
Philips: 69 cl, c.
Photodisc: 23 cr; 26 bl; 98 br; 173 b.
Psion: 79 cr.
Redferns: 132 tr (Jon Super); 131 tr (Henrietta Butler).
Science and Society Picture Library: 45 c; 109 tc, 110 c (National Museum of Photography, Film & TV).
Science Photo Library: 12 b; 24 bl (Dale Boyer/NASA); 28 tr (Sheila Terry); 29 tr; 30 cl (Doug Allan); 31 br (Dr Arthur Tucker); 34 tr (Andrew Syred); 35 br (Tony Craddock); 42 bl (Peter Menzel); 46 tr (Astrid & Hanns-Frieder Michler); 49 tr (Francoise Sauze); 54 tr (BSIP VEM); 54 cl (Blair Seitz); 55 tr (Chris Knapton); 59 b (Rosenfeld Images Ltd.); 60–61 c (Alex Bartel); 62 bl (Peter Menzel); 64 tr (Martin Bond); 65 tr (John Mead); 67 bl; 68 bl (Tony Craddock); 69 tr (Sandia National Laboratories); 70 bl (TEK Image); 76 bl; 83 tr (B. Kramer/Custom Medical Stock Photo); 87 bl (Philippe Plailly/Eurelios); 88–89 tc (NASA); 90 bl (Geoff Tompkinson); 93 cr (Volker Steger); 96 tr (Martin Bond); 99 bl (Royal Observatory, Edinburgh); 102–103 tc (NASA); 105 bl (Guy Felix/Jacana); 105 bc (Eye of Science); 106 b (William Ervin); 112–113 bc (David Parker); 115 tl (CNRI); 115 c (Biophoto Associate); 115 cr (Lawrence Berkeley Laboratory); 117 bl (Alex Bartel); 118 bl (Will & Deni McIntyre); 118–119 tc (David Parker); 119 br (Colin Cuthbert); 120 bl (Adam Hart-Davis); 122–123 tc (Dr Arthur Tucker); 124 tr (Lawrence Berkeley Laboratory); 125 bl (American Science & Engineering); 127 tr (Rafael Macia); 128 br (Crown copyright/Health & Safety Laboratory); 133 bl (C. S. Langlois, Publiphoto Diffusion); 136 cr (Dr Jeremy Burgess); 137 tr (Saturn Stills); 140 tr (Bernhard Edmaier); 142–143 t (David Leah); 144–145 t (Rosenfeld Images Ltd.); 148 cr (Pascal Goetgheluck); 152 bl (John Howard); 153 cr (Lawrence Livermore National Laboratory); 157 tr (R. Maisonneuve); 159 br (Pascal Goetgheluck); 160 bl (Rosenfeld Images Ltd.); 166 bl (Pascal Goetgheluck); 169 tr (David Parker); 170 tr (CNRI); 171 tr (Peter Menzel); 176 tr (Simon Fraser); 178 tr (Simon Fraser/Northumbrian Environmental Management Ltd.); 179 br (US Department of Energy); 181 bl (Hank Morgan).
Scipix: 151 tr.
Sony UK Ltd.: 69 cr; 78 tr; 84 bl; 85 tr; 101 br; 133 cr.
TRH Pictures: 167 tl (Short Brothers plc).
Virgin Atlantic Airways: 79 b.
Volkswagen: 19 br.
Woodfall Wild Images: 71 c (Paul Kay); 141 b (David Woodfall); 163 br (Heinrich Van de

OXFORD
UNIVERSITY PRESS

Great Clarendon Street, Oxford OX2 6DP

Oxford University Press is a department of the University of Oxford. It furthers the University's objective of excellence in research, scholarship, and education by publishing worldwide in

Oxford New York

Auckland Cape Town Dar es Salaam Hong Kong Karachi Kuala Lumpur Madrid Melbourne Mexico City Nairobi New Delhi Shanghai Taipei Toronto

With offices in

Argentina Austria Brazil Chile Czech Republic France Greece Guatemala Hungary Italy Japan Poland Portugal Singapore South Korea Switzerland Thailand Turkey Ukraine Vietnam

Oxford is a registered trade mark of Oxford University Press in the UK and in certain other countries
Text copyright © Oxford University Press 2001

The moral rights of the author have been asserted

Database right Oxford University Press (maker)

First published 2006

British Library Cataloguing in Publication Data

Data available

ISBN-13: 978-0-19-911510-5
ISBN-10: 0-19-911510-9

10 8 6 4 2 1 3 5 7 9

Printed in China by Imago